Disarming States

Disarming States

The International Movement to Ban Landmines

KENNETH R. RUTHERFORD

Praeger Security International

AN IMPRINT OF ABC-CLIO, LLC
Santa Barbara, California • Denver, Colorado • Oxford, England

Library of Congress Cataloging-in-Publication Data

Rutherford, Ken, 1962–
Disarming states : the international movement to ban landmines / Kenneth R. Rutherford.
p. cm. — (Praeger security international)
Includes bibliographical references and index.

ISBN 978–0–313–39396–9 (hard copy : alk. paper) — ISBN 978–0–313–39397–6 (e-book)
1. Land mines (International law) 2. Arms control—International cooperation. I. Title.
JZ5645.R88 2011
341.7′3—dc22 2010039770

ISBN: 978–0–313–39396–9
EISBN: 978–0–313–39397–6

15 14 13 12 11 1 2 3 4 5

This book is also available on the World Wide Web as an eBook.
Visit www.abc-clio.com for details.

Praeger
An Imprint of ABC-CLIO, LLC

ABC-CLIO, LLC
130 Cremona Drive, P.O. Box 1911
Santa Barbara, California 93116-1911

This book is printed on acid-free paper ∞

Manufactured in the United States of America

Contents

Preface: Second Chance

It was a typically hot and dry day in the Somali desert. I arrived at the white, concrete three-room office at the edge of the city of Lugh—as usual—early in the morning before the heat chased people backed to their abodes, huts, and tents.[1] It was Thursday, and I needed to achieve certain project tasks and run a few errands before the end of the day because the next day—Friday—was the Islamic holy day, when most Muslims took time to rest and worship, and did not go to work.

On that morning, December 16, 1993, I was a humanitarian loan officer in Somalia servicing a community devastated by years of drought and war. I had taken the Somalia position over better-paying posts in more-attractive locations because of the tremendous human suffering that I had seen on television, because I had spent much of my recent life working with former nomads affected by drought and war, and because my parents encouraged public service. When processing and disbursing the loans to Somalis to assist them with their lives, I made it a point to say that the money came from the people of the United States of America.[2]

I was so determined to get as much accomplished that day in order to travel to Kenya on Friday so I could call my fiancée, Kim, who was living with my brothers in Boulder, Colorado. She was preparing to join me in Africa, and ask her whether I should continue my job in Somalia or accept a position as an assistant director of the Peace Corps in Uzbekistan. The Somalia security situation was deteriorating rapidly and cascading into greater violence because of the "Battle of Mogadishu" two months earlier

(October 3, 1993), which was captured in the book and movie *Blackhawk Down*. Americans were being killed and kidnapped. American military forces were withdrawing from Somalia. Emotionally, I could not look at this situation objectively and that was when I had always called on Kim. She was making plans to come to Kenya to be close to me and was not happy about my continuing in Somalia. She had been trying to hide that fact, and I had felt an emotional pull and humanitarian impulse to stay in Somalia and help the people in need.

On that Thursday, I was to meet with all of the donkey cart owners in Lugh. The donkey carts were an important part of Lugh society because they provided water throughout the city, which did not have running water. At 9 a.m., only 29 of the 50 donkey cart owners had appeared at the credit union. I decided to postpone the meeting, as I realized that many of the donkey cart owners were traveling long distances from rural areas. Little did I know that within an hour a donkey would help save my life.

My staff pointed me to three recently returned Somali refugees sitting on the credit union steps to request financial help for their rural businesses. One such business is the manufacturing of limestone, which is an extremely common construction building block in the region as it is tough, is long-lasting, and normally occurs in easily accessible surface areas. I decided to visit their project site, which also would allow more time for the donkey carts to come to the credit union.

The lime producer applicants got in our Toyota Land Cruiser's back seat, while the three credit union directors and the union's manager, Abdulahi Farah Ali, got in the second row. I sat in the front seat between my driver Abdual Raman and Somali counterpart Mohamed Hassan Duale. We drove toward the project site, which was several miles outside of Lugh. During the drive, as usual, I worked on my to-do list for the day—tasks like dismantling the project's chicken cages at the airport so they would not be looted during my time in Kenya. I was also arranging a possible Maasai wedding for Kim and me. I was probably more excited about that idea than Kim and our families. They thought I was crazy.

As I was sitting in the middle front seat of the Land Cruiser, I angled my legs to the right because of the stick shift and focused on my papers while the Somalis talked among themselves. I looked up from my papers and the car started to slow to avoid a donkey cart on the right side of the road. As we neared it, I returned to reading when the Land Cruiser suddenly shook and filled with dust after hitting a landmine (see photo P.1). I could not see the papers on my lap. They had disappeared. As the dust cleared, I could see a foot on the floorboard. I wondered to myself, "Whose foot is that?"

I tried to step out of the cab, but my legs would not move. I grabbed the steering wheel and pulled myself out of the vehicle and crashed down to the ground. As I looked down at my legs, I saw that foot again because it

Photograph P.1

Author's Toyota Land Cruiser after hitting a landmine near Lugh, Somalia, on the road to Wajid. December 16, 1993. (Courtesy of author.)

was still attached. And I saw a lot of blood. Since I was an Eagle Scout, I instantly recalled my first aid merit badge and raised my legs to stop the bleeding, putting them on the driver's seat. There was that foot again, hanging down to my right knee attached by my torn skin and frayed ligaments. You know the calluses on the bottom of your foot that you never see? I saw those calluses and thought it odd. With a determination and a calmness that remain a mystery to me, I tried to put my foot back on. But it was not cooperating. It kept falling off. And I kept trying to put it back on.

Then I noticed that the handheld radio, the one I always kept in my briefcase for security reasons, was lying nearby. That day I had attached it to my belt clip and it had fallen off when I dragged myself out of the cab. I calmly crawled for the radio, whereupon Abdulahi handed it to me. As soon as I grabbed it, I announced my call sign, "Kilo romeo, kilo romeo," and said, "we have hit a land mine. We are bleeding. I am O-positive. Send for an airplane."

I monitored the radio traffic. I heard the UN radio operator reply to check the scene before calling for an airplane. My calm voice disarmed the radio operator and the community, and they thought I was all right. They did not know I could not get my foot back on.

I interrupted his message and blurted out, "Bloody hell! We are bleeding to death! Could you please hurry up and call an airplane?" I did not tell them about my foot, which was still not cooperating.

I kept trying to put my foot back on, but not because of the pain. I was not in pain. It just looked so odd to have a body part hanging in the air, and I wanted to put my body back together. For some strange reason, I thought to myself that if I *could* put my foot back on before the rescuers arrived that they would not notice and everything would be OK. I had added a new item to my to-do list: getting my foot back on.

Have you ever done sit-ups for 15 minutes in a row? Well I did in a Somali desert, sitting up to reach my foot and try to put it back on. After countlesssit-ups, I could not do another one. All I could do was to lie there and stare at my foot while coughing up blood. It was all over my shirt and my chin. I knew I was dying.

I began thanking God for a wonderful life. I had a wonderful family, the best of friends, went to excellent schools, and had lived in an awesome community. I said, "God, if this is the way you want me to check out and leave, I am ready and willing." I looked up at a clear blue Somali sky with white puffy clouds and thought that would be my last view of Earth. I was comfortable, calm, and ready for my next life.

But I did not die then. So I said, "God, did I make the right decision in coming to Somalia? My father was against it. Kim was against it." With God's encouragement, I quickly shut that off and knew that I had made the right decision in coming to Somalia. And what a privilege it had been to help so many people who were in desperate need. I was happy and peaceful.

I still did not die. And the rescuers still had not arrived.

As I was lying on my back against the dry, hard ground of Somalia thinking that this is the end of the line of my life, initially, I did not have time to be afraid nor fear death, but felt it was coming. The rocky ground became my death bed. For me, the last sensations of this life were the taste of blood and the sight of a clear Somalia sky with white puffy clouds. The lovely day had dramatically changed to an abomination. My life would never be the same.

Then I thought of Kim, and it struck me that I had never loved someone as much as I loved her and that it would be nice for us to have a life together. I was not ready to die, and I said, "God, I just changed my mind. I want to marry Kim, have children with her and become a professor. Whatever comes after that is icing on the cake. I commit to you that if these things happen that I will be the most grateful servant, never asking for anything more."

What I did not know was that the power of gratitude was keeping me calm, collected, aware, and alive. People who are traumatically injured often become hysterical and uncontrollable. In my case, those moments were some of the most calm and peaceful in my life.

Finally, the rescuers, including Islamic fundamentalist gunmen from the local militia, arrived, and one of the first ones down the hill asked me if I was OK. I asked him, "Could you put my foot back on?" I meant it in a humorous way because I already realized that it would be nearly impossible to have a normal foot again, and that it psychologically hurt too much to cry.

The gunmen picked me up by the shoulders as others picked me up behind the knees because below them there was nothing to grab except bloody tatters of my feet. Because of the awkward holds, I was in a cradle position, and going uphill. It was a rough twenty to thirty yards to a waiting United High Commissioner for Refugees (UNHCR) Suburban rescue vehicle. A few others got on the other side of the vehicle to grab me from inside. They could not because there was nothing to grab.

Eventually, I was placed in the back of a white pickup truck of the local Islamic fundamentalist militia. With my head on the lap of an Islamic soldier, I leaned against the back of the truck cab while my right hand was being held by the soldier's right hand, as his left held his machine gun. My left hand was held by another soldier sitting on the side of the pickup truck; he held a machine gun as well. I looked up and into their eyes as we all squeezed each other's hands. Meanwhile, people holding my right leg kept trying to keep my foot on and maintain balance in the bouncing truck.

I thought it was terrific that Somali Islamic fundamentalist soldiers were trying to save my life and comfort me during what could possibly be my last moments on Earth. I especially realized how ironic this was while several hundred miles away, in Mogadishu, other groups of Islamic fundamentalists were fighting with Americans. In contrast, these soldiers were trying to save my life by racing me to the local hospital and risking their own lives by driving over the same road on which I had hit a land mine.

The pain set in quickly once I was placed in the truck and was dependent on others. I looked as the dirt road converged with the Lugh's main road. The credit union was just south of the intersection, while Lugh's main town was north, including the region's lone hospital. As the truck turned north from the intersection, I raised myself and looked out to see the road and the credit union, which were blocked by the large number of donkey carts still waiting for me to return and review their loan applications.

The hospital courtyard was filled with people who had heard about the accident when the honking rescue cars and trucks had sped through the city to the scene. Lying in the back of the pickup, I remember Somalis touching my legs and arms saying, "Sorry." I thought, "Who is going to help them? Who is going to continue the credit union work here? We have over 400 loan applications still to process for Lugh alone. Is this the end?"

I was lifted out of the truck bed and onto a gurney, and then taken in through the hospital's doors into a medium-sized, bare white concrete room, which was full of Somali medical personnel and a few trained international medical staff—Francis Kizito, a Ugandan Kenyan doctor; Willis Ouma, a Kenyan doctor; and Tamera Morgan, an American nurse.

A woman pressed my head to the bed by placing her hands firmly on my forehead. I kept struggling to deal with the pain, as the clinic did not have pain medicine, and trying to raise myself so that I could look at my mutilated feet. I could not believe that they were so destroyed. Two men held my arms down in a cross position to keep me from moving too much as the staff tried to prevent me from bleeding to death.

Dr. Kizito had started an IV in the field, but this one IV access point was not enough to keep me alive. So after re-adjusting the field tourniquets that I began, Morgan restarted two new large bore lines in both antecubital spaces and started normal saline, wide open. While she was doing that, Dr. Ouma applied pressure dressings. Morgan also administered IV valium to help produce amnesia and an IV dose of promethazine, a drug that enhances the effects of other sedating drugs.

After a few hours at the clinic, I was air evacuated to Nairobi. During the flight, I remember moaning and mumbling "Oh my God" so much from the pain that I thought the Irish pilot, Joe Moran, must have hated me since I was probably giving him a headache. In the plane, I almost died. To keep me alive, Morgan and Joris Vandelanotte, a Belgium doctor based in nearby Mandera, Kenya, saved my life by not only providing excellent emergency medical care, but also taking blood from each other via gravity into empty saline bags. They then changed the needle and "piggybacked" the blood line into one of my existing IV normal saline lines.[3] Moran later commented that while he had conducted more than 100 emergency evacuations during his 30 years of flying in Africa, he remembers this particular flight because of the amount of blood loss from my mutilated legs overrunning his Twin Cessna 402 plane.[4] I could not hear them, but Morgan and Vandelanotte were telling Moran to fly lower as my blood pressure was dropping dramatically and my blood was barely perfusing enough to keep my vital organs alive. Moran lowered the plane's flying attitude from around 10,000 feet to several hundred feet in order to raise my blood pressure to keep me alive. "We were clipping treetops," Moran, said humorously years later, "it was cowboy flying, but I was good at it."[5]

Upon arriving at Nairobi's Wilson Airport, I was transferred to the general hospital, where I started begging the staff to save my right leg, knowing very well that it was gone, but trying to protect my left leg. I figured that if I let my right leg go easy, then it would be much easier for them to cut off my left. I was twisting and struggling from the pain. The professional, patient, and efficient Kenyan hospital staff then strapped both my arms stretched out to each side as if preparing for a crucifixion. The last thing I remember before the operation was a nurse apologizing as he cut away my maroon T-shirt—the one that I wore at my going away party in Colorado that my family and friends had given before my departure five months earlier.

I woke up with the medical staff's hands holding down my shoulders explaining that they had to amputate my lower right leg to save my life. I was then flown to Geneva, where I received three surgeries on my left foot over one week at l'Hôpital de la Tour, and finally to Colorado, where I recovered. My left leg was amputated three years later after a total of 12 surgeries.

After my accident, Kim and I married. I applied and was accepted to graduate school at Georgetown University, where I earned my Ph.D. in government, in order to follow the footsteps of my father, who was a professor. At that time, the International Campaign to Ban Landmines (ICBL), a global coalition of hundreds of non-governmental organizations (NGOs), was actively involved with the International Committee for the Red Cross (ICRC) in pushing for an international prohibition on the use of anti-personnel landmines (APLs) in order to stop the humanitarian devastation they were causing.[6]

As I entered graduate school, I was still unsure about my role in alleviating the global landmine crisis and had no intention of participating in the movement. However, during my graduate school days, I was invited to participate in the ICBL that was instrumental in achieving a global comprehensive agreement to ban APLs, known as the 1997 Mine Ban Treaty (MBT).[7] I traveled the world with undergraduate exams in my backpack to grade at night after the landmine conferences and events ended. By participating in the ICBL, I realized that my accident and recovery was not unique but a common story in many mine-infested countries (see photo P.2).

I anticipate that this book is one of the most comprehensive studies on the mine ban movement and the MBT's formation to date. While focusing on a particular global movement and widely used military weapon, the book describes a grass-roots movement that captured the world's attention. It also raises wider questions about the role of civil society in global politics, especially in an area at the heart of state sovereignty—weapons. I believe that the MBT's creation and the ongoing discussion on other issues such as cluster munitions and child soldiers show the importance of NGOs working with governments to address security issues.

There are two broad questions that this book describes and addresses: How did the campaign achieve its success and how can we apply the lessons of the campaign to ban landmines to other global challenges and situations? In addressing these questions, other questions need to be asked, such as why did the landmine issue take off when it did? What was inherent in the nature of the issue that appealed widely to numerous constituency groups? How did it muscle its way past many other legitimate issues to get on the global and governmental agendas?

Photograph P.2

Public service announcement for Physicians Against Land Mines (PALM), a NGO whose mission was to end the death, dismemberment and disability caused by land mines. Founded in 1996 by Dr. William Kennedy Smith, PLAM sponsored public information initiatives, advocate reforms in international law and numerous disability programs. PALM educated the public through advertisements, such as the one reprinted here, featuring Ken Rutherford, designed by advertising company Leo Burnett, for use in magazines, bus shelters and inside buses and trains. Several magazines—including *Harper's, Atlantic Monthly, Bomb*, and *People*—had donated space for this ad campaign. In 1998 PALM became the Chicago/Washington D.C. based, not-for-profit organization "Center for International Rehabilitation" (CIR) and initiated its Rehabilitation Engineering Research Center on Landmine Victim Assistance. (Courtesy of the Center for International Rehabilitation. Used by permission.)

The answers to these questions are relevant not only to landmines but to other global issues, some of which do not get on the international political agenda. This project is a result of my own experiences and from viewing the campaign to ban landmines from the academic perspective, which increased my supposition that the movement was a unique political event.

When I went to Somalia in 1993 as part of the international relief effort, I did not realize that the world was in the midst of a global landmine crisis. I also did not realize that at that time, UN Secretary-General Boutros Boutros-Ghali was discussing the global landmine catastrophe. He wrote that landmines are easy to use and are inexpensive, sometimes costing less than three dollars, but very difficult to eradicate: There was a mine-clearing accident for every 1,000–2,000 mines destroyed, and each mine cost between $300 and $1,000 to clear.[8] Somalia, in particular, was one of the most severely affected countries. According to a study that I later read, Somali mothers leashed their babies to trees so they would not crawl into minefields with more than one million mines randomly deployed throughout the country.[9]

But in retrospect, I came to understand that my accident in Somalia was actually a blessing for me in many ways. It allowed me to focus on what was important in life and not waste energy on trivialities. Far from making me reflective or wise, my accident made me appreciate what we can do with our limited means and talents. Focusing on our beliefs and resources, we can accomplish amazing things. The global movement to ban landmines is one of them. It is story that I have wanted to share.

Ever since my last day in Somalia, I wake up every day as landmine survivor. Yet, notwithstanding my own predispositions that may enter into this book at times, I attempt to be impartial, affirming, in one piece, an across-the-board story and record the references when necessary. Nonetheless, while I believe my view is fair-minded, it is not really objective as the success of the ICBL, ICRC, and MBT in alleviating the negative humanitarian impact of landmines proved what many of us were saying in rallying the world to address the landmines problem. As an additional reference for interested readers, I have included an extensive bibliography for those interested in furthering their interest on the landmine issue. Also, while the story ends with the achievement of the MBT in 1997, I briefly summarize its achievements since then in Chapter Six and list additional informational sources for current landmine information in the bibliography.

Less than two decades after an event might seem to be soon to write an analysis and history, but now is a good time to write a book about the international movement to ban landmines. It has taken only a short time for relevant documents to be made available. In addition, my personal association and social contact with many governmental officials, ICBL members, and ICRC staff provided primary sources. I participated in the movement first as a landmine survivor, then as a campaigner, and finally a leader on promoting social and economic assistance to those affected by landmines. In writing this book, I have attempted to distill the essential facts from a mountain of information, to identify the key lessons.

I have relied principally on published material, unpublished correspondence, and papers, including personal notes and correspondence. The book also draws upon formal interviews and informal conversations that I conducted. Finally, the book includes my personal observations and experiences as a landmine survivor, campaign participant, and cofounder of the Landmine Survivors Network—which was the first organization by and for landmine survivors—as a consultant working for the U.S. Defense and State Departments and in my position as the Director of James Madison University's Center for International Stabilization and Recovery, which publishes the *Journal of Explosive Remnants of War and Mine Action*, the world's only journal about explosive remnants of war and landmine mine action and the longest continuous source of landmine information in the world.

Acknowledgments

Disarming States: The International Movement to Ban Landmines could not have been written without the assistance and encouragement of many organizations and people.

It also would have been difficult to finish this project without research grant funding from the Missouri State University (MSU) Graduate College and the support of its Dean, Dr. Frank Einhellig, in the form of a faculty research grant, and Provost, Dr. Belinda McCarthy. Also important to the project's realization was the editing assistance Jeff Sjerven, who stayed with the project despite his many demands. I am especially indebted to Cory Kuklick, Cameron McCauley, and Dr. Robert Rutherford for reading the complete manuscript with an eye to detail and substance. I would also like to thank my MSU graduate assistants, Steve Henry and Jeff Bernhard, for their research help and organizing the book's extensive bibliography.

I would also like to recognize three special colleagues, who I had the very good fortune to have had as my Georgetown University professors and also happen to be my dissertation committee members—Dr. Andrew Bennett, Dr. Christopher Joyner, and Dr. George Shambaugh. They worked with me for years on developing this manuscript through their classes, guidance, and many conversations.

At Praeger Press, I would like to express my gratitude to my editor, Steve Catalano, who, from the beginning constantly authenticated this project's importance and, true to his word, worked most efficiently to help complete it.

The writing of *Disarming States: The International Movement to Ban Landmines* was facilitated by the services of archivists and librarians around the world. I thank the librarians at the Library and Archives Canada in Ottawa, the Pearson Peacekeeping Centre in Clementsport, Nova Scotia, the Dag Hammarskjöld Library at United Nations in New York, and the United Nations Depository and Government Documents Libraries at MSU. I especially thank MSU's extraordinary librarians Bryon Stewart and Ann Fuhrman, who would "volunteer" as a driver to bring my students to visit the U.S. Department of Defense Humanitarian Demining International Training Center (HDTC) at Ft. Leonard Wood, which is one of the world's premier landmine instructional centers, and experience first-hand the challenges of humanitarian demining.

At Ft. Leonard Wood, special thanks goes to its public affairs officer Mike Warren for always providing first-class hospitality, then HDTC Director Paul Arcangeli who suggested the field trip idea and continues to make a difference in helping the world to walk safely. The HDTC team ensured a top quality educational experience for my students, who

Photograph A.1

Missouri State University students and staff receiving landmine in-classroom and hands-on training at the Humanitarian Demining Training Center (HDTC), Ft. Leonard Wood, Missouri. HDTC is the premiere U.S. military establishment for the collection of information and the training of U.S. personnel in humanitarian demining operations. The HDTC is the Department of Defense Center of Excellence for humanitarian demining-training and was set up in 1996 in order to expand U.S. efforts in humanitarian demining abroad. (Courtesy of author.)

always left their presence grateful to meet the heroes directly responsible for reducing mine casualties around the world and freeing land for productive use (see photo A.1).

The HDTC is part of the U.S. Government response to the global landmine crisis. Also important to its response is the State Department's Weapons Removal and Abatement (WRA) team, including Jim Lawrence, Stacy Davis, Mark Adams, Dennis Hadrick, and John Stevens. Their dedication to help people to walk the Earth in safety and commitment to humanitarian landmine action and conventional weapons destruction makes their office one of the global leaders in combating the threat of landmines.

Through the extraordinary courage and life-saving skills of Joe Moran, an Irish pilot with the African Medical and Research Foundation (AMREF), Tamara Morgan, an American trauma nurse with AMREF, and Joris Vandelanotte, a Belgian doctor with Medecins Sans Frontieres (MSF), I was able to survive a landmine accident in Somalia. Back in the United States, Don Henderson was second to none in terms of his unconditional friendship and compassion during my years of recovery. Jerry White was a valuable peer supporter, who had the vision to use our landmine experiences to launch the Landmine Survivors Network to help victims, in doing so, andreceiving support, praise, and partnerships at the highest levels.

My earnest appreciation to all the people made invaluable suggestions, gave freely of their time and expertise and all working to address the global humanitarian problem caused by landmines: Samy Abdul, David Atwood, Col. Dennis Barlow (U.S. Army Ret.), Sharif Baasser, Liz Bernstein, Ambassador Lincoln Bloomfield, John Borrie, Kerry Brinkert, Anne Goldfeld, Steve Goose, Mark Gwozdecky, Paul Hannon, Peter Herby, Ambassador Rick Inderfurth, Ratana Khum, Bob Lawson, Holly Myers, Tim Rieser, Sean Sutton, and Mary Wareham.

Any errors in the book are mine alone and should not be associated with them.

I am indebted to the following individuals and organizations for giving permission to use their or their organizations' photographs in this book: Cambodia Campaign to Ban Landmines, Dr. Anne Goldfeld, Ambassador Rick Inderfurth, International Campaign to Ban Landmines, Colin King, Office of Senator Patrick Leahy, Dr. Will Kennedy Smith, Survivor Corps, Dr. Wade C. Roberts, and Mary Wareham. In particular, I would like to thank two incredibly skilled photographers: Luke Powell, who has taken wonderful photographic images of Afghanistan's beauty (www.lukepowell.com), and Mines Advisory Group photographer Sean Sutton, the world's first full-time photographer covering landmines, and arguably the world's foremost "battlefield archeologist" (www.maginternational.org/multimedia/).

United States Senate

WASHINGTON, DC 20510-4502

APPROPRIATIONS
JUDICIARY

March 28, 1994

Ken Rutherford
c/o Donna Thompson
386 Park Avenue South
New York, NY 10016

Dear Mr. Rutherford:

I heard that you were injured by a landmine in Somalia, and that you recently described your experience in a television interview. Although I did not see the interview, you certainly impressed several people who told me about it.

I have been working against the proliferation of landmines for several years, after establishing a fund in the foreign aid program to assist people who have lost legs and arms from landmines. Last September my amendment to cut off exports of anti-personnel landmines from the United States passed the Senate 100-0. It was followed by a United Nations resolution calling for a global export ban, which was adopted unanimously by the General Assembly. With momentum building in many countries to stop the harm to civilians from landmines, this is a crucial year for international action.

As chairman of the Subcommittee on Foreign Operations I plan to hold a public hearing in the Senate on the landmine problem on Friday, May 13, 1994. I expect this to be the only comprehensive hearing on this subject in the Congress this year, and I would be very appreciative if you would be willing to testify. Your presence would be very helpful in describing the indiscriminate effects of these weapons, and the impact they have on the lives of people who have been injured by them.

The hearing is scheduled to run from 10:00am - 1:00pm.

I look forward to hearing from you.

With best regards,

Patrick Leahy

PATRICK LEAHY
United States Senator

VERMONT OFFICES: COURT HOUSE PLAZA, 199 MAIN STREET, BURLINGTON 863-2525
FEDERAL BUILDING, ROOM 338, MONTPELIER 229-0569
OR DIAL TOLL FREE 1-800/642-3193

PRINTED ON RECYCLED PAPER

Photograph A.2

Senator Patrick Leahy invitation to author to testify at the Global Humanitarian Crisis hearing. (Courtesy of author.)

My deepest gratitude to Senator Patrick Leahy and his foreign policy aide Tim Rieser for inviting me to testify at the 1994 U.S. Senate Hearing "The Global Landmine Crisis," which fundamentally altered the direction of my life. Per the invitation letter (see photo A.2), they were visionary leaders before the global landmine movement became popular and remain influential champions in striving for the continued assistance to victims, those who care for them and their families, and those removing landmines from the land.

In preparation for the Senate hearing testimony, I was surprised and shocked at discovering the large-scale humanitarian devastation caused by landmines. After the hearing, Senator Leahy and Rieser's friendship and inspiration provided me with the moral backing to start fighting to

Photograph A.3

Ken, Kim, Hayden, Campbell, Duncan, and Lucie Rutherford. (Courtesy of Marla Rutherford.)

help survivors, including paying attention to their personal stories. At every occurrence meeting victims, they listened intently to each word and then communicate across the foreign language wall a depth of feeling that clearly reassured them.

The international movement to ban landmines story as relayed in this book would not have been possible without a love story. Throughout out my rehabilitation, family members were wonderful supporters: So a big thanks to Robert, Ann, Eric, Douglas, Xenia, and Marla Rutherford and the Schwers family and Austin Kim, who was my fiancée at the time of my landmine accident, married me. In the beginning of our marriage, she courageously guided me through my frequent hospitalizations, and then patiently tolerated my lengthy absences while I was working overseas on the landmine issue and, when at home, the many early mornings and late nights working on this project over the last decade. Our children, Hayden, Campbell, Duncan, and Lucie now conduct their own regular landmine and disability awareness programs among their classmates and friends. This book is dedicated to them (see photo A.3).

Acronyms

ACDA	Arms Control and Disarmament Agency (United States)
AP	Anti-Personnel
APL	anti-personnel landmines
ARC	American Refugee Committee (United States)
AT	anti-tank
BWC	Biological Weapons Convention
CALM	Campaign Against Land Mines (New Zealand)
CCM	Convention on Cluster Munitions
CCW	Convention on Conventional Weapons
CD	Conference on Disarmament
CTBT	Conventional Test Ban Treaty
CWC	Chemical Weapons Convention
DFAIT	Department of Foreign Affairs and International Trade (Canada)
DMZ	Demilitarized Zone (Korea)
EU	European Union
GGE	Group of Governmental of Experts
ICBL	International Campaign to Ban Landmines
ICRC	International Committee of the Red Cross
IDA	Institute for Defense Analysis (United States)
HI	Handicap International (France)
HRW	Human Rights Watch (United States)
LSN	Landmine Survivors Network (United States)
MAC	Mines Action Canada (Canada)
MAG	Mines Advisory Group (United Kingdom)
MBT	Mine Ban Treaty
MI	Medico International (Germany)
NATO	North Atlantic Treaty Organization
NGOs	non-governmental organizations

NPA	Norwegian People's Aid (Norway)
NSC	National Security Council (United States)
OAS	Organization of American States
OAU	Organization of African United
PHR	Physicians Against Landmines (United States)
QUNO	Quaker United Nations Office
SD	self-destruct
SN	self-neutralizing
UK	United Kingdom
UN	United Nations
UNBRO	United Nations Border Relief Operation—Khmer Refugee camps on the Thai/Cambodia border
UNDHA	United Nations Department of Humanitarian Affairs
UNGA	United Nations General Assembly
UNHCR	United Nations High Commissioner for Refugees
UNICEF	United Nations Children's Fund
UNIDIR	United Nations Institute for Disarmament Research
UNOCHA	United Nations Office for the Coordination of Humanitarian Affairs
UNSGA	United Nations Secretary-General
UNTAC	United Nations Transitional Authority in Cambodia
US	United States
USAID	U.S. Agency for International Development (United States)
USCBL	United States Campaign to Ban Landmines (United States)
UXO	unexploded ordinance
VVAF	Vietnam Veterans of America Foundation (United States)

CHAPTER 1

Overview: Why Ban Landmines?

For the first time a weapon which has been in widespread use by armed forces throughout the world is being withdrawn from arsenals due to its appalling human, economic and social costs. And for the first time the use, development, production, stockpiling and transfer of a weapon are being prohibited in one decisive step. This reflects an important insight with implications for the future development of international humanitarian law.

Statement of Cornelio Sommaruga, president of the International Committee of the Red Cross, "A Global Ban on Landmines: Treaty Signing and Mine Action Forum," Ottawa, Canada, December 3, 1997

OBJECTIVE

The twentieth century ended with the entry into force of the Mine Ban Treaty (MBT), prohibiting anti-personnel landmines (APLs). The treaty was an incredible accomplishment: It was the "first time the majority of the nations of the world will agree to ban a weapon which has been in military use by almost every country in the world."[1] It also did not have the support of many major powers; unlike most multilateral disarmament agreements (see Table 1.1). Even as late as 1994, there was a consensus among all states that landmines were legal. In March 1995, Belgium became the first state to pass a domestic law providing for a comprehensive APL ban.[2] Less than thirty-two months later, on December 3–4, 1997, Belgium was joined by 121 states in signing the MBT.[3] On March 1, 1999, it became the fastest major multi-lateral weapons treaty ever to enter into force.[4]

Academics, diplomats, and representatives of non-governmental organizations (NGOs) consider the MBT's genesis and negotiations an innovative model for the future development of international law. Even the

Table 1.1

International Arms Control Conventions

Convention	Major Power Influence	Issue Initiator
1869 St. Petersburg Declaration	YES	Russia[a]
1899 Hague Conference	YES	Russia[b]
1907 Hague Conference	YES	Russia[c]
Biological Weapons Treaty	YES	Great Britain, USSR, United States[d]
Chemical Weapons Treaty	YES	Japan, Great Britain, United States, USSR[e]
Nuclear Non-Proliferation Treaty	YES	Canada, United Kingdom, United States[f]
Mine Ban Treaty	NO	NGOs

[a]Declaration Renouncing the Use, in Time of War, of certain Explosive Projectiles. Saint Petersburg, 29 November/11 December, 1868.
[b]Russian Circular Note Proposing the First Peace Conference, August 12, 1898, in James Brown Scott, *The Reports to the Hague Conferences of 1899 and 1907* (Oxford: Clarendon Press, 1917), 1–2.
[c]International Peace Bureau, http://www.ipb.org/org/history/history.html.
[d]On July 10, 1969, Great Britain became the first state to submit a plan to ban biological weapons. Two months later, the USSR proposed a similar plan, which included chemical weapons. The United States supported the British plan, which became the foundation for the Biological Weapons Convention. Arms Control and Disarmament Agency.
[e]Chemical Weapons Convention Proposals were floated by Japan (1974) and Great Britain (1976), but coordinated international action did not occur until bilateral talks broke down between the United States and USSR in the early 1980s, when each supported multilateral discussions. Organization for the Prohibition of Chemical Weapons, *Chemical Disarmament: Basic Facts* (Organization for the Prohibition of Chemical Weapons: The Hague, 1998), 5.
[f]On November 15, 1945, Canada, the United Kingdom, and the United States proposed the creation of the United Nations Atomic Energy Commission "for the purpose of 'entirely eliminating the use of atomic energy for destructive purposes.' " Arms Control and Disarmament Agency, http://www.acda.gov/treaties/npt1.htm.

Nobel Committee recognized this unique coalition by awarding the International Campaign to Ban Landmines (ICBL) and its coordinator, Jody Williams, the 1997 Nobel Peace Prize, in part for helping create a fresh form of diplomacy.[5] Specifically, the committee was referring to the fact that the MBT was initiated by NGOs and then driven by a unique partnership with mid-size states and international agencies during a fifteen-month period to develop political momentum toward prohibiting APLs, otherwise known as the Ottawa Process. Unlike most multilateral disarmament agreements, it did not have the support of major powers such as China, Russia, and the United States.

As evidenced by the Nobel Peace Prize, there has been tremendous celebration of the international ban landmine movement's success. There is also much ambiguity, however, in determining the reasons it was successful. At first glance, the claim that mid-size state and NGO collaboration played an important role in the creation of the MBT may not appear unique, but there are very few comprehensive single volume studies that have analyzed and traced a successful state and NGO coalitional effort that eventually cumulated in international law.[6] More broadly, analysis and research of the NGO role in working with states, especially those that are mid-size, on security and weapons issues are minimal. In addition, the role in this case of a partnership between mid-size states and NGOs, and the conclusion of the MBT in the absence of sponsorship by a hegemon and in the absence of support from leading states, constitutes a substantial challenge to international relations theories that suggest hegemonic leadership is necessary for regime formation.

This book reveals the critical role that NGOs played in facilitating the MBT prohibiting APLs and how they enhanced their credibility in an area traditionally at the heart of state sovereignty—weapons procurement and use. While banning weapons may not be unique in international relations, this book explores how NGOs emerged as a powerful force in the process and developed partnership with mid-size states in order to achieve an effective MBT.

Cynics have commented that the achievements of the MBT mean little because major states, which were the primary producers, exporters, and users of APLs, did not sign it. While there is an element of truth in this observation, it does not resolve the puzzle of how NGOs and their partnership with mid-size states were successful despite their focus on banning a popular weapon with opposition by major states.[7] In addition, the MBT has had a significant impact on alleviating the humanitarian suffering caused by landmines. For example, Dennis Barlow, who was the Director of Humanitarian Policy in the Office of the U.S. Secretary of Defense and the first leader of the Humanitarian Demining Task Force in the Pentagon, believes that

> [t]he MBT has undeniably had an incredible effect on tamping down the use of APLs globally. Even the casual or jaded observer would have to admit that the chill in manufacturing, transfer, and use of APLs is directly or indirectly attributable to the Ottawa Treaty. Further, the treaty has developed an oversight system for the destruction of landmine stockpiles, which generally have been eliminated in a transparent and pervasive global context. But I think the real value of the MBT was that it signposted the way for international cooperation among diverse—and sometimes antagonistic—players. I cannot think of any other worldwide challenge

which has been met by the kind of cooperation, communication, and coordination which has hallmarked its efforts.[8]

The book also provides a starting point for studying the role of NGOs in global security issues. This is especially important now as there has been a tremendous flurry of NGO and mid-size state collaborations focusing on challenging state security practices, such as prohibiting cluster munitions, restricting small and light weapon use, and bringing greater clarity and transparency to the arms trade.[9] The broader implication of this study is that, under certain conditions, NGOs and possible partnerships with mid-size states may contribute to creating international legal rules, which in turn can change state behavior. One of the book's practical policy implications is that NGOs may be needed on international issues that governments are unwilling and unable to address unilaterally, especially if there is major state opposition. More importantly, these lessons can portend the potential success or failure of these important initiatives, which are, in general, not initiated, but opposed by major powers, such as the United States, Russia, China, and India (Table 1.1).

The MBT is unique in history. It bans a weapon in widespread use, and it is a blend of arms control and international humanitarian law. It is also the first time that civilized society has found a partnership with governments around the world to eliminate a conventional weapon. The treaty requires both negative and positive sanctions. Negative sanctions include no production and use, and positive sanctions include destruction of stockpiles, de-mining, and victim assistance.The remainder of this chapter provides a brief overview of the grounding of the international landmine-ban movement and the process by which it achieved the prohibition. Each of these topics will be covered in more detail in subsequent chapters.

ARMS-PROHIBITION BACKGROUND

As far back as we can go, we see that war is tremendously brutal: from the Mongol curved sword scimitar designed to slash victims from horseback to the use of catapults by Byzantine and Muslim forces to launch Greek fire and containers full of lime to choke the enemy. Long since the days of these weapons, military forces have embraced technological advances that have brought dizzying changes to warfare. With the advances have come new temptations for military leaders to gain an unfair advantage.

The law of armed conflict will always wrestle with the unclear balances between military demands and humanitarian standards. Yet after every war, the global community fields complaints from governments and civil society about many tactics and weapons. In addition to these developments, there have been commensurate efforts as far back as we can go to reduce the violence of war through controls, prohibitions, and restrictions.

If a persistent problem is identified, the international community, in most cases and in one form of another, suggests changes to rules. Banning certain weapons for humanitarian reasons is not unique in international politics. For example, the Laws of Manu prohibited Hindus from using poisoned arrows, while the Greeks and Romans customarily observed a similar prohibition. The Lantern Council of 1132 declared that the cross-bow and arbalest were "unchristian" weapons. Modern codification of humanitarian law is based on the 1868 St. Petersburg Declaration when Russia hosted a multilateral conference that produced an agreement banning bullets weighing less than 400 milligrams. Nearly thirty years later, the global community convened at the 1899 Hague Peace Appeal Conference to ban certain weapons that were indiscriminate and caused unnecessary suffering through declarations that called for the banning of exploding bullets and chemical gas, and the cessation of the practice of dropping explosives from hot air balloons. In 1925, states signed a treaty further calling for a chemical weapons ban. Between the 1949 Geneva Conventions and the 1997 MBT, two international agreements banned whole categories of weapons. The first international agreement banning not just the use but the production, stockpiling, and transfer of a whole category of weapons was the 1972 Biological Weapons Convention (BWC). It was the first time the global community banned a whole category of weapons, not just their use. The second international agreement was the 1992 Chemical Weapons Convention (CWC), which banned the development, production, possession, and use of chemical weapons.

So on the one hand, we understand that war is brutal, and on the other you have groups of people trying to reduce the harm caused by wars. The principles of modern international humanitarian law are housed in the 1949 Geneva Conventions. They strive to limit the effects of warfare by distinguishing between non combatants and combatants by establishing the principle of proportionality, and by prohibiting the use of weapons that cause superfluous injury or unnecessary suffering.

In addition to weapon prohibitions, this time period also witnessed the development of further restrictions on the use of weapons and tactics. One of these major principles of international humanitarian law is the distinction between civilians and soldiers that was originally outlined in the fourth Convention of the 1949 Geneva Conventions.[10]

THE INTERNATIONAL MOVEMENT TO BAN PERSONNEL LANDMINES

The subject of this book are APLs, which are time-delay weapons that are target-activated, typically by pressure-sensitive fuses or tripwires. They are primarily used by armed forces to channel, delay, or restrict enemy movement and are usually manually planted below the ground

Photograph 1.1

Chinese Type 72 anti-personnel mine. To the left. The mine as it appears when new compared with the current appearance (right) in Cambodia. (Courtesy Colin King. Used by permission.)

(see photo 1.1), placed above ground, usually with trip wires (see photo 1.2), or scattered by air vehicles, such as missiles or planes. When detonated, APLs rely on fragmentation or blast to induce casualties. Some APLs, when triggered, shoot up from the ground and explode to create casualties in a circular area, usually killing the individual responsible for pressuring the mine and injuring others in the radius.

Beginning in the early 1960s, the modern military scene started changing as guerrillas, liberation fighters, rebels, and warlords started using landmines more frequently and for wider purposes. The users typically were non-state actors in civil wars, and training and recordkeeping were poor. Regardless of the user, most APL use dramatically affected noncombatants, both at the time of use and, more seriously, after the hostilities had ceased.

- The genesis of APLs as a contested issue started in the nineteenth century during the American Civil War. In 1864, Union General William Sherman witnessed one of his officers losing his leg to a primitive landmine and commented that its utilization "is not war but murder."[11]

Photograph 1.2

PMR-2A—The Yugoslav PMR-2A is a stake mine; basically a grenade on a stick, initiated by a trip wire. This mine was photographed in Kosovo. (Courtesy Colin King. Used by permission.)

- The potential long-term humanitarian problem caused by landmines were also somewhat recognized in the Allies' Armistice Demands on November 10, 1918, stating that the Germans had an obligation for the "clearance of mine fields and occupation of all forts and batteries, through which transit could be hindered."[12]
- Landmines drew attention in the early 1950s, when the ICRC conducted discussions on preventing the great damage to civilian during World War II and the increase production in the armaments industry. [13]
- The introduction of APLs as an issue on the international arms control agenda took place in the 1970s, when the ICRC hosted discussions on a range of weapons that eventually produced the two 1977 Additional Protocols.

The landmine-ban issue was born when NGOs and international agencies operating in developing countries identified landmines as a major obstacle to their work and decided to cooperate to prohibit their use. They viewed APLs as hindering post-conflict reconstruction, seriously undermining infrastructure, and denying land to civilian use. They also considered landmine use a violation of humanitarian legal principles, in part because they cannot target their victims. According to the International Committee of the Red Cross (ICRC), landmines killed or injured more than 24,000 people every year in the 1990s, which by itself may not be illegal, but a significant number of the victims are civilians.[14] In 1993, American Red Cross President, Elizabeth Dole, called for an end to the indiscriminate use of APLs estimating that "[e]ach month, 800 people are killed and 450 people injured by landmines" including "[l]ittle children" that are "maimed, long after the fighting is over, by landmines that are scattered like deadly toys where they live and play" (see photo 1.3).[15]

Even the U.S. government highlighted the global APL crisis when the State Department estimated that between 59 million and 69 million APLs were deployed worldwide thereby making them "one of the most toxic and widespread pollution[s] facing mankind."[16] For example, nearly eleven years after the 1979 Soviet withdrawal from Afghanistan, where APLs were indiscriminately and randomly used, 150 to 300 civilians were still being injured by landmines each month, resulting in nearly 4 percent of the country's population being disabled by mines and unexploded ordinance (UXO).[17]

Photograph 1.3

Elizabeth Dole, president of the American Red Cross, hosted a press conference, featuring Princess Diana and Ken Rutherford, to raise half a million dollars for landmine victims. Headquarters of the American Red Cross, Washington, D.C., June 17, 1997. (Courtesy of author.)

Although it is not as codified as humanitarian law, international environmental law may also provide a legal basis to ban landmines.[18] These environmental legal rules were violated during the 1991 Gulf War in Kuwait and Iraq, where direct and indirect damage to the environment, some of which is irreversible, was caused by the use of landmines.[19]

Arguments were also made that APLs are destroying one of the earth's most critical and fragile resources—its agricultural land. Areas infested with APLs become economically unproductive and uninhabitable (see photo 1.4). In Cambodia, it was estimated that nearly 25 percent of the country's most fertile areas are not cultivatable because of landmines.[20] While in Afghanistan, nearly a decade after the Soviets withdrew and major fighting had ceased, "more than 223 square kilometers of Afghanistan's agricultural land has been contaminated with landmines," which is all the more critical when only 12 percent of the country's land area is cultivatable.[21]

By no means are agriculturalists the only labor grouping affected by the environmental damage caused by APLs. Nomadic populations are just as likely to be negatively affected as farmers are (see photo 1.5). In Afghanistan, the Kuchi nomads interviewed for a study reported animals lost to APLs equaled 60 percent of the then-current stock.[22] Also in northern Somalia,

Photograph 1.4

The desperate need—as soon as it is cleared, people cultivate the land. Luena, Angola 1995. (Courtesy Sean Sutton. Used by permission.)

Photograph 1.5

Deminer and Flock: The man in the foreground was removing an anti-tank mine. Musa Qala is in the desert northwest of Kandahar, Afghanistan. The entire area is irrigated by a qarez system. Underground water channels bring the water for miles under the desert from a point on the slopes of a mountain, where the water table rises high enough to be tapped. These underground tunnels are also useful for guerilla warfare. A great deal of the destructive impact of the Mongol invasions was their systematic destruction of the irrigation systems. (Courtesy Luke Powell. Used by permission.)

the traditional nomadic pasture lands "are littered with camel carcasses, and stone mounds mark the graves of herders."[23]

Nevertheless, until NGOs formed the ICBL, APLs and mine warfare remained "a relatively unknown subject outside the mine community."[24] The ICBL's goal was to create a "strong public and professional taboo—to stigmatize the APLs and remove it from the world's arsenals."[25] At the time, most government officials dismissed that as a utopian dream. Some in the defense establishment countered that "[m]ine warfare is important because it is likely to be used in the future even if strategic deterrence successfully prevents nuclear war."[26]

Little did they all know that during the next five years, APLs would explode on to the international political scene, forever changing how global politics is conducted. According to Mark Gwozdecky, Coordinator of the Mine Action Team in the Canadian Department of Foreign Affairs and International Trade (DFAIT), and central to the MBT negotiations, the international arms control agenda "was bare of anything new and important" and therefore arms control negotiators were undistracted from the NGO call for an APL ban.[27] At the time, he says that

> [t]here was no meaningful negotiation happening after late 1996 when the Ottawa Process got going. Every bureaucrat can argue that one is working busily on things but in fact there was little more than mopping up activity going on with regard to Chemical Weapons Convention (CWC) and Conventional Test Ban Treaty (CTBT) and certainly nothing as globally important as the APL convention negs [negotiations].[28]

John Borrie, a New Zealand diplomat, at the time is also supportive of the main point being made here:

> Many talented disarmament practitioners could see the limitations of Cold War era ways of doing disarmament and arms control, and became receptive to news approaches like the Ottawa process as these obstacles became glaringly apparent in the context of AP II [Additional Protocol II also known as the Landmines Protocol] negotiations. In other words, the agenda was a lengthening one—the challenge was how to move on it.[29]

It was difficult for the ICBL and ICRC to change people's thinking about a weapon that had been widely used for decades. But the idea for a MBT prohibition sprang from failure of the consensus-based Convention on Conventional Weapons (CCW) that restricted, but did not prohibit, landmine use.[30] The attitudinal shift among several governments is reflected in their changing discourse concerning landmines. Rather than discussing the military aspects of mine use, much of their language focused on victims and the negative humanitarian effects. Opening up the debate to humanitarian discussion allowed significant access to the public policymaking process for non-traditional foreign and security policy actors, such as foreign affairs and development officials, humanitarian and religious groups. Their humanitarian focus, based primarily on experience in the field, gave them credibility in the discussions. The humanitarian focus of their arguments also allowed them to deflect criticism claiming that they were playing politics with national security.

The effects of APLs—from emplacement to injury—are obvious. According to a leading academic scholar on how and why weapons are addressed by society, APL injuries are "unlike the more often complex attributions of responsibility for other tragedies such as starvation."[31] The short chain between cause and effect allows parameters of the discussion to be narrowed. Moreover, the solution to the APL problem is relatively easy to understand for diplomats—"ban landmines"—thereby also making it easier for state diplomats to manage.[32] One prominent NGO activist wrote that because "the impact of the use of APLs is visible and shocking," the ICBL

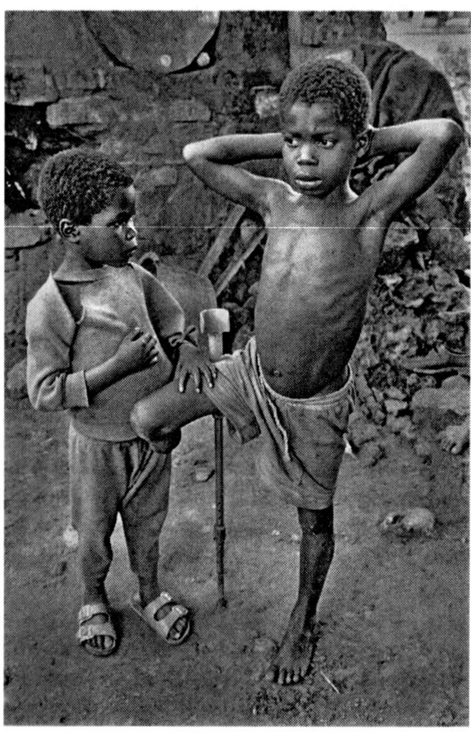

Photograph 1.6

Many towns in Angola were surrounded by minefields denying people access to land, food and water. Edwardo nearly died after stepping on a mine. (Courtesy Sean Sutton. Used by permission.)

was able to generate "public opinion which has been so important in moving governments to taking action of the APL problem."[33] The impact was enhanced by the stories detailing bodily harm to landmine victims, who were typically innocent civilians, injured by landmines while performing daily, but necessary tasks for survival (see photo 1.6).

Another important factor in the rise of the APL issue was how the ICBL and ICRC expanded the debate to address the security of both combatants and noncombatants; previous APL discussions had been confined to combatant security in a range of battlefield situations. Even though they realized that APL retained a military utility, the ICBL and ICRC wanted to concentrate efforts on the humanitarian consequences of APL use. A major challenge facing the ICBL and ICRC was overcoming government and military opposition to prohibiting mines. They are inexpensive and easy to learn how to use, making them appealing to cash-strapped governments and militaries, but they are also expensive to clear since personnel need to be trained and equipped to do the work. According to ICBL Coordinator Jody Williams:

> Manufactured cheap Chinese mines [sell for] three dollars. The average cost of removing the mine [is] $300 to $1,000 per mine. [That is], by the time you train

the people, by the time you supply them with the equipment, by the time you deploy the hole system and the logistics of setting up a national de-mining program. On the other hand, if you destroy those 100 million mines while they are still in stockpiles of the world, a dollar a mine is the average.[34]

Yet another factor drawing attention to APLs is that technological advances in deployment capabilities allowed for thousands of APLs to be deployed in minutes and that the mine users were either unwilling, unable, or not trained to consider the effects of mine use in civilian areas or post-conflict effects. For example, Patrick Blagden, a UN demining expert, said that in his thirty-four years in the British Army, the post-conflict effects of APL use were neither discussed nor taught.[35]

By the early 1990s, it became evident to many NGOs working in APL-infested areas that the protocol was not working properly. Increasing civilian APL casualties and land denial due to APL infestation indicated that states and other international actors had disregarded the Protocol and that it was an inadequate response to the growing humanitarian crisis caused by APLs. It was also evident to the NGOs that major states opposed addressing the landmine-ban issue in a multitude of national, regional, and international forums, such as the Conference on Disarmament (CD).[36] In April 1996, the First CCW Review Conference in Geneva ended without significant movement toward a ban.

The First CCW Review Conference ended with the adoption of the amended landmines protocol in May 1996.[37] The amendment included "extending its scope of application to cover both international and armed conflicts, by prohibiting the use of non-detectable APL and their transfer, and by prohibiting the use of non-self destructing and non-self-neutralizing mines outside marked areas."[38] While the amended protocol was the best that could be achieved under consensus rules, the ICBL and ICRC decided that a non-consensus negotiating forum outside the UN auspices provided a better avenue to achieving a global ban quickly.[39] Steve Goose of Human Rights Watch and one of the major ICBL leaders stated, "[y]ou don't have to follow or work through the traditional rules and become a 'slave' to UN negotiations. It is possible to step outside the boundaries of traditional diplomacy."[40] The ICBL did not want to be held to the UN consensus-based rule system, which holds "treaty negotiations to the lowest common denominator."[41]

In October 1996, Canada, with the ICBL and ICRC's support, announced that it would host a landmine strategy conference in Ottawa. This conference launched the "Ottawa Process," which entailed fourteen months of government and NGO negotiations, which eventually cumulated in the signing of the MBT. The conference was attended by more than 50 states, all of which recognized "the urgency of halting all new deployments of APLs; increasing resources for mine-awareness, clearance and victim assistance programs; and concluding as soon as possible a legally binding international agreement to ban APLs, the first draft of which Austria undertook to produce."[42]

At the conclusion of the October 1996 meeting, Canadian Foreign Minister Lloyd Axworthy called for a conference to be held in December 1997 in Ottawa that would conclude with a comprehensive treaty banning APLs. Those states not supporting the treaty, either through the continued opposition to a ban or their support for an alternative forum such as the CCW or CD, were isolated by the "self-selection" process developed by Canadian officials who wanted to prevent diplomatic sabotage of the conference.

The new negotiating format was devised by a core of the "Core Group," with the Canadians and Norwegians playing lead roles in partnership with the ICBL and ICRC. The format was important because it allowed for those governments, especially mid-size states opposing their cold war major-state allies, to join together and sign the MBT without being blocked by veto of other states. Ironically, the UN stepped in to support the Ottawa Process rather than its own negotiating forums and in contravention of a majority of the permanent members of the UN Security Council. In fact, UN Secretary-General Boutros Boutros-Ghali's surprisingly strong statements criticizing the slow pace of the CCW Review conferences in fall 1995 and spring 1996 helped to add a sense of legitimacy and urgency to creating a non-UN track to ban landmines. He clearly stated that he desired a comprehensive ban to emanate from the conference:

> I wish to state again that we must eliminate landmines once and for all! We must ban their use! We must ban their production! We must destroy those that are stockpiled![43]

Boutros-Ghali's replacement as UN Secretary-General, Kofi Annan, continued to support an alternative APL-ban process rather than relying on the CCW and CD. By the time Annan became Secretary-General in 1997, the international movement to ban landmines was already under way. Rather than show irritation or disappointment in a non-UN process, Annan appeared quite pleased with the MBT.[44] At its signing, Annan stated that "I am proud and privileged to assume the duties of depositary of the Convention [MBT] and pledge to carry out this responsibility with passion and care."[45]

MAJOR STATE OPPOSE THE MINE BAN TREATY

According to the Political Science neo-realist school of international relations, the MBT achievement despite opposition by major states is understandable.[46] The end of bipolarity and the beginning of a multipolar international system signal the onset of irresponsible behavior by small and mid-size states because these governments no longer feel beholden to major states. Those states banning APLs are showing a lack of concern for their own security by not following the lead of the non-signatory major states, such as China, Russia, and the United States. By banning the use of APLs—weapons that retain a military utility on the battlefield—these states are acting foolishly. Meanwhile, major states continue to feel responsible for their own security requirements and therefore refuse to give up APLs. While most smaller and mid-size states support the MBT, major powers, such as China, India, Pakistan, Russia, and the United States, did not sign because it was perceived not to be in their interest to do so (see Table 6.4 in chapter six).

According to these scholars, the MBT is mitigating or, in other words, not significant. A leading member of the neo-realist school, Kenneth Waltz, argues that "[a] general theory of international politics is necessarily based on great powers" and "[s]o long as major states are major actors, the structure of international politics is defined in terms of them. States set the scene in which, they, along with non-state actors, stage dramas or carry on their humdrum affairs."[47] He also predicts that a multipolar system will be even more unpredictable than a bipolar system because major powers have less flexibility to balance the system, and weaker states have greater flexibility to act irresponsibly concerning their security interests.[48] According to this analysis, therefore, a treaty without major power support is meaningless. It contends that major states may not participate directly in the affairs of weaker states, but they "nevertheless set the terms of the intercourse, whether by passively permitting informal rules to develop or by actively intervening to change rules that no longer suit them."[49] In the meantime, weaker states "enjoy the freedom of the irresponsible since their security is mainly provided by the efforts of others."[50]

What is so important about the characteristics of the mid-size state and NGO partnership in the Ottawa process that resulted in the MBT is that it has changed state behavior in an area traditionally at the heart of state sovereignty: military methods and weapons. Contrary to neo-realist explanations, once mid-size states, international agencies, and NGOs established APL use as inhuman and uncivilized, their actions affected state behavior, including that of major powers, toward APLs. In addition, governments, such as Canada, banning APLs had to have conducted serious deliberations regarding how they would continue to assure their own security once foregoing mines."[51]

Some, however, may question the ban's effectiveness because the major states, which are the world's largest APL producers and users, did not sign. While it is true that China and Russia did not sign, most of the other major landmine producers have stopped production. This belies a rationalistic explanation that only states that did not produce them agreed not to sell them. Specifically, within two years of the MBT signing, the number of states producing landmines has:

dropped dramatically from 54 to 16. The 38 who have stopped production include a majority of the big producers in the 1970s, 1980s, and early 1990s—those who bear much of the responsibility for the tens of millions of mines now in the ground. Eight of the twelve biggest producers and exporters over the past thirty years have signed the treaty and stopped production: Belgium, Bosnia, Bulgaria, Czech Republic, France, Hungary, Italy, and the United Kingdom. Other significant producers that have signed include Germany, Croatia, Chile and Brazil.[52]

Even though the major states did not sign the treaty, mid-size state and NGO pressure, enforced by public opinion, encouraged them to unilaterally implement certain APL policy changes. Even as they continued to state their opposition to the MBT, the major states have instituted unilateral APL policy changes that closely reflect the MBT's objectives (see Table 1.2).

Table 1.2

Major States Changing Landmine Policies Since ICBL Founding in 1991

Major State	Treaty Position	Change in Landmine Policy Since ICBL Founding
China	Non-signatory	Unilateral landmine export moratorium.[a]
India	Non-signatory	Support for ban on all landmine transfers.[b]
Pakistan	Non-signatory	In light of humanitarian concerns, Pakistan observes "high standard of regulating use."[c]
Russia	Non-signatory	Unilateral landmine export moratorium.[d]
United States	Non-signatory	1. Unilateral landmine export moratorium.[e] 2. Cap on landmine stockpiles.[f] 3. Cessation of landmine use in 2006 if "suitable alternatives to APLs and mixed munitions" are identified and fielded.[g]

[a]"The Issue of Anti-Personnel Landmines," China National Defense White Paper, *op. cit.*
[b]"India Calls for Int'l Consensus on Banning Landmines," Xinhua English Newswire, November, 15, 1998.
[c]BBC Worldwide Monitoring Source, Radio Pakistan external service, March 17, 1999.
[d]"Yeltsin affirms support for ban on mines," Reuters, October 29, 1997, http://www2/nando.net/newsroom/ntn/world/102097/world6_468_norrames.htm; "Landmines: A media round-up," British Broadcasting Service, December 2, 1997, http://news.bbc.co.uk:80/hi/english/world/monitoring/newsid_36000/36510.stm.
[e]"Suspension of Transfers of Anti-Personnel Mines," U.S. National Defense Authorization Act for Fiscal Year 1993, U.S. Federal Register, Volume 57, p. 228, November 25, 1992.
[f]Statement by the Press Secretary, The White House, May 16, 1997.
[g]President Clinton letter to Marissa A. Vitagliano, August 31, 1998.

Such unilateral policy announcements reflect a nonconventional approach to international law, and, in particular, seem to bode well for the MBT's potential effectiveness. These actions, especially from major states, are caused by "the failure of the international legal system, coupled with fundamentally changed circumstances since the time when the relevant texts were agreed." [53] While the major states thought they had unique military responsibilities requiring APL use, after the MBT signing they implemented more restrictive APL policies, thus signaling movement toward supporting the MBTs objectives.

GOING FORWARD: BOOK OVERVIEW

This book is the first comprehensive, single-volume narrative of the global movement to ban APLs. There have been other publications on this movement, but not in a comprehensive manner as discussed here. The edited volume, *To Walk Without Fear*, provides an excellent campaign analysis from an insider's perspective for governments, NGOs, and academics, but the effort was not chronologically or organizationally connected, as it told individual stories and experiences without linking the different chapters. In 2004, I co-edited *Landmines and Human Security: International Politics and War's Hidden Legacy* for SUNY Press, whose contributors included activists, scholars, government officials, and journalists providing their own individual insights, but there was not a chronological or organizational linkage among the chapters. Similarly, ICBL and USCBL leaders, Jody Williams, Steve Goose and Mary Wareham co-edited *Banning Landmines: Disarmament, Citizen Diplomacy and Human Security* that includes a range of contributors that primarily focus on selected issue-areas, such as implementation and compliance, during the first ten years after the MBT entered into force.

In 2000, ICRC lawyer Louis Maresca and consultant Stuart Maslen, co-edited *The Banning of Anti-Personnel Landmines: The Legal Contribution of the International Committee of the Red Cross 1955–1999*, a massive legally detailed volume of ICRC history with APLs, and in 2004, Maslen produced an excellent legal analysis in *Mine Ban Treaty*.

This book focuses on explaining how and why the APL issue rose on the world's political agenda in the late 1980s and intensively negotiated in the mid-1990s, especially since there was never before a sustained effort to ban APLs. It provides a nice complement to Leon Sigel's *Negotiating Minefields: The Landmines Ban in American Politics*, which, as the title suggests, takes an informative U.S.-centric perspective on the politics of the global landmine ban movement. In this book, I cover the entire history of the global APL-ban movement from before the ICBL's formation in the early 1990s up until the MBT signing in 1997. I have not, however, gone in-depth into the history of mine use or beyond the MBT achievement in 1997.

The additional material required will be covered in a future book project, because to recount the history would only prove anticlimactic and detract from the strategic importance of APL-ban movement.[54] I made the exclusion in an effort to bring APLs to the forefront of global campaign politics and international law—a position I believe it justly deserves.

The book is organized in three sections: The first section, chapters two and three, focuses on voices from the field and details how the ICRC and ICBL brought the landmine issue to international attention. These chapters briefly examine the APL movement's origins, including the role of U.S. Senator Patrick Leahy in pushing the U.S. government to a leadership position during these early years of the movement. The APL issue was born when the humanitarian NGOs working in APL-infested states decided to form the ICBL and work with the ICRC after they identified APL as a major obstacle to their work. It describes how the global APL-ban movement generated international attention by frequently and prominently featuring landmine victims coupled with strong advocacy and research skills. It also highlights how working with high-profile individuals, the movement was able to change state conception of APL use in a very short time.

The second section, chapters four and five, details how the ICBL and ICRC recruited mid-size states to the movement's goals in order to build up the numbers of states supporting a ban, which could then counterweigh major-state opposition. Mid-size states, such as Austria, Canada, Norway, and Switzerland, were especially important to the coalition because they supported MBT drafting and, more importantly, funded many NGOs and the ICRC to conduct their landmine work. It also discusses the final MBT negotiations and challenges in ensuring a comprehensive treaty.

The book concludes with chapter six, which examines the global landmine movement from a broader political perspective focusing on its impact, if any, on international relations concerning the role of NGOs and weapons. If NGOs play a significant role in getting the international community to deal with the APL issue, it becomes more relevant to examine the conditions under which NGOs affect the international political agenda. The broader implication is that under certain conditions, NGOs can contribute to setting the international political agenda, especially in seeking to obtain legal prohibitions on weapons, which in turn can effect state behavioral changes.

The underlying importance is that there are many global issues that are important but that are never placed on the world's political agenda. The tentative conclusion, which will be described further in the book's final chapter, is that global movements comprised of NGOs may be a necessary but not sufficient condition. Friendly states were necessary to help get international issues addressed, but the actual negotiations were conducted by a relatively small group of individuals that worked well together across previous political divisions.

CHAPTER 2

The Founding of the Global Landmine Ban Movement

PART ONE: 1989–1991 VOICES FROM THE FIELD

The 1980 Convention on Conventional Weapons (CCW) Landmines Protocol was designed to reduce civilian casualties by limiting the ways anti-personnel landmines (APLs) could be used. Despite these limitations, APL use continued to grow—more than 65 million mines were deployed from 1980 to 1995—leading to increased civilian APL injuries.[1] The major causes of the widespread increase in landmine use were the development of delivery systems allowing professional armies to lay landmines quickly in a wide, unsystematic fashion through aerial deployment, and the increased use of APLs by nonprofessional military forces who manually laid landmines by the millions for surprise attacks and to disrupt civilian life.

The primary reason for the increase in civilian casualties is that a deployed APL will continue to function, or "attack," long after a conflict ends, and so victims are usually noncombatants getting on with their lives after the war rather than soldiers during the war. Finally, the APLs themselves are unable to distinguish between combatants and noncombatants or strike specific targets.

The dramatic surge in landmine causalities remained unnoticed by the global community for several reasons. First, landmines were killing and maiming people one by one or in small groups, mostly in developing countries. Second, most landmine accidents were taking place in rural areas after wars ended, which further distanced landmines from governments and the media. Third, much of the Cold War's armed conflict was fueled by the U.S.-USSR rivalry in their quest for zero-sum political victory. Fourth, during the Cold War, many non-governmental organization (NGO) and United Nations (UN) humanitarian personnel did not have access to APL-infested areas because of instability and politics; that left them either unaware of the problem or unable to properly assess the effects of landmine use.

Meanwhile, the legality of APL use was comparatively ignored because of increasing fears of nuclear war. Compared with other controversial weapons, such as biological and chemical weapons, poison gas, and nuclear weapons, landmine use remained an obscure issue for governmental policymakers until the early 1990s, when the alarm was sounded. According to Lt. Col. Burris M. Carnahan, there was only one U.S. military manual regarding the use of APL and international humanitarian law by the early 1980s.[2]

As an example of the ignorance of the humanitarian devastation caused by landmines at high government levels, a comprehensive 1991 APL study in Cambodia, which was one of the most heavily landmine-infested countries and home to the highest percentage of mine survivors in the world, concluded that "[n]o one interviewed during the trip, with the exception of Red Cross workers, had ever heard of the UN protocol on mines [Landmines Protocol]."[3]

World awareness of the landmine threat grew after the Cold War ended, when humanitarian personnel called attention to the tremendous civilian casualties caused by landmines. For the first time, humanitarian personnel were allowed to enter previously closed-off areas, such as Afghanistan and Cambodia, where most of the fighting had ended. To these few individuals operating in the field, it became clear that the Landmines Protocol was not achieving its objectives and that it needed to be revised or replaced by a new international law to protect civilians. They saw villagers killed and injured while trying to farm their mine-infested fields and herders suffering similar fates taking their animals to pastures littered with landmines. These first-hand and personal experiences relayed by relief and development personnel led to international action toward banning landmines. The humanitarian workers reported back to their headquarters in Geneva, New York, and other Western cities that even though the wars had ended, landmines continued to take lives and harm economic and political stabilization and reconstruction projects. For example, the International Committee of the Red Cross (ICRC)'s medical staff "began to sound the alarm, warning that the mines' impact on civilians had reached intolerable levels."[4] These workers also became the primary sources of APL information since they were the only people who had enough first-hand experience to have "dirt under their nails," according to one diplomat.[5]

For the next few years, the global community was continually shocked by the APL contagion. Increasingly, humanitarian work in mine-infested countries involved producing limbs, clearing ground, and caring for mine victims. The problem caught the attention of the media, which covered the medical challenges facing mine victims and difficulties confronting people working to clear mines.

Drawing much attention to the APL crisis were the refugee-repatriation efforts in Afghanistan and Cambodia in the early 1990s after their respective peace agreements. Complicating efforts to reduce mine casualties among returning refugees was the lack of mine awareness among personnel in the UN High Commissioner for Refugees (UNHCR). It was especially slow in addressing the APL issue despite the fact that the top ten countries hosting landmines (more than 45% of then-current estimates) also held 47 percent of UNHCR persons of concern, including refugees and internally displaced persons (IDPs).[6] Despite this fact, there was "little corresponding UNHCR literature on how landmines affect UNHCR persons of concern."[7]

The time marker for the beginning of the end of government ignorance on the global APL crisis was the April 1988 Geneva Accords settling the Afghanistan conflict. The task to rebuild Afghanistan fell to the UN Office for the Coordination of Humanitarian Affairs (UNOCHA), which immediately tried to address the repatriation needs of the tens of thousands of Afghan refugees in neighboring countries, especially Pakistan, who were unlikely to return or, if they did, would be physically threatened or killed by landmines.[8] According to an ICRC study in its hospital in Peshawar, Pakistan, that treated Afghan patients, in the last six months in 1992, more than "85 percent of the 528 mine-wounded were engaged, when wounded, in non-military activity such as farming, traveling between villages or tending cattle; 77 percent were returnee refugees."[9] Another ICRC medical study of its hospitals treating returning Afghan refugees also confirmed that landmines were devastating the UN's repatriation efforts:

> [I]n 1992 44 percent (1,530) of the wounded admitted (3,461) were due to mines. From April to July 1992, the proportion of mine-wound victims increased substantially on the Afghanistan border due to the partial return of refugees to Afghanistan encouraged by the fall of Kabul to the Mujhideen.[10]

Therefore, UNOCHA targeted the landmine infestation as a problem that needed to be solved in order to reach the peace accord's objectives. It was the first time in history that the landmine was recognized as a hindrance to peaceful reconstruction. According to Afghani Sharif Baaser, who is the UNICEF Program Specialist in Mine Action and Small Arms,

> [i]n Afghanistan, the mine impact became obvious as the UN and other humanitarian organizations started to expand their activities beyond the main cities.

It was the first time that the UN came across this problem. Aid delivery and other essential projects such as water and irrigation projects were blocked by landmines, and in a way the UN was dependent on demining to get its work done and therefore came up with innovative ideas and programs to solve the problem (see photo 2.1).[11]

One of the first humanitarian workers into Afghanistan was Rae McGrath, founder and director of the Mines Advisory Group (MAG), a UK-based organization that focused on demining and landmine-awareness programming. Based on his landmine-clearing experience, McGrath, with funding from the European Union (EU), started writing about the "deaths and injuries caused to innocent people, and the denial of ground for agricultural and other civilian purposes as a result of the presence of mines."[12] He also wrote an EU concept paper for humanitarian mine clearance that would utilize local resources. McGrath's previous military experience and renowned expertise with landmines and other munitions served as an important catalyst for getting many EU members and associated military officials on board with addressing the APL problem. Meanwhile, as McGrath and his MAG personnel were removing mines, mines were also turning up for sale in the Afghani bazaars, where locally lifted mines were being sold by desperate farmers for as little as fifty cents.[13]

Photograph 2.1

Sunrise at Kandahar: Minefield, Ward 6, Kandahar, Afghanistan, October 2000. (Courtesy Luke Powell, 2010. Used by permission.)

In 1991, MAG, released the *Afghanistan Mines Survey,* touted as the world's first "comprehensive survey of the impact of landmines on people, their animals, their agricultural land, irrigation systems, farming implements and access routes" (see photo 2.2).[14] The information provided the global community with the first comprehensive overview of the humanitarian devastation caused by APLs. McGrath categorized the Soviet use of APLs in Afghanistan as "a classic example of this genocidal tactic—in some areas virtually all mountain grazing land was remotely mined and the whole agricultural infrastructure bought to a halt by the wide-scale mining of fields, karez and surface irrigation systems."[15]

After the Afghan refugees started returning to a peaceful Afghanistan, the ICRC hospitals serving Afghans in Peshawar and Quetta, Pakistan, started witnessing huge increases in mine-injured as a percentage of the overall patient population and subsequently became beleaguered by the problems associated with landmine injuries. Other field studies concluded "that victims of mine blasts are more likely to require amputation" than other types of weapon injuries.[16] Another study found that mine victims are more likely to remain in the hospital longer.[17] These factors put other burdens on already stretched medical infrastructure in many developing countries where landmines were present.[18]

Photograph 2.2

Boys on Bicycles: Gabreel Village, Enjeel District, Herat, Afghanistan, April 30, 2003. According to Powell, "two boys on bicycles would have been quite the anachronism in Herat the 1970s." (Courtesy Luke Powell, 2010. Used by permission.)

For example, by 1995, nearly half the patients at the ICRC Peshawar hospital were mine victims, with civilians accounting for 34 percent and the majority being under the age of 16. More than 75 percent of the mine-injured patients claimed to be returning refugees, and 37 percent of these had returned in the three months before their mine injuries.[19]

The upsurge in mine casualties further depleted the already minimal medical resources in Afghanistan and along its border with Pakistan (see photo 2.3). On average, landmine injuries require more blood units and repeated surgical care than other munitions injuries.[20] The ICRC medical staff records showed that "[a]s many as 85 percent of all amputations performed in ICRC hospitals are for victims of landmines."[21] Moreover, 30 percent of landmine patients require blood transfusions averaging 120 units and 75 percent require blood transfusions averaging 320 units if they require an amputation. In contrast, only 15 percent of fragment injured patients require blood transfusions and, if they do, then they require around 50 units.[22] Another ICRC blood-use study of its hospitals "found that, overall, for every 100 wounded, 44.9 units of blood were required, while every 100 mine injuries required 103.2 units."[23] According to the ICRC, landmine

Photograph 2.3

Landmine Victim. Chil Stoon, Kabul, Afghanistan, October 2000. (Courtesy Luke Powell, 2003. Used by permission.)

victims are more likely to require amputation, which meant they were more likely to remain in the hospital longer (see photo 2.4).[24]

Soviet medical personnel in Afghanistan during the 1979–1988 occupation also came to the same morbid conclusion that landmine injuries were different from other munitions injuries. In addition to dying from the loss of blood and limbs to a mine blast, the Soviets learned that many mine victims died from shock and internal injuries. The Soviets became so well-read in treating mine injuries that they determined that a new way of treating mine injured patients was required. Soviet medical personnel

> [L]earned that normal treatment time periods may not apply and, although surgery was often necessary, it was better to make sure that the patient was stabilized before doing any surgery. The Soviets also discovered that performing multiple surgical procedures at the same time, though increasingly common under ideal circumstances, was not a good idea and should only be done by exception to save the patient's life. With landmine injuries, surgical procedures should be done sequentially, rather than simultaneously.[25]

The ICRC and other humanitarian groups operating in other countries had similar experiences with landmines. For example, in a cluster survey of 174,489 people living in 32,904 households in 206 communities in

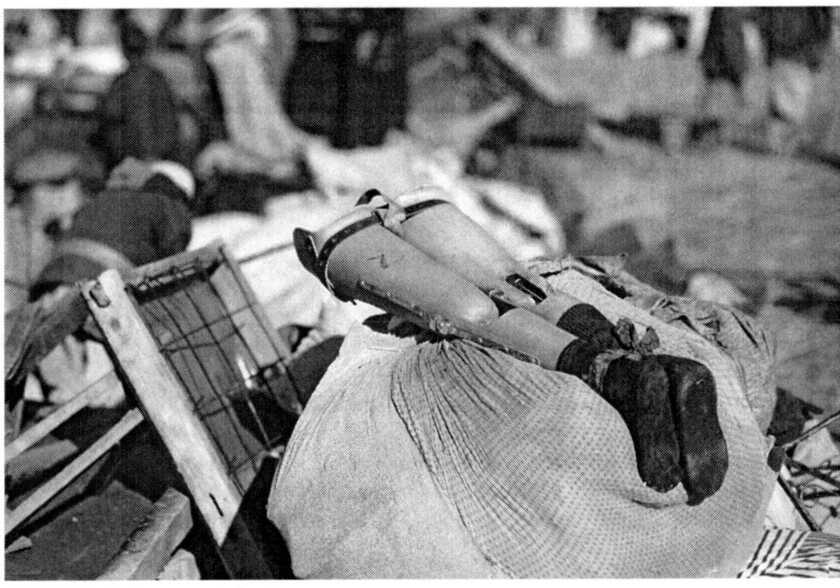

Photograph 2.4

Legs. Shamali Plain, Kabul Province, Afghanistan, 2002. (Courtesy Luke Powell, 2010. Used by permission.)

Afghanistan, Bosnia, Cambodia, and Mozambique, the study concluded that landmines "seriously undermine the economy and food security" and "kill and maim civilians at an increasing rate." The results found that

> "[b]etween 25 percent and 87 percent of households had daily activities affected by landmines. Based on expected production without the mines, agricultural production could increase by 88–200 percent in different regions in Afghanistan, 11 percent in Bosnia, 135 percent in Cambodia, and 3–6 percent in Mozambique. A total of 54,554 animals were lost because of landmines, with a minimum case value of $6–5m, or nearly $200 per household. Overall 6 percent of households (1964) reported a landmine victim; a third of victims died in the blast. One in 10 of the victims was a child."[26] In addition, the study found that "[i]ncidences have more than doubled between 1980–3 and 1990–3, excluding Bosnia."[27]

The ICRC also found that of the patients entering its hospitals in Afghanistan, the Pakistan-Afghanistan border, the Thai-Cambodian border, and Sudan from January 1991 to July 1998, more than 30 percent of the weapons injuries "occurred in the contexts other than inter-factional combat" and more than 42 percent of these patients were civilians. More specifically, of the 18,877 patients, 4,686 were mine injuries, of which 1,445 (30.8%) were civilians.[28] The ICRC hospital in Kabul had a higher proportion of mine-injured civilian patients with 262 of the 476 total patients having mine injuries. It should also be noted that those injured in the rural areas were usually admitted more than six hours after the injury and thus could potentially already be dead from blood loss or delayed medical care.[29]

Highlighting the global nature of the landmine problem, MAG expanded its mine-clearance operations in Afghanistan to northern Iraq. The logistical difficulty and political sensitivity of implementing the mine clearance operation were challenging.

> MAG started bringing metal detectors and other mine-clearance equipment in suitcases to the region through Syria. It would then ship the baggage over land and across rivers into northern Iraq. MAG also shipped equipment on a French Hercules plane that would arrive in the United Kingdom (UK) to pick up and deliver the MAG equipment, because the UK government didn't want to get involved at the time and would not offer air transport. At one point the UK government was not going to let the French plane take off and only allowed it do so after McGrath threatened to take the story to the media. In contrast, then-French President François Mitterrand's wife, Danielle, who was a strong supporter of the Kurds, intervened on behalf of MAG in order to get them their demining equipment.[30]

Meanwhile, the United States' largest private international private relief group, CARE, was also significantly and negatively affected by landmines. The landmines were causing humanitarian devastation in

46 of its 64 programming countries and severely hindering its ability to operate. For example, in one year four CARE staff were killed, and more than $425,000 worth of vehicles were destroyed in mine explosions.[31]

After Afghanistan, Cambodia became the next country to expose the landmine crisis to the global community. The October 23, 1991, Cambodia peace agreement signed in Paris ceasing decades of armed conflict created the opportunity to provide international development aid for war-affected communities, and indirectly address the global mine crisis. Similar to UNOCHA, which was designed to coordinate Afghan relief efforts, the UN established the UN Transitional Authority in Cambodia (UNTAC) to coordinate Cambodia's recovery; the authority also considered landmine infestation to be a major obstacle to achieving its work.

Compounding the landmine challenge for UN officials in Cambodia was the fact that the landmine crisis "was a relatively new issue for the United Nations in 1991 when it began planning for UNTAC's deployment in Cambodia."[32] According to a Canadian diplomat involved in the Cambodian landmine issue, "National contingents within UNTAC were reluctant to undertake the hazardous and costly task of mine clearance."[33] For example, in December 1991, UN officials wanted to repatriate more than 360,000 refugees from the Thai border camps, but they would not do it until the roads were clear of mines.[34] From 1984 to 1992, the ICRC's Khao-i-Dang Hospital on the Thai-Cambodia border witnessed 3,452 patients injured by mines.[35] According to Ratana Khun, Chief of Secretariat for the Public Cambodian Mine Action Center,

> UNTAC had come to Cambodia and found that the mine crisis was a major problem to proceed with elections and in hindering the development process after the election, so it decided to start mine clearance programs in 1992.[36]

With the peace agreement in place, there was freer movement of refugees and internally displaced persons back to their homes, and as a result, there was a dramatic spike in mine injuries. Soon after the official ending of fighting, the Battambang Orthopedic Centre treated 1,466 landmine injuries from October 1991 to July 1993.[37] In Mongkol Boreri in northwest Cambodia, 51 percent of the ICRC patients in the preceding four months of the peace agreement were mine-injured, while in the four months after the agreement this figure was increased to 61 percent.[38] In a *New York Times* op-ed, Joel Charny, the Asia regional director of Oxfam America, and Anne Goldfeld, a fellow at Harvard Medical School working with the American Refugee Committee (ARC) in the Thai-Cambodian refugee camps, wrote that "People risk eyesight, limbs and their lives foraging for something salable or edible in the minefields. As a Cambodian has said, you will know the Cambodian of the future by his one leg."[39]

The first major report on Cambodia's landmine crisis was *Landmines in Cambodia: The Coward's War* published in September 1991 by two U.S.-based NGOs, Asia Watch (a program within the Human Rights Watch (HRW) organization) and Physicians for Human Rights (PHR), an American organization representing about 5,000 physicians.[40] They issued their report jointly on landmines in Cambodia that the international community to consider "unconditional ban on the manufacture, possession, transfer, sale and use of land mines and other devices that detonate on contact in all international and internal conflicts."[41] After collecting and analyzing nationwide data from clinics and hospitals, they found that the wide-scale public health problem due to APLs resulted in Cambodia having "the highest percentage of physically disabled inhabitants of any country in the world." It also found that nearly 50 percent of APL victims died before reaching medical help, and that most landmine victims were civilians "who stepped on mines while gathering firewood, harvesting rice, herding animals, or fishing."[42] In addition to these grim statistics, they claimed that the "Cambodian conflict may be the first war in history in which landmines have claimed more victims—combatants and noncombatants alike—than any other weapon."[43]

The three-member team was also informed by a U.S. government-funded mine-clearance team that they "had dealt with 6,000 antipersonnel devices in a one-kilometer stretch of ground close to an old Vietnamese military post and 3,800 mines in another two-kilometer section."[44] One of the report's authors remembers when they sat in a hut in Cambodia "taking down interviews and gathering data, and we wondered aloud if we'd ever be able to raise people's consciousnesses about this terrible problem. We did."[45] They found that out of the country's "8.5 million inhabitants over 30,000 are amputees, and a further 5,000 or so amputees live in refugee camps along the Thai border."[46] In fact, one out of every 235 Cambodian was an amputee due to a mine injury.[47]

The report's authors also called upon the UN and ICRC to re-evaluate the effectiveness of the 1980 CCW landmine protocol and urged governments to "seek advice from representatives of relief, medical, de-mining and military organizations."[48] Furthermore, governments "should base their review on epidemiological data on the use of land mines and their effects on civilian populations in countries that have recently experienced or are in the grip of international or internal conflict."[49] After receiving a copy of *The Coward's War*, Prince Sihanouk of Cambodia called for an APL ban while speaking at the UN concerning the Cambodian Peace Agreement.[50]

Back in the United States, no one was talking about the landmine issue at the policy level until April 10, 1991, when Anne Goldfeld testified before the Asia Pacific Sub-Committee of the House Foreign Affairs Committee. She called for the immediate institution of a mine ban and urged the congress to formulate and adopt "[t]he outlawing the use of land mines as a weapon of war," thereby becoming the first American to call for a landmine ban before congress.[51]

Goldfeld's testimony came after she had returned to Cambodia from January 1–8 as part of a delegation with the Women's Commission for Refugee Women and Children 10 months after she had left the Thai-Cambodian border.[52] She would later write in the *New York Times*, "Because of heavy fighting between the resistance and Government, at least 180,000 Cambodians have been displaced. About 1,000 people a month area killed, mutilated, or blinded by landmines alone."[53]

The year before in the fall of 1989, Goldfeld, an infectious disease specialist and research fellow from Harvard University worked as the medical coordinator for the American Refugee Committee (ARC)'s program at the largest encampment of refugees along the Thai-Cambodian border, Site II. As resistance forces opened up mine infested and contested land outside the camp as their conflict with Cambodian government forces escalated, the mine injuries steeply increased and Goldfeld was at the front line of treating the wounded (see photo 2.5). As she would later write,

The first time I saw a landmine victim was in the fall of 1989 on the Thai-Cambodian border, where I worked as a doctor in a refugee camp. Although I had cared for

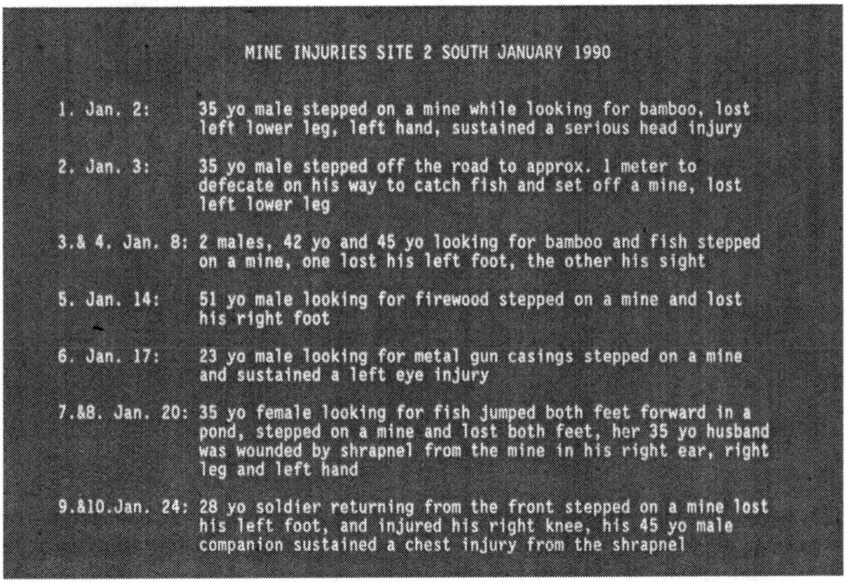

MINE INJURIES SITE 2 SOUTH JANUARY 1990

1. Jan. 2: 35 yo male stepped on a mine while looking for bamboo, lost left lower leg, left hand, sustained a serious head injury

2. Jan. 3: 35 yo male stepped off the road to approx. 1 meter to defecate on his way to catch fish and set off a mine, lost left lower leg

3.& 4. Jan. 8: 2 males, 42 yo and 45 yo looking for bamboo and fish stepped on a mine, one lost his left foot, the other his sight

5. Jan. 14: 51 yo male looking for firewood stepped on a mine and lost his right foot

6. Jan. 17: 23 yo male looking for metal gun casings stepped on a mine and sustained a left eye injury

7.&8. Jan. 20: 35 yo female looking for fish jumped both feet forward in a pond, stepped on a mine and lost both feet, her 35 yo husband was wounded by shrapnel from the mine in his right ear, right leg and left hand

9.&10.Jan. 24: 28 yo soldier returning from the front stepped on a mine lost his left foot, and injured his right knee, his 45 yo male companion sustained a chest injury from the shrapnel

Photograph 2.5

Documentation of land mine injuries in January 1990 in site 2 south on the Thai-Cambodian Border—the beginning of the global awareness campaign. (© Anne Goldfeld. Used by permission.)

many trauma victims during my medical training, nothing had prepared me for this terrible sight. Both of the men's legs were blown off and his upper leg bones stuck out jaggedly from surrounding flesh; a lower leg dangled by a tendon.[54]

To prevent further injuries, Goldfeld started one of the world's first known landmine-awareness programs for civilians, which was launched in January 1990 at Site II. She had illegally smuggled a camera into the camp and she remembers,

when a mine victim was brought to the Site II hospital on January 2, 1990, the medics blocked the doorways of the operating room so I could photograph the scene with no risk of being discovered by the Thai military. A young man had stepped on a mine while foraging for bamboo to sell and sustained devastating injuries to his legs, hand and head. All of us in the room were determined to somehow show the world the excruciating pain and senseless injury we were witnessing. When I showed the photos to the UNBRO [United Nations Border Relief

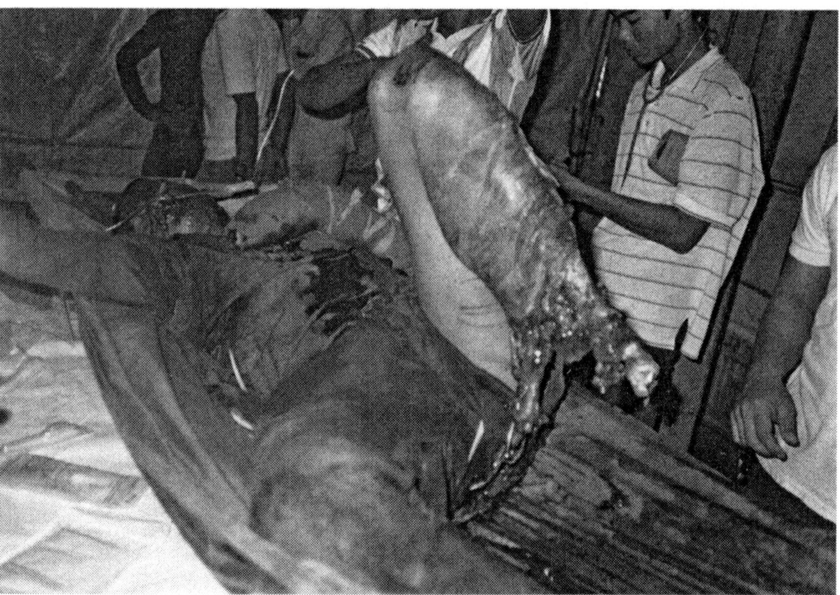

Photograph 2.6

The beginning of the mine injury prevention campaign. **A young man had stepped on a mine while foraging for bamboo to sell and sustained devastating injuries to his legs, hand, and head. The medics blocked the doorways of the operating room so Dr. Goldfeld could photograph the scene with no risk of being discovered by the Thai military. According to Goldfeld, "All of us in the room were determined to somehow show the world the excruciating pain and senseless injury we were witnessing." January 2, 1990. American Refugee Committee (ARC) site 2 south hospital on the Thai-Cambodian border. (© Anne Goldfeld. Used by permission.)**

Operation—Khmer Refugee camps on the Thai / Cambodia border] medical staff to urge them to do something about this, I was told this wasn't a medical problem. I was astounded. A Thai UN camp officer then helped me to enlist artists in the camp to paint large posters of the photos I had taken and these were posted around Site II's perimeter in an effort to help get the message to people in the camp of how dangerous it was to go outside the fence (see photo 2.6).[55]

The photos of persons injured by landmines were placed on fence posts "to remind people of the dangers that lie ahead with the purpose to educate people not to go beyond the fence to forage in mine fields."[56] Goldfeld "reasoned if they knew this is what happened to one of their neighbors, they would take it seriously."[57]

Susan Walker, also an American working with the refugee population along the Cambodia-Thai border, would translate her on the ground landmine experiences to advocate for a landmine ban by 1993. She was working as a rehabilitation specialist with the French-based NGO Handicap International (HI) helping to provide services to more than 5,000 Cambodian amputees, most of them mine victims (see photo 2.7). One of Walker's jobs was to prevent mine injuries, and she concluded that the best way "to prevent a mine accident—and it is not an accident, it does exactly what it is intended to do—is to ban landmines."[58]

Photograph 2.7

Victims include all persons directly impacted by landmines as well as their affected families and communities. Landmine survivor family near Battambong, Cambodia. 1996. (Courtesy of author.)

In recognition of her work with victims in the camps, the director of the HI prosthetic workshop presented Walker with a replica prosthetic leg of one of her favorite patients, a Cambodian girl who had lost a leg to an APL and learned to walk again with HI's assistance. Walker was told that "you will now leave us and we want you to take this as a remembrance of us . . . [and] [w]e ask you to go and tell the world to please not send us antipersonnel mines that kill and maim our children."[59] For nearly the next two decades, Walker carried the prosthetic leg to global landmine conferences advocating for an APL ban and victim assistance. Many times she shared the following story explaining her involvement:

> I have experienced the horror of a 34-year-old Cambodian man being killed by an antipersonnel mine 400 meters from me, leaving behind a wife and three small children and have carried a 19-year-old Cambodian boy to the hospital two hours after he was blown up by an AP mine. It is because of experiences like this that many of us are involved.[60]

In addition to being the training ground for Goldfeld and Walker, the mine infestation in Cambodia produced a leader that would start a global-movement culminating in a new international law prohibiting landmines. In November 1991, Bobby Muller, the founder of the Washington, D.C.–based Vietnam Veterans of American Foundation (VVAF), opened a prosthetics and orthopedics clinic and training program in Kien Khleang, near Cambodia's capital of Phnom Penh, to build prosthetics and train technicians to serve the country's large amputee population. The following year, VVAF opened a similar rehabilitation clinic for the physically disabled in Vietnam.

Approaching the landmine issue much like a scientist trying to prove a difficult theory, Muller started with an untested idea and brainstormed ways to make it work to create and implement effective policy to alleviate the landmine crisis. In the 1980s, he visited Cambodia and was shocked by the large numbers of landmine victims and the lack of medical care to serve them.[61] He commented that "Vietnam was brutal, but it wasn't the absolute insanity that took place in Cambodia. Here the landmine became the principal weapon of war."[62]

The discussions and arguments for a ban were ad hoc, scattered, and unorganized idealistic chatter until October 1991, when VVAF executive director Muller and Thomas Gebauer, director of the Frankfurt-based Medico International (MI) met for lunch at La Tomate, a small Washington, D.C., restaurant, near DuPont Circle. They talked about how their humanitarian work was hindered by landmines, and the possibility of banning their use. They also decided to make the first serious bid for a global movement to ban APLs. While their organizations conducted humanitarian work in Cambodia and El Salvador, where MI was conducting rehabilitation operations, they noticed something odd about their patients—they were being injured by landmines long after the wars had ended.

Muller had originally started VVAF in part to focus on helping to prevent the causes and alleviate consequences of war, but his organization's rehabilitative and prosthetic work faced serious challenges posed by landmines, igniting his desire to ban their use. Similarly, Gebauer's organization focused on helping people with disabilities in developing states. He also stated that APLs should be banned "on the grounds of the experience of war-disabled in Cambodia, Vietnam, El Salvador, and Kurdistan."[63] Both of them realized that the APL-ban idea was already floating in the international community, but nobody was acting on it, especially not in a coordinated fashion.

The following month, Gebauer and Muller agreed to explore the possibility of creating a global campaign to ban landmine by bringing "together the NGO voices that were increasingly being heard on the issue in a coordinated effort to ban landmines."[64] One of the factors pushing Mueller and Gebauer was the recent publication of *The Coward's War* coupled with Cambodian Prince Sihanouk's call for a ban. According to Muller, these events "propelled us to begin our campaign and take the position of a complete ban."[65]

Gebauer suggested that Muller hire as the campaign's coordinator Jody Williams, who was deputy director of the Los Angeles–based Medical Aid for El Salvador. At the time, she was developing and directing humanitarian relief projects. Muller invited Williams to "see about the possibility of grouping together a coalition of non-governmental organizations to try to do something about this evil weapon—landmines."[66] Williams accepted Muller's invitation, agreeing to a three-month contract. She viewed the campaign

> as a tool to deal with not only the landmine itself, but a means to address much broader issues of war and peace. It's a prism through which to look at the laws of war. It's a prism for how we are supposed to conduct ourselves in civilized nations. I just thought it was a marvelous way to expand my own thinking.[67]

Williams immediately started exploring the possibility of a global ban on APLs, forming an advisory board and a planning conference to launch the campaign.[68] After numerous calls, faxes, and meetings with NGOs and Tim Rieser, foreign policy aide to Senator Patrick Leahy, she concluded that there was support for a global APL ban campaign if someone would volunteer to organize and launch it.[69]

As it turned out, accepting Muller's offer to lead the ICBL was a historic decision for Williams and the world. She was the right person at the right time to lead the ICBL and to achieve tremendous political success. She had cut her advocacy and organizational teeth on the tough, and sometimes life-threatening, human rights work in Central America in the 1980s. While her work as ICBL coordinator would not be as life-threatening, it would prove to be tough and gritty.

PART TWO: 1992—THE PARTNERING OF THE MOVEMENT

VVAF and MI's call for a landmine ban was strengthened by ad-hoc statements and activities of other NGOs and organizations. As a result of its Afghan and Cambodian medical experiences, the ICRC decided that it had "to take a definite stand and become active on the issue."[70] In 1992, based on its medical field experience and pushed by its medical personnel in the field who were "operating, again and again and again on victims," most of whom "were not combatants," the ICRC began discussing the humanitarian problems caused by APL "with military commanders, diplomats, and legal and medical experts to develop a view of what could be done on the legal level."[71]

The ICRC contribution to the ICBL's call for a ban and working collaboratively was significant because Williams was worried "about stepping on anybody else's toes (such as the ICRC given their historic role in this kind of work) by being too strident about what we are doing."[72] By late spring 1992, events in France helped sustain the political momentum toward addressing the landmine issue. Handicap International (HI), a French NGO based in Lyon, experienced in providing medical treatment to civilian populations injured by landmines, including along the Thai-Cambodian border, called for a ban in May at a landmine conference it hosted in Paris. In doing so, it exceeded its mandate of helping "handicapped individuals who were victims of conflicts and/or in underdeveloped countries."[73] Nevertheless, the three HI co-directors decided that they no longer could ignore the indiscriminate use of landmines and the horrible injuries they inflicted on people where HI field projects were based.

At the conference, HI released an updated and French edition of *The Coward's War* and distributed it to all European Parliament members, including the president of the European Parliament, Simone Weil, two Belgian senators, who subsequently took up the APL ban cause in their respective legislatures, and to all French Parliamentarians through Michel Noir, who was the mayor of Lyon.[74] HI also initiated a call for the collection of signatures to "Stop the Coward's War" to persuade policymakers to support an immediate APL ban.[75]

After the May conference, ICBL Coordinator Jody Williams asked HI about its specific goals related to landmines and its interest in banning landmines. She also wanted to know if HI could "lobby the French government to call for an international conference to re-examine and amend the 1980 Convention on Conventional Weapons (CCW) including the Landmines Protocol."[76] HI agreed to Williams's request and subsequently acted as a "permanent link" among French "political leaders and high-ranking officials on one side, the media, public opinion and members of Parliament on the other."[77] During the summer of 1992, HI Director Philippe Chabasse met with French Foreign Ministry officials sympathetic to greater legal restrictions on mines. That meeting resulted in a ministry review of existing international humanitarian law, which concluded that the CCW offered the most promising avenues for further restricting the use of landmines.

Williams also continued to contact the UN and other international organizations, including the newly created UN Department of Humanitarian Affairs (UNDHA), and individuals from thirty-five mine-producing and mine-infested countries to create global political pressure to prohibit mines.[78] As an institution, the UN was slow to respond to the ICBL, but individuals employed by the UN were pleased to support the call to ban landmines. Secretary-General Boutros Boutros-Ghali, for example, wrote that it was increasingly "evident that peace building after civil or international strife must address the serious problem of landmines, many tens of millions of which remain scattered in present or former combat zones."[79] Also in early 1992, UNDHA hired former British military engineer and ordnance-clearance expert Paddy Blagden to develop a strategic plan for the UN's approach to the landmine issue.

By August, Williams had put together a committee of prominent individuals to serve as advisers for the campaign.[80] She also had secured commitments from a small group of key international non-governmental organizations (NGOs)—Handicap International (HI), Human Rights Watch (HRW), Mines Advisory Group (MAG), Medico International (MI), Physicians for Human Rights (PHR), and Vietnam Veterans of America Foundation (VVAF)—to agree to a landmine strategy meeting on October 6 in the New York City office of HRW. Also invited to participate at the New York meeting were two organizations that would play an important role in an APL ban years down the road, UNDHA and the ICRC. Both organizations did not think a ban was feasible despite the dangerousness of the landmine problem. For example, Yves Sandoz, the director of ICRC's Department of International Law and Relations, stated that in the near term the ICRC would focus on encouraging states to ratify the CCW Landmines Protocol because "for the ICRC to announce a prohibition is not possible, that is not the way we work."[81]

It was at this meeting that the decision was made to design "a public launching of the ban campaign" known as the International Campaign to Ban Landmines (ICBL).[82] The group's first major decision was approving VVAF's Jody Williams as the ICBL coordinator.[83] Muller had already hired Williams, who was primarily based at her home in Vermont, and provided office space in the VVAF Washington, D.C., office.[84] She quickly became the ICBL's dynamic, energetic, and unifying force. The central organizational features of the ICBL consisted of no overall budget, no permanent operations headquarters, no legal incorporation, and no permanent employees, except for Williams's position as coordinator, which VVAF funded with much of the fundraising done by Williams herself. In addition, no member could be directed to perform particular actions.

The participants agreed to coordinate campaigning efforts and co-sponsor the first NGO conference on landmines in London in 1993 and also called for the following:

- An international ban on the use, production, stockpiling, and sale, transfer, or export of APLs; and
- The establishment of an international fund, administered by the United Nations, to promote and finance landmine awareness, clearance, and eradication programs worldwide; and
- Countries responsible for the production and dissemination of APLs to contribute to an international fund.

The six founding members of the ICBL mirrored the wide range of problems caused by landmines around the world. (See Table 2.1). First, they had the ability to conduct landmine-specific research, as all were

Table 2.1

Founding ICBL Members and Their Expertise Areas

ICBL Founding Member	Landmine Expertise Area	Landmine Infested State Area	Country
Handicap International (HI)	Physical Rehabilitation	Cambodia, Vietnam, Mozambique	France
Human Rights Watch (HRW)	Human Rights (documenting impact on civilians, and laws of war)	Angola, Cambodia, El Salvador, Kurdistan, Mozambique, Nicaragua	USA
Medico International (MI)	Physical Rehabilitation	Angola, El Salvador	Germany
Mines Advisory Group (MAG)	Demining	Afghanistan, Cambodia, Kurdistan	United Kingdom
Physicians for Human Rights	Medical Support and Human Rights	Bosnia, Cambodia	USA
Vietnam Veterans of America Foundation (VVAF)	Physical Rehabilitation	Angola, Cambodia, Vietnam, El Salvador	USA

based or had access to operations in mine-infested states. They were also interconnected through their landmine expertise, such as prosthetic and de-mining programs, or legal and medical research. According to MAG's Rae McGrath, the ICBL was on a mission: "There was no theoretical opposition to arms or any sort of disagreement on what we are aiming at . . . we had already seen from our joint experiences in the field what the problem was and what the solution should be."[85]

Back at VVAF headquarters in Washington, D.C., Muller became fast friends with Senator Patrick Leahy, a Vermont Democrat, who also had become interested in the landmine issue. In 1985, Leahy and his wife, Marcelle, who is a nurse, visited the border of Honduras and Nicaragua, where they met a young Honduran boy who lost his leg to a landmine. The boy told the Leahys that he did not know who put the landmine there. In retelling the story, Senator Leahy said that it did not make any difference whose mine it was—that boy's life was ruined. Leahy immediately wanted to alleviate the suffering caused by APLs by assisting victims and supporting laws to curtail their use with the goal of eventually banning them.

After returning from Central America, Leahy studied the issue and made good on his promise to work toward restricting the U.S. use of

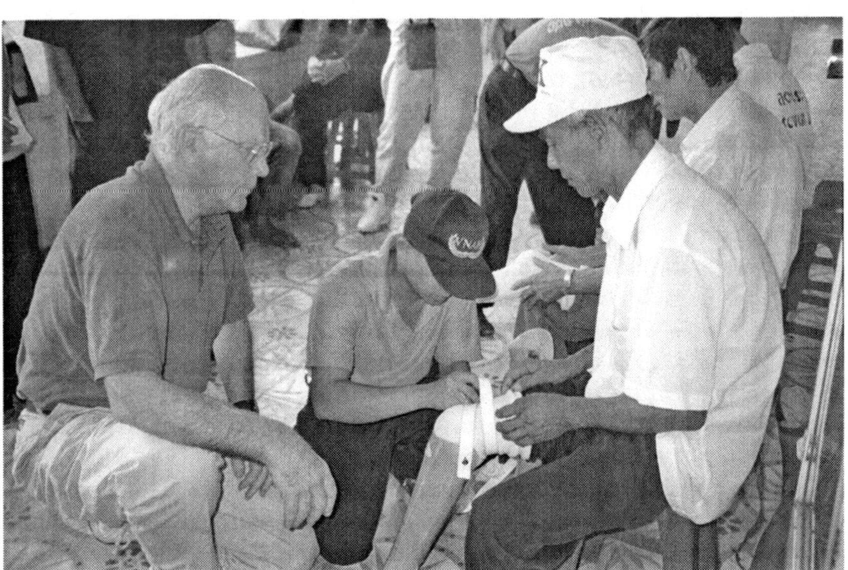

Photograph 2.8

Senator Patrick Leahy visiting landmine survivors at the Vietnam Assistance for The Handicapped, Project II, which was funded by the U.S. Agency for International Development. November 1996. (Office of Senator Patrick Leahy. Used by permission.)

landmines as a step toward a comprehensive ban. After speaking to his senior foreign policy aide Tim Rieser, a key member of his staff, about his experience with landmines and ways to help war victims, Leahy soon introduced legislation in Congress to start a fund for war victims. That resulted in the appropriation of $5 million to create the War Victims Fund, housed at the U.S. Agency for International Development (USAID) and established with congressional bipartisan support in 1989 "to provide prosthetics to amputees in developing countries (see photo 2.8)."[86]

Senator Leahy also worked with Representative Lane Evans (D-IL) and Muller to start curtailing landmine exports through congressional legislation known as "Leahy-Evans Landmine Moratorium Act," which was included in the National Defense Authorization Act.[87] The moratorium placed a one-year prohibition on the sale, transfer, or export abroad of all APLs, including mixed APL and anti-tank (AT) systems. Leahy's export moratorium legislation received endorsements by nine of the largest American overseas relief organizations.[88]

Two months later, on October 23, President George H. W. Bush signed into law the Leahy-Evans export moratorium as part of the fiscal 1993 defense authorization bill.[89] The United States thus became the first country to enact a one-year renewable moratorium on its sale, transfer, and export of APLs and it was also the first law in the world to successfully stop the trade of APLs.

The Leahy-Evans moratorium also helped legitimize the ICBL by indicating that the world's only military superpower was considering the elimination of one of its weapons unilaterally and voluntarily. The moratorium also spawned significant attention for the mine issue and propelled the ICBL globally into political circles as a credible source of information for a justifiable cause.

In France, the Leahy-Evans moratorium gave impetus to HI's efforts to lobby the French government to request that the UN secretary-general call for a review of the 1980 CCW, specifically its Landmines Protocol and that French President Mitterrand publicly call for all landmine supplier countries to stop exporting landmines. Citing the Leahy-Evans export moratorium, the European Parliament issued a landmine resolution for a five-year moratorium on the export of APLs.

Through the fall of 1992, the founding members of the ICBL continued to produce valuable and informative landmine research, which they effectively disseminated to both the public and policymakers (see Table 6.2). Their publications proved an important and remarkable magnet in drawing attention to the landmine issue. For example, in October HRW, through its Middle East Watch program, released a report on landmines in Kurdistan, titled *Hidden Death*. The following month, PHR released its report, *Hidden Enemies: Landmines in Northern Somalia*. Both reports spotlighted the humanitarian devastation caused by landmines and further solidified the ICBL as the pre-eminent international source of expert landmine information and analysis. Finally, to keep up with landmine announcements and activities, the VVAF issued in December the first *Landmine Update*, which would become a regular quarterly update on the ICBL and a way to provide country updates on respective governmental landmine positions.[90]

PART THREE: 1993—MOBILIZING THE MOVEMENT

The beginning of 1993 illustrated how the ICBL and governments could effectively work together to ban APLs. Soon after President Bill Clinton took office in January, Leahy urged the new administration to review the 1980 Landmine Protocol for the purpose of seeking Senate ratification and to pursue, with other countries, ways of strengthening it. It was Leahy's hope—expressed in letters to Senate colleagues—that with the active involvement of the Clinton administration, the United States could achieve real progress toward a verifiable international agreement prohibiting the sale, export, or transfer of antipersonnel weapons, and further limit their use, production, and deployment.[91] Leahy already had secured support from all the military veteran senators and others who had visited mine-infested countries.[92]

Leahy also sent a letter to HI encouraging the organization's activism and the French government's signal that it might call for a review of the CCW. A country other than the United States had to call for the review, because, as Leahy noted, "the United States is in the embarrassing position of not having ratified the protocol, [and therefore] we cannot ourselves call a review conference."[93] HI interpreted the letter as a signal from Leahy "to encourage the association in its effort to convince the French government to ask for the convening of an International Review Conference."[94] Thus, in February, HI and MAG, with the assistance of the French Institute of International Relations, co-sponsored a landmine symposium with the goal of convincing "the members of the French cabinet of the public's concern in the landmines problem, and of the urgent need to make a clear stand on this topic."[95] During the conference, organizers used Leahy's letter of support for the symposium "to 'persuade' a rather reluctant [French] Foreign Ministry to take a public stand on the issue, which they have done" ... and it also announced "that a letter has been sent to the Secretary-General officially requesting a review conference of the 1980 convention [CCW]."[96]

Several days after the conference ended, French President Mitterrand accompanied his wife, Danielle, to visit Cambodia, where she was concerned about the humanitarian tragedy caused by landmines. After arriving in Phnom Penh, the country's capital, Mitterrand received over 22,000 signatures from the HI petition initiative in support of its call to "Stop the Coward's War," and to consider the "urgent need of an international conference to end slaughter of civilians in times of peace."[97] A parallel initiative was another HI letter and 15,000 signatures to President Mitterrand sent through Mrs. Mitterrand, requesting support for calling the review conference.[98] The day after receiving the signatures in Cambodia, on February 11, President Mitterrand called for the review of the CCW. He officially recognized France's "voluntary abstention" from the export of landmines and called upon other states to do the same.[99]

Leahy's legislation was not as welcome across the Channel in the United Kingdom, where a British government official stated that it was "not contemplating separate legislation to cover the export of APLs similar to that recently adopted by the U.S. Congress." Douglas Hogg, Foreign and Commonwealth Office, Minister of State, responded to parliamentarian requests to adopt Leahy's export moratorium legislation that the UK's "stringent controls on the export of defence equipment, which include controls on all mines, are sufficient to stop the sale of these weapons to countries which may use them in an irresponsible manner."[100]

During the third week of April, the ICRC hosted a two-day landmine symposium in Montreux, Switzerland, for more than sixty government, military, mine-producer, and NGO representatives to discuss ways to alleviate the suffering caused by APLs. The symposium came in response to its Medical Division, whose field personnel had raised the alarm about mine casualties; the purpose was to "collect the necessary facts and ideas to coordinate future action by bodies that are interested in improving the fate of mine victims and in undertaking preventive action."[101] For example, the current research done by ICRC medical doctor Robin Coupland showed that 58 percent of the mine injuries in northwest Cambodia were noncombatants and that military activities accounted for only 26 percent of the casualties.[102] In addition, most common landmine injures demand more surgical time and transfusion service: These patients "require more operations, and more such patients require blood transfusions, than patients with other injury patterns."[103] Coupland wrote that

> [T]here is a lack of reliable information on the full effects of antipersonnel mines. Military medical authors may not acknowledge antipersonnel mine injuries at all; if they do so it is only in the context of combat casualties. Had they expressed concern about these weapons outside a military context this humanitarian problem might have been recognized earlier.[104]

At the symposium, ICBL representatives wanted a ban, while the ICRC delegates believed that a more realistic and achievable solution should be considered. The lead UN demining expert, Paddy Blagden, presented information on behalf of the UN that that the carnage caused by APLs worldwide would not end anytime soon given that 200 million APLs could be scattered in at least sixty-four countries.[105] He estimated that a fiftyfold increase in the world's mine-clearing capability was needed to "stabilize" the situation.[106] Such an effort would require training 170,000 to 200,000 new mine clearers worldwide, costing $1.02 billion to $1.2 billion every year.[107] He warned, however, that under current practices, accidents happened at an astonishing rate: "A fiftyfold increase in manual mines clearance would probably cause a death and injury toll among mine clearers of about 2,000 per year, a rate that in the long term may not be supportable."[108] A case in point was Kuwait. Within the first week after the 1991 Gulf War, all five Kuwaiti mine-clearing experts were killed attempting to clear landmines.[109] By 1995, nearly 100 international mine-clearance experts had been killed in Kuwait.[110]

The ICRC symposium's participants agreed that there was a need for further research into the military use of APLs and its humanitarian impact.[111] They also agreed that there should be global action to limit and control APLs, but, noticeably, they did not support the ICBL's call for a ban.

In the United States, unilateral APL controls led by Leahy and his congressional allies continued. On July 22 Leahy and 34 senators introduced a bill to extend APL moratorium for an additional three years. The bill affirmed that it is the policy of the United States to seek verifiable international agreements prohibiting the sale, transfer, or export, further limiting the manufacture, possession and use, and eventually, terminating manufacture, possession and use of APLs.

The moratorium extension request garnered additional momentum with the July release of the U.S. State Department report *Hidden Killers: The Global Problem with Uncleared Landmines*. Leahy's moratorium legislation in October 1992 had generated intense action at the State Department, which resulted in the influential and seminal publication. The report provided detailed statistics—though actually only best-guess estimations—of the global landmine crisis. The U.S. government-issued report estimated that there were 90 million emplaced APLs in sixty-two countries, and that between 600 and 1,200 people were maimed or killed each month, thereby making them "one of the most toxic and widespread pollution[s] facing mankind."[112] Since the report was produced by a government and not an ICBL member, its official confirmation and political impartiality on the issue lent further credibility to the ICBL's claims that APLs should be banned for humanitarian reasons.

After the report's release, the National Security Council (NSC) directed the Department of State to establish an Interagency Working Group on Land Mines and Demining to help develop and coordinate humanitarian de-mining policy in an effort to assist clearance efforts in mine-affected countries.[113] Also, in part, due to the report's startling conclusions—calling landmines "one of the most toxic and widespread pollution[s] facing mankind"—the Leahy-Evans Export Moratorium was extended three years, passing the Senate by a 100-0 vote.

The purpose of Leahy's legislation was to challenge major landmine-producing countries to follow the U.S. example and adopt their own production moratoriums. Over 300 types of APLs were being produced and exported by more than 44 countries, including the United States, which despite its vast military production output, is not a major landmine exporter.[114]

Leahy was convinced that only international cooperation could address the global landmine crisis. But technological advancements allowed more states to deploy more mines and systems to deliver them faster and at greater volume. Landmines could be deployed through aerial dispersal, such as by airplane and artillery, which leads to greater deployment in a shorter time. Some more advanced remote delivery systems could deploy thousands of APLs in minutes.[115] Not only had technology resulted in more APLs and faster deployments, but they also were being deployed more indiscriminately, since accurate recording is not possible with aerial delivery systems.[116]

The rising humanitarian concern with mines had no effect on the weapons industry producing and promoting faster delivery methods. Scatterable systems evolved rapidly after the Vietnam War by including a mix of APL and anti-tank mines and thus blurring the line between them. By the end of 1993, twenty-two countries had produced scatterable systems.[117] During this period, modern militaries expanded this technology by packaging APL and anti-tank mines together, because studies showed that sowing APL with anti-tank mines significantly slowed down enemy minefield breaching and protected the anti-tank mines from enemy lifting.[118]

Government, industry, and military officials wanted to preserve the right to produce landmine systems. In 1993, for example, the Chinese firm China North Industries Corp. revealed that it was nearing completion of a remote-control scatterable mine-laying system operated from a truck for the export market. Each truck had eight launchers with each having a 36-tube capacity organized in six rows of six tubes. Each tube was capable of deploying 5 AT, 15 AP (Anti-Personnel) fragmentation, or 45 AP explosives per tube, all of which could be remotely launched by someone in the truck's cab.[119]

American business executives also wanted to preserve the scatterable landmine market. They lobbied American policymakers for a relaxation of the Leahy export moratorium, in part to claim the potentially large market. Toby Watson, president and chief executive officer of Alliant Techsystems, wrote a letter to Leahy voicing concern about the landmine export moratorium. His concern was twofold.

> First, I believe that an extension of the current moratorium's blanket prohibition will open the way for the proliferation of foreign-produced, technologically

inferior mines that will actually increase the risk of death or injury to noncombatants.... Unlike mines manufactured in many countries throughout the world, those produced by Alliant Techsystems have highly sophisticated and reliable automatic self-destruct or self-neutralization mechanisms. These mechanisms, which are designed into the product and cannot be overridden or circumvented, enable the mine to destroy or neutralize itself if it is not detonated within a predetermined time following deployment. As a result, there is no after-battle threat to noncombatants and no need for expensive and elaborate mine clearing operations.[120]

Second, as Chief Executive Officer of the largest supplier of munitions to the Department of Defense and a major producer of mines, I am concerned about the adverse effect the moratorium will have on jobs not only in my country, but elsewhere in an already weakened defense industry.... The potential market for sales of self-destructing mines to close U.S. allies is estimated to be between $400 million to $600 million over the next five years. The moratorium, however, had closed the door to any exports of U.S. mine systems, leaving foreign competitors to vie for contracts that Alliant Techsystems or other U.S. firms might be in a strong position to win.[121]

Later in the summer, Leahy received more landmine industry pressure. In August and September, C. M. Welch, the chairman of Delaware-based Mohawk Electrical Systems, wrote Leahy a few times to protest the export moratorium because it would cover Claymore mines. In his August letter, he outlined several reasons why the M18 Claymore should be exempted from the ban. The September letter focused on the U.S. loss of jobs and damage to the U.S. economy if the moratorium was passed. He believed "that an extension of the moratorium on mine exports could result in the loss of as many as 2,000 positions among the U.S. contractors and subcontractors that produce mines and mine components, including Alliant Techsystems."[122]

The American industry's claim regarding lost sales was not without merit. The moratorium immediately affected mine producers. In April, New Jersey's Emoco Inc's application to export 300 extended-range trip wire sensors for use in German APLs was denied due to the APL export ban.[123] Also, during the previous ten years (FY 1983–1993), U.S. foreign military sales of antipersonnel landmines totaled 33,586 mines at a cost of $26,526,669.52.[124] According to Steve Goose, director of the Washington office of the HRW Arms Project, "estimates suggest that manufacturers have probably produced an average of between five and ten million APL per year in recent decades, roughly ten times the production volume previously reported in the trade press. Combined global production for traditional APL is probably worth between $50 million and $200 million annually."[125]

In May, more than 50 representatives from more than 40 NGOs met in London at the first ICBL International Conference on Landmines to discuss how to expand the movement and continue to build political momentum toward a landmine prohibition. The founding members "recognized that ultimate success of the campaign depends upon broad public support which as yet is generally lacking."[126] The ICBL members committed themselves to target their recruiting efforts to particular geographical areas. For example, Oxfam America "offered to help fund development of such participation in those regions where it works," while World Vision International committed itself to using "its network to develop national partner participation."[127] Beyond expanding the campaign, the participants also focused on key steps that entailed expertise in legal, policy, and technical matters. These steps included developing "a technical definition of the weapon to be outlawed," developing "a draft alternative [landmines] protocol calling for a ban on a/p mines," and investigating specialized and non-specialized bodies to bring to the landmine issue.[128]

The ICBL members felt that the call for a prohibition was the minimum requirement for participation in the campaign but also that the "campaign should maintain the necessary flexibility to be inclusionary as part of the strength of the effort to date has been its ability to include NGOs from a wide spectrum of issues and appreciate the contribution each can make by working through its own constituency based upon its own mandate."[129]

The conference participants also selected an ad-hoc steering committee that consisted of HI, HRW, MI, MAG, PHR, and VVAF, with VVAF acting as the coordinator. These six organizations, all the founding ICBL members, "had organized the conference and had served as a catalyst to the campaign by virtue of having made serious, ongoing organizational and financial commitment to the effort."[130] The committee was mandated to make decisions on behalf of ICBL. Discussion concerning the development of a more formalized campaign structure was set aside since many of the NGOs present had not yet taken a position on the campaign, much less signed on to the call.[131]

One of the most well-received presentations was by MAG's Rae McGrath, who based his presentation, "The Reality of the Present Use of Mines by Military Forces," on his personal experience in clearing mines in many countries. He stated that "there had been no discernable change in the use of mines since the adoption of the 1980 Convention, since the existence of that instrument was unknown to most users."[132] According to McGrath, the ICBL

> is not a crusade against war, nor a disarmament issue—there are intrinsic properties specific to landmines which separate them from other weapons, and the key issue is not their physical effects, although this obviously has relevance, but their random and uncontrollable nature . . . MINES are random because, once emplaced or disseminated, it is the victim who causes the mine to explode by a normal, human, and most commonly, non-military function—the mine cannot be directed

exclusively at a specific individual or group although there may be an intent that the mine damages a specific target. Landmines are UNCONTROLLABLE for several reasons, but primarily as a result of their design . . . disseminating mines determine that the operator is remote from the actual location where the mines are laid.[133]

At the end of its meeting, the ICBL produced a *Joint Call to Ban Antipersonnel Landmines*, which had three prongs: establishment of an international APL ban; establishment of an international fund to promote de-mining; and persuasion of both landmine-producing and landmine-using countries to contribute to the fund.[134]

Meanwhile, Jody Williams continued her aggressive networking to galvanize and broaden campaign support. On August 4, she wrote UNICEF consultant Stephen Lewis, who was advising UNICEF Executive Director James Grant, asking for his support for the ban. In turn, Lewis suggested to Grant that supporting the ban "was consistent with its aggressive efforts to press for the ratification and implementation of the Convention on the Rights of the Child."[135] Then on August 16, 1993, UNICEF informed VVAF that it had decided "to advocate for the ban on landmines" thus becoming the first UN agency to call for a landmine prohibition.[136]

Two months later, on October 6, U.S. Ambassador to the UN Madeleine Albright notified Leahy that the Clinton administration "had decided to pursue the issue of landmines during the 48th UN General Assembly." The United States would call "on states to observe a moratorium on exports of APLs is a necessary first step in the right direction" and "complements other U.S. initiatives, including your own."[137] One of her stated reasons for her personal interest was based on her visits to Somalia and Cambodia a few months before, where she "had the opportunity to learn firsthand of their terrible consequences" and realized "[t]hat something must be done."[138]

Ambassador Karl Inderfurth, who was the U.S. representative for special political affairs to the UN, with the rank of ambassador become seized with the negative effects of APLs and proved to very helpful throughout in pushing Leahy's anti-APL agenda at the UN. He had accompanied Albright on the peacekeeping trip to Cambodia and Somalia and had personally witnessed for the first time the humanitarian harm caused by landmines.[139] In Kisamayo, Somalia, they participated in an outdoor meeting with local clan leaders, who told them about the increasing numbers of landmine casualties. Inderfurth immediately "realized the extent of the mine problem" and "registered that as part of the scene in Somalia."[140]

From Somalia, Albright and Inderfurth flew on to Cambodia, where they participated in a round of government visits, including meetings with King Norodom Sihanouk, U.S. Ambassador Charles Twining and Cambodian Co-Prime Minister Hun Sen. A main and lasting impression of the visit was that they "saw and discussed that a lot of people were missing limbs caused by landmines."[141] On the plane flight leaving

Photograph 2.9

Ambassador Karl Inderfurth addressing members of the United Nations Security Council. February 1995. Working closely with Senator Patrick Leahy and his senior foreign policy aide Tim Riser, Inderfurth spearheaded U.S. landmine advocacy efforts at the UN. He was appointed by President Bill Clinton as the Special Representative of the President and Secretary of State for Global Humanitarian Demining in 1997. (Courtesy Ambassador Karl Inderfurth. Used by permission.)

Cambodia, he and Albright discussed the landmine issue asking questions, such as "What can we do?" and "What is the UN doing?" and then they resolved "to look at what could be done at UN and within the U.S. government about the landmine problem."[142]

In November, Leahy was invited by Albright and Inderfurth to introduce legislation at the UN First Committee (Disarmament) meeting to encourage states to agree to implement a moratorium on mine exports on November 30 in a first step to reduce their proliferation (see photo 2.9). Once in New York, he was concerned to learn that the final resolution that he was to introduce was drafted by the State Department without his consultation. There was some negotiation before he introduced the resolution, when Leahy voiced his concerns to Albright and Inderfurth about watering it down. Leahy said that he "would be extremely disappointed if the present U.S. draft resolution was watered down from its call on states to "agree to" an international moratorium to simply asking members to "consider a" moratorium. In my opinion, countries which are opposing the present U.S. draft should be isolated, forced to oppose or abstain, and exposed to what I anticipate will be a major international campaign to persuade them to join us and others in a moratorium.[143]

Leahy introduced the U.S. resolution calling on all states "to agree to a moratorium on the export of anti-personnel mines that pose grave dangers to civilian populations." Department of Defense officials insisted on this reference to grave dangers to civilian populations, which they construed to implicitly exclude self-destruct mines—the only mines produced in the United States, while the State Department believed this phrase was sufficiently vague enough to leave the issue open for further debate during preparations for the UN conference to review the Landmine Protocol.

Leahy ended his remarks by stating that the export moratorium called for by the resolution is an "important first step" because "people everywhere want to put an end to this human tragedy caused by landmines."[144] After introducing the resolution, Leahy stayed at the UN to continue his personal lobbying and to meet one-on-one with the representatives of Italy, Brazil, and Indonesia to convince them to support the U.S. resolution. These were important countries because Italy was one of the world's largest exporters of landmines and Indonesia was head of the non-aligned countries.

The U.S. actions at the UN regarding APLs was supported by the November release of HRW Arms Project and PHR's joint publication *Landmines: A Deadly Legacy*, which provided a detailed account of international landmine production and trade and, most importantly, detailed a strong case for why APLs should be banned under current international humanitarian law.[145] One of the key contributor's, HRW's Steve Goose, stated that one of the publication's goal was "to portray anti-personnel mines as even worse than chemical or biological weapons."[146]

On December 7 the Department of State sent a telegram to 53 missions in identified landmine-producing countries, instructing U.S. embassy officials to "draw from background information and talking points" to be reviewed by the department in order to encourage them to adopt, without delay, an export moratorium. In its telegram, the Department of State estimated that "there are 85–110 million unexploded landmines in 63 countries, 65 million of which were placed within the last 15 years."[147]

The U.S. resolution was adopted unanimously by the UNGA on December 16. This important first step toward addressing the global landmine crisis established the United States as the leader in the growing effort to stop the carnage caused by APLs.

Also on December 16, the UNGA adopted the French resolution calling for the UN secretary-general, in his role as CCW depository, to convene a conference to review the CCW, especially the Landmines Protocol.[148] As a signal that that the international community was willing to address the landmine ban issue, the French resolution was unanimously adopted. The French government had been spurred by HI and other members of the French Campaign to Ban Landmines and ICBL, along with Leahy's encouragement.

In explaining the French actions, Williams later wrote that she believed that President Mitterrand pushed for the review to get "the NGOs and French public . . . off his back."[149] She also was informed by a Swedish diplomat that the combined local HI and ICBL pressure "pushed the French government to make the official request for the review conference of the treaty."[150]

The United States was one of only three countries to abstain from the French resolution calling for the review conference. In light of the U.S. resolution banning the export of APLs, adopted unanimously by the UNGA that same day, Leahy was "very surprised and disappointed" to learn that the United Sates had abstained, while 162 countries voted for it.[151] Apparently and inexplicably, the United States abstained because of hortatory language in the resolution, which expressed support for possible future talks on disarmament which could include the goal of ending the production, stockpiling, and proliferation of these weapons.[152]

According to Leahy, "[t]his retreat was due to last-minute lobbying by the Pentagon." To quickly "offset the damage caused by this inexplicable vote," he called on the Clinton administration, to strive "to ensure that the United Nations conference agenda is broad enough to consider fully all possible limits up to and including a total ban."[153] Responding to Leahy's inquiry about why the United States abstained, Clinton wrote that the United States had supported the resolution as a co-sponsor until "the addition of a last-minute amendment by Mexico that, inter alia, called for an end to the production of landmines, [and] the United States and twenty other nations withdrew sponsorship of the resolution and the United States abstained from the vote. While we fully support the overall thrust of the resolution, we could not vote for it because U.S. Armed Forces continue to require landmines to accomplish certain military missions."[154]

In addition, Albright informed Leahy that she shared his "dismay" over the U.S. absentition, but her quarrel was with the situation leading to the U.S. abstention and not the abstention itself. She notified Leahy that "Mexico proposed an amendment which we believe divided the First Committee needlessly over a resolution which previously enjoyed unanimous support, including U.S. co-sponsorship. It was our [U.S.] view that the amendment, as written, focused the resolution inappropriately on a single paragraph of the Weapons Convention—that on the production, stockpiling and use of land mines—and furthermore served to prejudge the outcome of the review process."[155]

The UNGA resolutions helped establish the basis for a global APL comprehensive ban and were significant steps toward strengthening movement toward an international ban. Within the next 12 months, at least a dozen countries had stopped exporting AP mines. Many legal scholars claim that UNGA resolutions are generally viewed as having a significant influence on the "nature and substance of contemporary international law."[156] In particular, "votes and views of states have come to have legal significance as evidence of customary law."[157] In the other words, the unanimous or near-unanimous adoption of resolutions by UNGA members helped to dictate what international customary law is.[158]

During the month of December 1993, the movement saw strong action toward an APL ban in Italy, Canada, and Sweden. Italian NGOs launched the Italian campaign with a workshop in Rome. In 1993, pressured and supported by Canadian NGOs, especially human rights groups, the newly elected Liberal government in Canada transformed its foreign policy decision-making process to include more NGO consultations.[159] This policy change allowed a coalition of NGOs, working under the auspices of Mines Action Canada (MAC), to directly influence Canada's APL position by placing it on the government's agenda.[160] Initial Canadian NGO-government meetings "produced little common ground from which discussions could progress" once it was placed on the agenda.[161] However, these meetings gave the NGOs an opportunity to educate government officials on the humanitarian problem caused by landmines, thereby gaining legitimacy for their arguments and detracting from military and strategic arguments for opposing a ban.[162]

One of the first APL producer casualties was the Swedish manufacturing firm Bofors, which announced in December "that for 'moral' reasons it will stop manufacturing antipersonnel landmines as well as the export of fuses and explosives to buyers who might use the material to produce such mines."[163] It set a precedent by unilaterally announcing that it would cease "production of AP mines [APLs] as well as the export of components that others might use to make them."[164]

CHAPTER 3

Humanitarian Advocacy and Diplomatic Deadlock

1994—INTERNATIONAL LEGAL RE-ENGAGEMENT

By the start of 1994, Senator Patrick Leahy's efforts to get the Clinton administration to address the landmine crisis were paying off: Through Leahy's staff efforts, domestic interest in the issue grew steadily and received an added boost by a *New York Times* magazine cover story titled "It's the Little Bombs That Kill You," which stated on the cover "[t]here are more than 100 million of them [landmines], in 62 countries, waiting."[1] At the very least, Leahy believed that determined leadership by the United States could achieve significant limitations on the use of antipersonnel landmines (APL), including in internal conflicts, and export restraints by major suppliers. While this outcome fell short of the International Campaign to Ban Landmines (ICBL) goal of a comprehensive international ban, which Leahy doubted was practically attainable in the foreseeable future, his short-term strategy was already at a critical stage.

The central part of Leahy's strategy was to advocate a comprehensive global ban by trying to mobilize congressional backing. Support for his domestic landmine legislation bridged the gap between Democrats and Republicans resulting in wide-ranging congressional non-partisan sponsorship, which, at the same time, gave Leahy greater credibility and flexibility in his efforts to move the Clinton administration on the landmine issue.[2] He and his foreign policy aide, Tim Rieser, relentlessly worked with governments, non-governmental organizations (NGOs), and other interested parties in preparations for the Convention on Conventional

Weapons (CCW) Review Conference, especially its Landmine Protocol, including working to identify significant limitations in the protocol that could be pushed through at the conference that would take place in the fall of 1995 in Vienna. Leahy's advocacy goal was to prevent governments from settling into a comfortable path of slight modification of the CCW Landmine Protocol by making it as hard as possible for governments to settle for a few cosmetic changes and to encourage them to dramatically revise it to provide meaningful protection for civilians.[3]

That said, Leahy had achieved more progress on the APL issue than he had thought possible at the outset: His unilateral U.S. moratorium legislation and other advocacy activities called for the strongest possible APL regime within the CCW—without creating a perception that anything less than a total ban was a failure.

This was a difficult political line for Leahy to walk. On the one hand, it could sound like he was accepting beforehand a simple strengthening of the existing protocol, which, in turn, could play into the hands of the military bureaucrats around the world. On the other hand, he didn't want to be perceived as zealot for a chimerical outcome—a total global comprehensive ban—as the only measure of success, which could marginalize him in his attempts to rally the United States (U.S.) and other governments toward taking concrete measures toward a comprehensive ban. Leahy believed that the main reason his two landmine moratorium amendments won in the Senate was that they were within the bounds of what the U.S. military could tolerate. They banned exports—which are not important to the United States—but left production for U.S. purposes alone.[4]

In highlighting the increased political strain between supporting Leahy's export and production moratorium, Senator Ben Nighthorse Campbell (D-CO) wrote:

> I cosponsored Sen. Leahy's proposal last year to extend the moratorium on the export of landmines that legislation passed the Senate unanimously. This year, I decided to cosponsor Sen. Leahy's one-year production moratorium as well, in order to give U.S. negotiators greater credibility while pursuing a worldwide agreement on this issue. In fairness, I have to consider the views of U.S. Army officials. They argue against a ban on production and export of all landmines, making the point that many U.S.-made landmines deactivate themselves. I don't think, however, that a one-year moratorium will seriously affect the U.S. Army, and may give us a better chance to reach a worldwide landmine agreement.[5]

Having the support of the Clinton administration was crucial for Leahy's strategy, but it was far from solid. Although the administration supported his three-year extension of the export moratorium, the Defense Department continued to push for an exception for self-destruct (SD) and self-neutralizing (SN) mines.[6] The State Department's Legal Advisor's office, which negotiated the original Landmine Protocol, believed such an exception would be inevitable in any revision of the protocol. Leahy did not want to allow the administration to begin the effort by setting its sights that low.

Leahy concurred with the ICBL and ICRC's three major reasons why they strongly opposed any exception for SD or SN mines in any protocol revision: First, despite the availability of American SD mines, Third World countries would go on making and using their low-tech, inexpensive mines. Also, it was in these countries where most conflicts occur, and where U.S. and UN troops were likely to be sent in the future. Second, SD mines are an improvement over mines that remain active for decades, but during the weeks or months they are active they cannot distinguish between combatants and civilians any better than other mines. Even if they are used against what is a military target today, in a week or a month the same piece of land or stretch of road may be occupied by civilians. Third, SD mines are often scattered by air, some at a rate of hundreds per minute. It is impossible to aim them precisely, or to record where they land, and they impede the mobility and threaten the safety of U.S. forces.

Anticipating further inter-administration landmine control discussions generated by the Leahy legislative initiatives and public lobbying of high-level administration officials, the Joint Staff and State Department's Arms Control and Disarmament Agency (ACDA) worked on confidential landmine position papers in February.[7] As part of this process, a landmine utility study was commissioned to the Institute for Defense Analysis (IDA) by the Office of the Under Secretary for Policy. One of the study's findings was that "landmines do have military utility in high intensity mechanized land warfare" and concluded that the utility of landmines in high-intensity conflict does not override consideration of landmine arms control.[8]

In preparation for the CCW review conference, States Parties initiated and formed a group of experts to prepare detailed suggestions for revising the Landmine Protocol amendments with the objective of strengthening prevention or limitations on APL use. This group, officially known as the Group of Governmental of Experts (GGE), met four times to consider proposals to prepare for the Review Conference in October and with the purpose of reducing the humanitarian suffering caused by.

While the UNGA request excluded NGOs, including ICBL members from participating in the GGE meetings, the ICRC was asked to help facilitate the Geneva meetings that took place in the UN rooms at the Palais Nations. The ICRC was also invited to participate as were selected UN specialized agencies, such as UNDHA, UNHCR, and UNICEF.[9] During the four GGE meetings, an important battle over negotiations took place among the delegates regarding a possible ICBL participatory role in the upcoming CCW Convention.[10] Despite Leahy's lobbying for the inclusion of ICBL experts "who have considerable experience on these issues" in the experts meetings because "their input during the preparatory discussions would be very valuable," the ICBL was excluded from participating in all the experts meetings.[11]

- The first GGE meeting (February 28–March 4, 1994) took place in Geneva. Attending were 26 of the 39 state parties and 23 of the 29 signatories, who started setting the Review Conference agenda. As part of this work, the group requested background documents, which included two ICRC reports on why the CCW should be amended and consideration of other proposals relating to the existing and future CCW protocols. The group also discussed organizational details, including an agreement that all decisions would be taken by consensus, and appointed its officers, including Swedish Ambassador Johan Molander as the experts' group chair.[12] At the meeting, the ICRC offered several amendments for the governments to consider, including proposals to restrict certain types of mines and for further regulations on how mines are used.[13]
- The second session of the GGE meeting took place on May 16–27, 1994, in Geneva, where it discussed suggested amendments, including a proposal submitted by Australia, Sweden, and the Netherlands that suggested a new article be introduced "with the aim of denying access to antipersonnel landmines by States not adhering to the protocol, and allowing exports and transfers of antipersonnel landmines only for those types that are detectable and self-destructing or self-neutralizing."[14] The GGE also discussed an ICRC landmine report, which it had commissioned earlier that concluded a ban was the best way to alleviate the global landmine problem because of the technical complexities of restricting self-destruct mines.[15]
- On August 8–19, 1994, the GGE met for the third time with mixed results. At this meeting, the group decided that it could not reach a consensus on extending the scope and application of the landmines protocol and thus recommended that the CCW Review cover it in the fall.[16] Most significantly, the Swedish government submitted a proposal for a "[p]rohibition on the use, development, manufacture, stockpiling, and transfer of certain mines and booby traps" thus becoming the first government during the review process that formally called for a comprehensive ban.[17]
- The fourth and final GGE meeting, held January 9–20, 1995, adopted the heavily bracketed "Chairman's Rolling Text," which recognized that APLs are the cause of most of the humanitarian devastation caused by mines.[18] The GGE defined an APL as "a mine primarily designed to be exploded by the presence, proximity, or contact of a person and that will incapacitate, injure or kill one or more persons."[19] The experts also put forward several proposals of modest control measures to the Review Conference, including APL detectibility, that remotely delivered mines should include an SD capability and that mines that are not fenced or guarded must also include an SD feature.

Throughout the spring of 1994, the ICBL continued to gather political momentum leading in to its May Second NGO International Conference on Landmines in Geneva.[20] More than 110 representatives from 75 NGOs were present, doubling the size of the ICBL's first NGO meeting in London the previous year.

In the Conference's keynote presentation, ICBL co-founder and Vietnam Veteran of America Foundation (VVAF) director Bobby Muller urged that ICBL members move the campaign forward by courting public support rather than focusing on government and military representatives. Otherwise, he said, "We will lose."[21] His thrust was for the ICBL to focus on the humanitarian aspects of the issue rather than discussing it from a disarmament point of view. His argument was buttressed by the ICRC, which produced a series of documents and papers educating both NGOs and states about the humanitarian consequences of APL use. Coincidently, the U.S. State Department contributed to the changing discourse on APLs by stating in its *Hidden Killers* report that landmines "may be the most toxic and widespread pollution facing mankind."[22]

The ICBL conference's discussions centered on whether the ban was a utopian goal or whether the campaign should focus more on improving the existing landmines protocol.[23] Members agreed that the ICBL message to governments should be "that a complete ban on landmines is the only solution to the global crisis."[24] Some ICBL members also questioned the ICRC position, since that organization had not come out with an official call for a ban, even though the ICRC president declared his support for a ban and it had suggested one to the GGE. When an ICRC delegate was asked at the ICBL meeting whether the ICRC's "call for the ban" was an official ICRC position (or whether he considered "the ICRC position slightly different or clearly different?") the ICRC delegate replied, "I wouldn't go into semantics and say whether it's an official endorsement."[25]

The ICBL steering committee also recommended that the campaign be extended beyond the APL ban call itself and bring in the related issues of mine-victim assistance and de-mining. In this regard, the ICBL's informational materials were broadened to include human rights issues as a way to outreach to non-arms control constituencies and expand membership in and support for the campaign.

The conference also integrated for the first time what would become a fixture at ICBL meetings: progress reports of national campaigns and activists regarding their successes and failures, and lessons learned in their efforts to convince governments to ban APLs. For instance, national campaign reports were given by France, Germany, Italy, Mozambique, the Netherlands, New Zealand, Sweden, the United Kingdom, and the United States. HI Co-Director Philippe Chabasse explained the French campaign's successful lobbying techniques in courting the media, public opinion and policymakers to the APL-ban goal: It worked "to build up a base of journalists through regular contacts, mailing of information, and organizing press conferences and symposia in order to maintain media interest in the issue, and then recruited hundreds of people to pass out literature or gather signatures for a ban petition."[26]

The conference also saw the birth of another fixture: development of an ICBL six-month action plan, which outlined the campaign's activities and goals for the following six months. This plan, in turn, was made available to every ICBL member and those NGOs that wanted to participate in future ICBL actions. The main purpose was to give a lobbying and strategic roadmap to members once the conference ended so everyone knew how to move the landmine-ban issue forward.[27]

Meanwhile back in the United States, Leahy continued his efforts to get the government to move more aggressively. He focused on generating political will by convening the "The Global Landmine Crisis" hearing before the Senate sub-committee on foreign operations on May 13, 1994, in which two American landmine survivors, the author and Frederick Downs Jr., who received four Purple Hearts, the Bronze Star with Valor, and the Silver Star for his service in the Vietnam War, were invited to testify about the effects of landmines.[28] Since members of Congress are not going to lose re-elections over landmines, especially if they say they want to protect the troops, it was important for Leahy to put a human face on the landmine crisis and show the importance of it to Americans. The hearing was covered by national media with survivors being interviewed on the nightly news.[29]

At the hearing, Robert Muller, co-founder of the ICBL, testified that people

> cannot relate to the very broader issues of war and peace in the grand sense, but when you get the chance to talk to people about specifically what landmines are doing, they understand that and they get angry about that, and that is what has been driving the formation of an incredible worldwide campaign that has been coming together to deal with this weapon.[30]

The following month, Leahy introduced, along with more than 50 Senate co-sponsors, a bill that would require a one-year moratorium on the production and procurement of APLs by the U.S. government. This landmine legislation was the first time that Leahy hit a roadblock in getting Congress to support him. Significant Pentagon resistance developed as this "ban production" legislation was different from Leahy's export moratorium passed in previous years; those legislative measures did not directly affect landmine use and production.[31] For example, Sen. John McCain, who co-sponsored Leahy's export-moratorium legislation the year before, did not support Leahy's production and procurement legislation:

> A moratorium on the production and procurement of U.S. landmines raises some serious concerns that last year's export moratorium did not. Our servicemen and

women need landmines for their protection. Our forces deploy them responsibly and properly mark and record their location. And every indication is that U.S.-produced landmines are not the problem. Mine warfare is vital to military readiness . . . While we must take every step we can to curb problem exporters and users, I cannot support a moratorium on the production and procurement of U.S. landmines.[32]

Until this time, Leahy had experienced early and easy legislative victories partially because the media latched onto the landmine issue, and also because there was little congressional and Pentagon opposition. Few uniformed military personnel wanted to defend APLs, and several congressional members had had negative personal experiences with mines.[33]

By mid-summer, UN Secretary-General Boutros-Ghali started arguing that if the effects of APLs were more widely known, they "would undoubtedly shock the conscience of mankind—the same public reaction that led to the banning of chemical and biological weapons."[34] In July, the UN General Assembly (UNGA) adopted the secretary-general's report "Moratorium on the export of antipersonnel landmines" that noted, "Member states would have to take steps effectively to halt the proliferation and use of land-mines around the world" and recommended including APLs in the provisional agenda.[35] The UNSG report also stated that "[i]t is estimated that there are more than 110 million uncleared landmines in the world and that the removal of each one will cost between $300 and $1,000, while more than 800 deaths or injuries will result from them worldwide each month."[36]

Signifying rising global concern, officials attending the G7 summit in Naples, Italy, also discussed the APL issue for the first time on July 10. At the summit's conclusion, the chairman stated "[w]e assign priority to the problems of antipersonnel landmines, including efforts to curb their indiscriminate use, halt their exports, and assist in their clearance worldwide."[37]

Three weeks after the G8/G7 summit, the Italian Campaign to Ban Landmines successfully effected government change on August 2, 1994, when the Italian Senate required the government to ratify the CCW Landmines Protocol and to initiate policies that would ban the production and export of APLs. Founded in December 1993, the Italian Campaign to Ban Landmines had quickly garnered national attention by "a series of appearances on the most widely watched Italian television talk show," including an appearance with the Italian minister of defense, who "appeared with campaign representatives and voiced his support for a ban on landmines."[38] The ICBL Coordinator Jody Williams was most impressed with the Italian campaign's success in shutting down landmine production at the Valsella plant, which was one of the leading landmine producers in the world. The Italian campaign organized a

17 km walk to the Valsella plant to call for a ban on landmines. In one of the most moving moments of the march, women workers from the plant stood up and added their voice to the call for a ban. The mayor also announced that the town council had voted unanimously, in a special meeting, to join the Italian Campaign to Ban Landmines.[39]

Back in the United States, Senator Leahy's legislative actions were partially responsible for resulting in two significant U.S. policy actions. First, in August, the Clinton administration sent the CCW, including its Landmine Protocol, to the Senate for ratification. The second, and more significant policy action, occurred the following month, after several months of discussion within the administration on different positions, when on September 26, 1994, Clinton addressed the UN General Assembly, calling for "the ultimate goal of the eventual elimination of antipersonnel landmines."[40]

This was the first time that a major world leader had called for a ban, and it served as a touchstone for the continued work of Ambassador Inderfurth and the U.S. delegation at the UN on addressing the APL issue. Since the enactment in October 1992 of the unilateral moratorium on exports of APL, the United States had provided crucial leadership in a global effort to stop the humanitarian crisis caused by landmines. Much was achieved since then. At least 17 countries have declared their own export moratoria after the lead by the United States, and there had been a remarkable growth in public support around the world for banning landmines.

While the speech should have ended the debate about the need for a comprehensive ban on APLs, Clinton complicated its achievement by also announcing a new landmine-control initiative. He urged other states to support, as a first step toward the elimination of antipersonnel landmines, an agreement to reduce the number and availability of these weapons. Clinton stated that the

eventual elimination of a less-visible, but still deadly threat: the world's 85 million antipersonnel land mines—one for every 50 people on the face of the Earth. I ask that all nations join with us and conclude an agreement to reduce the number and availability of those mines.[41]

The administration had just conducted an expedited and intensive review to determine the parameters of what the United States would propose for a regime, both in the near term and the longer term. The president did not have to mention landmines in the speech, but he did so given the pressure from Congress led by Leahy's legislation that called for a one-year moratorium on production that would affect stockpiles and use.

Leahy informed Clinton administration officials that he was pleased that it adopted the goal of eventual elimination, which at least is symbolically important, but that he did not support Clinton's proposed regime that he believed promoted production, export, and use of SD and SN mines. He let Clinton know in a letter that he co-wrote with Congressman Lane Evans, an Illinois Democrat. They wrote that if APLs

> are to be eliminated, all countries must create new international norms that label landmines as inhumane weapons and reject them as acceptable means of warfare. Potential users need to know that they risk political censure if they use landmines, as they do with chemical weapons. This stigmatization goal will not be achieved by promoting the Clinton administration's regime that insists on certain mines, those produced in the U.S., are acceptable. While the regime would not significantly reduce the use of cheap, conventional mines by poor countries and insurgent groups, it most certainly would end the U.S. export moratorium and the moratoria of at least a dozen other nations by exempting self-destruct/self-deactivating mines. It could also well result in the U.S. again becoming a leading exporter of landmines, rather than a leading voice for ending the proliferation of landmines.[42]

With Clinton's speech and Boutros-Ghali's advocacy, the landmine issue started moving fast at the UN. At the First Committee meeting in early November, Leahy introduced the U.S. resolution with the call for the eventual elimination of APL.[43] It also recognized in operative paragraph 6 "that States can move most effectively towards the ultimate goal of the eventual elimination of antipersonnel land-mines as viable and humane alternatives are developed."[44]

Several delegations took a contrary view by speaking in favor of continuing the right of landmines for self-defense. The Finnish representative stated that "Finland considers it very important that the recommendations by the General Assembly should not be construed as somehow prejudging the outcomes of the ongoing negotiations . . . it is with this concern in mind that Finland reserves its position on operative paragraph 6." Speaking after Finland, the French delegate also expressed his government's displeasure in not being able to co-sponsor the resolution because "[u]nfortunately it could not do so, because of the mention in operative paragraph 6 of the eventual elimination of antipersonnel land-mines" and that its inclusion "would have a negative effect on negotiations under way in the GGE" by "further complicating" their work.[45]

Brazil, Iran, Turkey, and Pakistan also expressed reservations about operative paragraph 6. Iran and Turkey believed that it was an asprational political goal, while Brazil and Pakistan argued that APLs are defensive weapons, which, if "[p]roperly used . . . are an effective means of deterring attacks, and thus have a definite place in the defensive arsenals of States." Australia also stated that it "is one of the many countries, some of them sponsors of the draft resolution, that believe that antipersonnel mines can be a legitimate conventional weapon."[46] Despite the opposition by these delegations, the First Committee recommended the U.S. resolution to the UNGA, which adopted it with 74 cosponsors without a vote.[47]

The year 1994 ended with the U.S. State Department's publication of *1994 Hidden Killers: The Global Landmines Crisis* report that more intensely spotlighted the humanitarian devastation caused by landmines. It estimated that 80 million to 110 million APLs were buried in 64 countries and they "maim or kill an estimated 500 people per week worldwide."[48] The report's findings and implications contributed to the increasing global discussion regarding the problem of APLs exacerbating regional conflicts, hindering post-conflict reconstruction, seriously undermining infrastructure, and denying land to civilian use, thereby leading to overuse of existing land. It also increased the casualty numbers over its 1993 report based on more up-to-date research and awareness of the problem.[49]

1995—DIPLOMATIC STAGNATION AND ICBL "PHNOM PENH FORMULA"

On February 16, Leahy and Evans, a Marine veteran who served in combat in Vietnam, introduced a bill to place a one-year moratorium, beginning in 1999, on the use of antipersonnel landmines by the U.S. Armed Forces. In an attempt to support Leahy's legislation, Williams wrote to mine-ban supporters that

> [t]he importance of this legislation is far-reaching. The U.S. has been a leader on the landmines issue. How it acts to further the goal of eliminating landmines will affect other countries as well. Just as the U.S. export moratorium helped move 18 other countries to enact moratoria, this new legislation would signal to other countries that the U.S. is serious about further restrictions on the use of landmines.[50]

As expected, the Pentagon opposed the legislation by arguing that APLs were an integral part of its war-fighting methodology, and that a blanket prohibition on their use now would impede their military effectiveness. Not surprisingly, the Department of State also opposed the Leahy-Evans legislation. It believed that APLs were required "[t]o maintain U.S. military effectiveness and that of its close allies," especially since most allies "rely on APL as an important part of their military doctrine." It also informed Leahy that his legislation may "contravene U.S. NATO obligations that could have a negative effect on diplomatic relations and interoperability effectiveness with U.S. allies."[51]

Landmine manufacturers also opposed Leahy's legislation. The vice president for Alliant Techsystems, a major landmine producer, wrote that it supports a ban on "[t]he indiscriminate use of long-lasting antipersonnel landmines," but that the Leahy legislation should be amended "to provide for use of mines with built-in self-destruct or self-neutralization features as a practical way to achieve the goal of the UN protocol."[52]

The ICBL and Leahy's efforts received a significant boost on March 2 when Belgium became the first country to ban APLs. Most significantly as a NATO member, it raised a host of interoperatibility questions for other NATO members.[53] The Belgian announcement, coupled with the surprisingly fast-moving Leahy legislation, pressured Clinton to call for a review of U.S. landmine policy, which occurred on March 16 when Gen. John Shalikashvili, chairman of Joint Chiefs of Staff, ordered a review of the military's longstanding opposition to an APL ban.

Meanwhile, on March 16–17, 1995, ICBL members met in Rome to discuss future campaign organizational strategy, including participation at the fall CCW Review conference in Vienna. It was decided that in the lead-up to Vienna, ICBL members would work to expand the campaign into more countries.[54] Most importantly, the ICBL decided that the campaign's focus should remain on APLs, as opposed to other victim-activated weapons such as anti-tank mines or cluster bombs.[55] This issue of whether to include anti-tank mines in the campaign was contentious for ICBL members. Both the German and Italian campaigns targeted both kinds of mines, while the ICBL remained focused just on APLs. In Rome, the consensus agreement was that the ICBL "would continue to focus on APLs and that each national campaign or individual NGO can focus on other weapons as well."[56] According to Pierre Ryckmans and Vincent Stainer of Handicap International (HI) and the Belgium Campaign to Ban Landmines, one reason that Belgium became the first country to ban landmines was that the campaign "never attempted to include anti-tank mines in the ban," thereby avoiding stronger opposition from the military and great support for the antipersonnel ban.[57] Simplicity and singularity became the keystones for successfully promoting the international need to legally ban the use of landmines as a weapon of war.

Nearly three months later, from June 2 to 4, in Phnom Penh, Cambodia, the Cambodian Campaign to Ban Landmines and the NGO Forum on Cambodia organized and hosted an international conference devoted to "The Human and Socio-Economic Impact of Landmines: Towards an International Ban." More than 400 people from 42 countries attended the conference, which was the first international landmine conference held in a significantly landmine-infested country (see photo 3.1).[58]

The conference received letters of support from a range of world leaders, including Leahy, Pope John Paul II, and Anglican Archbishop Desmond Tutu. In his opening remarks, the Pope expressed "his ardent prayer that, with the support of relevant international groups, there will be a permanent ban on this type of weapon, which has such outrageous traumatic effects."[59] Meanwhile, the Archbishop wanted to add his "voice . . . calling for a categorical and unequivocal international ban on the production, sale and use of antipersonnel mines."[60]

The Cambodia conference was important because it was a major catalyst for broadening and expanding the ICBL membership, especially in the Southern Hemisphere which was important for the

Photograph 3.1

Mary Wareham (L) with Bobby Muller and Jody Williams of VVAF at the Cambodia conference, June 1995. (Courtesy Mary Wareham. Used by permission.)

campaign since many of these countries were the most intensely mined countries in the world.[61] Such expansion truly helped create a global movement, rather than one that was "North Atlantic dominated" and provided guidance, enhanced data collection, and dissemination by regional campaigners.[62]

The "Phnom Penh formula" included inventive campaigning and training tailored to local, regional, and cultural circumstances, such as escorting conference participants to prosthetics workshops and amputee vocational training centers, as well as visits to observe mine awareness and clearance teams at work.[63] For example, HI's Susan Walker, who worked for 15 years with landmine survivors on the Thai-Cambodian border, took a few ICBL leaders and campaigners to view a demining demonstration when a landmine accident occurred nearby.[64] She continued to frequently inform diplomats that if they were not inspired to ban landmines, they should "make one trip to a mine-affected country . . . [that would be] a bone-jolting ride on the back of a motorcycle to the far reaches of a mine-affected country to see what the reality is like for those living in mine-affected communities."[65]

Phnom Penh Conference on-site sessions were also held to educate campaigners on a range of advocacy issues and tactics. Among the ICBL training sessions were: *Using the Media and Campaign Awareness, How to Write a Media Release, How to Be Informed About Landmines, How to Start a Country Campaign,* and a *Case Study of a Successful Campaign—Belgium.*[66]

The formula itself originated from the non-violent peace walks known as Cambodian Dhammayietras, literally truth pilgrimages, which were designed to promote peace among the 4,000 to 7,000 walkers, comprised of Buddhist monks and lay people, and the communities that they walked through.[67] The 1995 Dhammayietra directly focused on the need to ban landmines as one of the most effective ways to create a peaceful environment in Cambodia.[68] Among the marchers were four soldiers from the different militias and armies fighting in Cambodia that had each lost limbs to landmines. They wrote a joint letter to launch national signature campaign to ban landmines and which eventually totaled more than 310,000 signatures.[69] Each Dhammayietra lasted around one month and usually attracted international media attention, such as from the *New York Times* and CNN. Most were peaceful but some marchers in previous Dhammayeitras were shot and killed by the warring factions.

The 1995 Dhammayietra was part of a larger walk from Auschwitz, Germany, to Hiroshima, Japan, to promote international peace during the 50th anniversary year of the atomic bombing of Hiroshima. The Cambodian Dhammayietra marchers met the international march at the Thailand border, and then accompanied them through Cambodia and on to the Vietnam border. Throughout the walk, the marchers made landmine presentations to communities along the route and collected signatures or thumb prints from bystanders on a landmine ban petition.[70] Many of the marchers subsequently became active ICBL members, and a few rose to ICBL leadership positions.[71]

The Cambodia Conference was also the first ICBL conference organized mainly by e-mail, as it quickly became the dominant communication medium in preparation for the Cambodia conference.[72] According to Williams:

> The switch to e-mail, actually was initiated by our Cambodian Campaign to Ban Landmines, which began using e-mail in the organizing of the third international conference in Phnom Penh . . . The developing world, in effect, forces us all to look at the speed, efficiency and cost-effectiveness of email. My own bills dropped from around $400–450 a month for telephone/fax bill to $20 for e-mail.[73]

The next international landmine meeting occurred the following month, July 5–7, at the Palais des Nations in Geneva, where the UN convened an "International Meeting on Mine Clearance." The UN's goal was to galvanize world public opinion by seeking financial and political support for its mine clearance programs.[74]

At the meeting, the United States continued to claim that APLs were a necessary weapon for its military. The head of the U.S. delegation,

Tim Connolly, principal deputy assistant secretary of defense for special operations and low-intensity conflict, said that "it is the position of the U.S. government that there is still, even in a post-Cold War environment, a military utility or need for antipersonnel land mines."[75] He also stated that the Department of Defense is "working aggressively . . . to find alternatives in the future to antipersonnel landmines."[76] This was very encouraging to Leahy because the Pentagon had maintained that the United States could move most effectively toward the goal of the eventual elimination of antipersonnel landmine as "viable and humane alternatives are developed." But he also said that he does "not believe this should be a precondition to a ban on these indiscriminate inhumane weapons."[77]

Turning to the House, in September, John Shalikashvili, chairman of the Joint Chiefs of Staff, sent a letter to Representative Ronald V. Dellums, of the House Committee on National Security, expressing his "significant concerns" that the legislation, as written, would place American personnel at risk.[78] Ultimately, the Senate would vote 67-24 in August to include the Leahy legislation to impose a one-year moratorium on the use of antipersonnel landmines except in demilitarized zones and along international borders.[79]

According to the top UN landmine expert, Paddy Blagden, the Shalikashvili letter included the typical military "punch line" that "landmines save the lives of American soldiers" despite the fact that "it will be difficult for anyone, either pro-military or pro-humanitarian to prove it."[80] He suggested that Leahy's office counter Shalikashvili's argument by questioning how the military has used its mines. He advised that the:

> main sticking point is that most armies base their continuing use of landmines on the fact that they always use them "lawfully." The short answer is that they do not. Perhaps you should be asking armies to indicate where and when they *have* used landmines in accordance with the protocols. The answer is they haven't, or have complied by using the escape clause in the protocol to avoid compliance. The only instance I can find of full compliance to the Protocols is by the East German Border Guards, who fenced and guarded their antipersonnel mines by fire, and now have pulled them up again.[81]

The VVAF provided added firepower at a National Press Club news conference on September 21 to release its seminal book, *After the Guns Fall Silent: The Enduring Legacy of Landmines*.[82] Co-authored by Shawn Roberts and Jody Williams, the book was the first socio-economic study of the humanitarian consequences of APL use and concludes that APLs should be banned. The book's release was coordinated to coincide with the CCW Review conference, which would begin the following week in Vienna.

The CCW Review Conference began in Vienna on September 25 with forty-four states participating and an additional forty observer states.

The ICBL presence at the CCW Review conference comprised more than 100 individuals representing seventy organizations from twenty countries. Several governmental delegations, such as those from Australia, Canada, and New Zealand, included NGO representatives.[83] Even though invited, U.S. NGOs did not join the U.S. delegation because "they would then be obligated not to disagree publicly with the official delegation position."[84] Unlike the GGE expert meetings, ICBL members and other NGOs were permitted to participate by observing the general sessions. In addition, HRW's Steve Goose and the ICBL leadership "created a separate NGO agenda in Vienna so as not to spend their time listening to government representatives debate whether a certain mine is better or worse than another."[85]

In the conference's opening address, Johan Molander, president of the Review Conference, welcomed the NGOs and informed conference delegates that "[w]e shall listen to them. Even if their views do not always coincide with those of governments, their participation and their experience can substantially contribute to our work."[86] He also gave the speaker's platform for one plenary session to twenty-two ICBL speakers, including landmine ban activists, landmine survivors, and de-miners.[87] Their credibility was enhanced when Molander stated that he appreciated the NGO presence and that governments are "indebted to them for their work 'in the field'—a phrase, which in these circumstances, takes on a particularly sinister connotation—but also for sounding the alarm and raising public awareness."[88]

Adding to the somber, yet urgent air to the packed conference hall, UN Secretary-General Boutros-Ghali addressed attendees via video recording to highlight the global mine crisis. He stated that "each year more than 20,000 human beings are wounded or killed by landmines" and that "most of them are not combatants: they are farmers, women and children." He further stated that while approximately 100,000 landmines were cleared each year, between 2 million and 5 million more landmines are laid during that same period. "Hence," he concluded, "landmine proliferation adds each year two or more decades to the eleven hundred years necessary to clear all landmines at current rates."[89]

Despite the call by Boutros-Ghali to ban landmines, nearly all of the delegations spoke of the need for further regulations as a step toward an eventual ban. Following is a sampling of national statements:

- Australia's Minister for Defense Science and Personnel Gary Punch announced that his country was replacing its long-life mine stockpiles with self-destructing mines as the "technology involved in producing and self-destructing and deactivating mines is simple, highly cost-effective, and already available."[90]

- The head of the Russian delegation, S. B. Krylov, said that Russia knew about the humanitarian consequences of mine use because thousands of its citizens had become "victims of the 'mine heritage' of World War II." As part of a global solution, Russia called for progress to be "minor though specific" toward lowering the APL threat. For example, Russia supported a ban on transfers to states that "are not parties to the Protocol, if the latter don't comply with the respective obligations of the future Protocol."[91]
- Li Changhe, head of the Chinese delegation, said that "we should not forget that mines are effective defensive weapons for many countries, especially the larger number of developing countries, to resist foreign aggression. It is a legitimate right for all states to use mines to fight against foreign aggressors."[92]
- Ambassador Mark Moher, Canada's permanent representative to the United Nations for Disarmament, stated Canada's support for the elimination of antipersonnel landmines, but added "[h]aving stated that objective it is equally clear that it will not be achievable for some considerable time into the future. Therefore what can we achieve now—at this Review Conference? In answering that question we must be bold enough to say what can be accomplished now; we must also be realistic enough not to demand too much and risk losing all. Diplomacy, especially multilateral diplomacy is after all (like politics) the art of the possible guided by principle."[93]

In conjunction with the events at the conference site, ICBL members conducted public-awareness activities throughout the UN Conference facility and Vienna itself. They started lobbying with a press conference at the Vienna Opera House, where the speakers included ICBL leaders and landmine survivors from Afghanistan, Cambodia, and the United States. Medico International (MI), a Frankfurt based NGO and ICBL co-founder, converted a flatbed trailer into a simulated minefield, and placed it in Vienna's downtown square.[94] Reporters, government officials, local youth, and tourists all tried their fate crossing the flatbed trailer that had layers of dirt and vegetation hiding sensors that would be triggered by a footstep. The implications were clear for the hundreds of participants and thousands of spectators.

Another ICBL event was the creation of a shoe pile in front of the Austrian Parliament that encouraged its president, Dr. Heinz Fischer, to declare his support for the ban.[95] As with shoe pyramids organized by HI in Paris, the shoes dramatically personified the unneeded shoes of hundreds of thousands of current and future landmine amputees.[96]

The ICBL also published "CCW News," which reflected its views and ran special features on particular activists, delegations, and national positions. The "CCW News" was often the only document produced on a daily basis at the conferences, and delegates read it diligently. It was also disseminated through fax and e-mail to the public, media, other NGOs, and policymakers around the world.[97] One of the most popular columns, titled "The Good, The Bad and the Ugly," "frequently roused the ire of governments," but "it also pressured them to bring their public statements in line with the realities of their negotiating positions—or vice versa."[98] The column capitalized on the cynical views of governments—agreeing that there is humanitarian suffering caused by mines but continuing to argue for landmine use—by using the media to promote landmine-victim stories, embarrass "bad guys," and isolate governments not supporting the ban.

In Vienna, the ICBL developed a "good list" that included 14 countries that supported a ban. This list proved useful to the ICBL as the conference negotiations drew to a close, since it "worked to convince the media and friendly governments that not only were the negotiations *not* moving toward a ban, but also that they were, in fact, weakening the already horribly weak CCW landmine protocol."[99] It was also circulated to the media, which publicized it, pressuring those governments.[100]

Also during the conference, landmine survivors from Afghanistan, Cambodia, and the United States presented Chairman Molander more than 100,000 signatures (see photo 3.2). The following year, two of the survivors—the author and Jerry White—launched the Landmine Survivors Network (LSN), which was the first international organization created by and for survivors to help victims of war rebuild their lives.[101] LSN also quickly became a leader in the ICBL advocating for the inclusion of socioeconomic assistance for survivors in any negotiated framework to ban landmines.[102]

The convention negotiations were stalled by the consensus voting rules that could not push the U.S./UK landmine control regime, based on SD and SN mines, and from other countries, such as China, India, Pakistan, and Russia, which thought that the negotiations were moving too fast.[103] For example, the China and Russia delegates said that they could not address some of the issues because they "had difficulties in obtaining any further instructions from their capitals regarding possible compromise."[104] China opposed a ban because it "holds that the landmine is a defensive weapon."[105] Meanwhile, other states opposed any restrictions in part to protect their lucrative mine industries,[106] while poorer or less technologically advanced countries are opposed to the "smart" landmine proposal for cost reasons.

The diplomatic negotiators participating in the conference achieved what they are best known for: compromise: Struggling to bridge deep divides over how to limit the humanitarian devastation caused by APLs, they agreed to disagree and to postpone proceedings as consensus rules prevented agreements from being passed. The decision was made to suspend the conference and an agreement was made for two additional sessions in Geneva to continue the negotiations: first, a technical session in January and then a concluding session to finalize the protocol in April.

Photograph 3.2

American landmine survivors Ken Rutherford and Jerry White with survivors from Afghanistan and Cambodia—presenting more than 100,000 signatures to Johan Molander, President of the First Review Conference of States Parties to the CCW. At the invitation of HI Co-Director Philippe Chabasse, landmine survivors delivered the petitions to President Molander. HI was responsible for coordinating the global signature campaign. (Courtesy of author. Used by permission.)

There are various interpretations of consensus-based voting, but all include a similar characteristic: All negotiating parties must approve (or at least not disapprove) the resolution in some form. Setting aside abstention votes, any resolution that draws less than one hundred percent support from all members does not pass, while any resolution without opposition signals that all parties agree to it. In other words, under consensus rules, resolutions are adopted only when no representative disagrees with it so robustly as to persist in blocking them.

Some of these challenges are described in the ICBL conference report produced after the conference:

> Going into Vienna, nations were discussing a self-destruct time limit of 7–90 days, with an acceptable failure rate of 1 in 1,000. The emerging consensus now seems to be 30 days and 1 in 20, though some nations have advocated 365 or more days and 1 in 10 failure rate. For self-deactivation, initial parameters of 30–365 days have given way to 120–200 days. Moreover, some nations, notably Russia, are insisting on a 15-year grace period for the new restrictions to take effect.[107]

One of the key sticking points to reaching a consensus decision was verification measures, which included fact-finding missions in states that were accused of violating the protocol. While NATO and Warsaw States were accustomed to intrusive verification regimes due to their experience with the Conventional Forces in Europe treaty, for the non-aligned states, such as China, Cuba, India, Iran, Mexico, and Pakistan, it was too intrusive and thus they could not support it. Another issue that quickly became important was increasing the treaty's scope to internal conflicts, especially since many landmines are used in conflicts of a non-international character. Some countries had specific concerns regarding non-interference and sovereignty regarding extension of the scope.

The deadlocked CCW meeting on landmines gave the ICRC the impetus on November 22 to announce the launch of its international media campaign to "stigmatize these barbarous weapons."[108] Developed by the international advertising firm BBDO, it was its first ever media campaign to help generate public momentum to stigmatize a weapon. It was also the first time the ICRC officially called for a weapons prohibition since its chemical weapons ban call after WWI.

The ICBL also remained active between the end of the Vienna Conference and the start of the January 1996 follow-up Geneva sessions. The ICBL decided on a two-tier strategy. First, the ICBL wanted to foster an international movement based on regional strategy that established "mine-free zones' as building blocks to a global ban."[109] It was also suggested that the ICBL needed "to continue growth and dynamism by reaching out to new organizations and constituents . . . such as religious institutions."[110] To accomplish this, it was decided at the Vienna meeting to begin planning preparations to host the next international NGO conference in Africa.[111]

The second strategy entailed persuading friendly governments to work together on moving the landmine ban platform forward in the international arena. Steve Goose:

> first proposed this strategy during one of the morning ICBL meetings in Vienna, touting the necessity to create a unified core group of governments supporting a ban. Some campaigners did not like this, thinking that we could not work successfully WITH governments, fearing that we would be used, or co-opted, or compromise our high standard for a ban. But the strategy was agreed to. With all the praise for the "partnership" that we have heard for so long now, it is easy to forget this was not an automatic thing, but was controversial for both the NGOs and governments involved.[112]

The ICBL pressured "those nations professing to support an immediate ban to take actions consistent with that position, actions both on the domestic front and in Geneva."[113] Most importantly, "NGOs should encourage 'ban' countries to form an informal working group in Geneva, and to meet regularly to discuss means of promoting a ban."[114] ICBL members were encouraged to keep contact with their country delegates to maintain a pulse on their country's landmine policies in order to prevent governmental consensus on how to deal with the landmine crisis.

Back in the United States, the U.S. Campaign to Ban Landmines (USCBL) reorganized in order to increase coordination and bring the headquarters to the East Coast and under the auspices of the VVAF. On December 13, 35 representatives from more than 20 American NGOs met as the USCBL at the offices of the Women's Commission for Refugee Women and Children (Women's Commission) in New York City.[115]

Since April 1995, the USCBL point of contacts were Women Commission board members Dr. Anne Goldfeld, one of the first Americans to call for a landmine ban, when she gave first-hand evidence of the humanitarian devastation of landmines in Cambodia before congress in 1991, and Holly Myers, who staffed the USCBL organization from her Palo Alto, CA, office.[116] They decided to begin a grass-roots effort that would be the beginning of the U.S. campaign after attending the 1994 2nd ICBL conference in Geneva, "where the lack of a coordinated U.S. campaign was evident."[117] According to Myers, she and Goldfeld:

> specifically set out to begin to mobilize a grass-roots country campaign, as there was no such effort in the U.S.; it seemed logical and necessary to multiply the more 'technical' efforts spearheaded in DC and to take up the lead of active campaigns in other countries.[118]

The USCBL was then based in the office of Myers in Palo Alto, California, and funded mostly with her personal funds.[119] Organizationally, the Goldfeld Myers worked under the auspices of the Women's Commission, which supported a global landmine ban because of "the disastrous impact of landmines on refugee and internally displaced populations worldwide."[120] Myers and a Stanford work study student, Melanie Charles, coordinated with Boston-based Goldfeld to return phone calls and answer letters from Americans interested in the landmine issue. Goldfeld recalls the many calls and letters from Americans outraged about the use of landmines. She particularly remembers "a right to life advocate in Vermont calling about landmines." "It is a life issue," the caller said. Another caller said he was a WWII veteran from the Sicily fighting and lent his support to the campaign.[121] According to Myers,

> [i]t is interesting to see how "crude" communication was in 1995; between campaign correspondents the year progresses from messages relayed mostly by fax to, toward the middle/end of the year, email. We had email at the PA [Palo Alto] office, which was hugely useful—but the public we were reaching out to still used

U.S. mail/written typed letter and (a small minority) faxes. I obtained an 800 number for the office, which proved very useful; interestingly, I was not able to obtain an "acronym" for the 800 number, as ATT had "run out" of numbers—and none were going to be available until introduction of the 888 exchange, planned for later that year. Newsletter design likewise was very crude—there are examples of more elegant design from that era, obviously, but we had to keep it simple, as we did not have a budget for a dedicated graphic designer. Compared with the lightning speed of internet activities as we now use them, it was all painfully slow and time-consuming.[122]

By the December 13th meeting in New York, Goldfeld and Myers had collected more than 13,000 signatures, through a petition and letter writing campaign they directed and organized, in just a few months.[123] At the meeting, there was disagreement regarding how the USCBL should be run, who should lead it, and where it should be located.[124] Jody Williams of the VVAF and the ICBL Coordinator and Steve Goose of Human Rights Watch Arms Project, and an important leader in the ICBL, wanted more campaign coordination "to get more groups to function as a real campaign, with real coordination and direction and common activities."[125] They viewed the work of the Palo Alto office as "a point of contact and clearinghouse."[126] This issue was pursued further in January 4 and 24, 1996, telephone conference calls that included Goldfeld, Goose, Myers, and Williams, among others, to discuss the USCBL's new organizational structure. The discussion resulted in a "consensus opinion" to establish a national coordinating office housed at the Washington, D.C. office of the VVAF.[127]

In the meantime, Goldfeld and Myers wrote a *Boston Globe* op-ed to bring a sense of urgency to Americans to support a landmine ban. They wrote

> . . . time is of the essence as the problem worsens daily—every year, 2 million to 5 million new landmines are laid while the international community clears a mere 100,000. Aren't 110 million in the earth horror enough? Why have landmines not already been banned? Is it because they affect the poor, the refugees, the voiceless? If landmines were blowing up thousands of citizens in our own country – if one in every 236 Americans were an amputee because of landmines, our citizenry would not tolerate their continued use.[128]

On February 15, Williams e-mailed individuals and organizations involved in the landmines efforts in the United States, updating the new U.S. organizational structure and asking for suggestions for members to the serve on the advisory committee in order "to arrive at a fair and balanced composition" in order "to have major sectors represented."[129] She also announced the hiring of Mary Wareham, the former convener of New Zealand's Campaign Against Land Mines (CALM), as the national

U.S. Campaign to Ban Landmines (USCBL) coordinator.[130] Wareham had "got involved in the landmine issue in late 1993" when she saw Williams "speak during her New Zealand tour."[131] While working on her MA in Political Science at the University of Victoria in Wellington, New Zealand, on the emerging movement to ban APLs, she had become involved with CALM and the ICBL. Nine months after graduating, she went to Washington, D.C. to work for VVAF on the ICBL after accepting the USCBL Coordinator offer from Williams.[132]

Despite there always being a rabid sense of being the underdog among the campaigners, the ICBL's hopes of achieving a ban increasingly rested on the strong bond between its leaders: Williams, Goose, and Carl von Essen from Radda Barnen (Swedish Save the Children) and government diplomats.[133] They discussed among themselves the need to bring pro-ban governments together as a bloc. During one of the daily morning ICBL meetings in Vienna, it was agreed that the ICBL would try to bring together a core group of truly pro-ban governments, and would at some point in the future host a meeting of the few openly pro-ban governments to discuss ways to cooperate.[134] Thus, ICBL leaders had been working with the Quaker UN Office in Geneva "for an informal off-the-record conference with diplomats to formulate a time frame to eliminate landmines" and in order to "put pressure on governments to do something."[135]

While governments might have been disappointed in the failure of the Vienna Conference to reach consensus on the Landmines Protocol, the ICBL remained undeterred, as it viewed "Vienna as part of an ongoing process that will lead to a ban."[136]

At the second CCW Review session held in January in Geneva, 43 governments participated, while another 33 attended as observers. ICBL representation was small, as it was billed as a technical session where no decisions would be made. ICBL members were active in lobbying including informing the delegates that since Vienna, the ICBL noted that "approximately 8,000 people, including at least five NATO soldiers in Bosnia, were killed or maimed by landmines," and that there were no technological solutions to the global landmine crisis.[137] ICBL members also passed out press kits, held press conferences, and screened the anti-landmine film "Silent Sentinels."

ICBL members had not made any preparations to host a first-pro-ban meeting because they were unsure whether or not they would have it the during the January session or later, and partially explains why some NGOs did not come to Geneva because they were not expecting a key meeting to take place.[138] During the Geneva meetings, Pieter van Rossem of Pax Christi Netherlands and a leader in the Netherlands Campaign to Ban Landmines also wanted to bring together the ICBL and those governments on the "good guys" list to discuss strategy for promoting an immediate ban, rather than the "eventual elimination" of landmines.[139] He ran his idea by Goose, eventually convincing him that the ICBL had little to lose. The main goal for the meeting was to search for ways to get beyond the stalemate induced by CCW consensus voting rules. According to Goose,

> At the January session, Pieter pushed for us to go ahead with trying to hold a "good guys" meeting. I was reluctant, because we had not prepared for it in ICBL (What we wanted out it, how we would run it, etc.), and had not prepped any governments for it, and some key NGOs were not in Geneva at the time. I wanted to wait for the April/May session. But Pieter convinced me it was worth a try.[140]

Van Rossem and Goose decided to bring together the ICBL and those 22 governments, who were on the "good guys" list as supporting a ban, to discuss strategy for promoting an immediate ban, rather than the "eventual elimination" of landmines."[141] As Williams and Goose later recounted, "A decision that turned out to be of pivotal importance ... was made to put a priority on getting avowedly pro-ban governments to self-identify and work together as a bloc ... as the only way to maintain movement ... and [move] the issue forward."[142]

The day after his conversation with Goose, van Rossem pursued the government outreach initiative by inviting several delegations on the "good guys" list to attend a special meeting the next day on the 17th. Van Rossem then chaired the ICBL-sponsored meeting at the Palais des Nations building. Of the 22 governments listed as supporting the ban, only eight accepted the invitation "to discuss bans at the national level and initiatives which might be developed for the third session of the CCW Review Conference beginning in April."[143]

Canada was added to the invite list the day of the meeting, as it did not make the ICBL's "good guy" list until that morning, when Ambassador Mark Moher announced that Canada had put in place a moratorium on the production, transfer, and operational use of APLs.[144] One of Canada's diplomats at the conference, Robert Lawson, decided to accept the ICBL's invitation to attend the meeting.[145] According to Goose, Lawson and the Austrian and Belgian ambassadors seemed the most enthusiastic about the bloc's chances to push for a ban.[146] Lawson said that "the meeting was largely structured around a brief exchange of views on national perspectives on the ban agenda" with "a general agreement on the need to enhance cooperation among pro-ban forces."[147]

In addition to Von Rossem and Goose, attendees included around eight ICBL representatives and Peter Herby, from the ICRC legal office. Near the meeting's end, when those attending were asked whether they wanted to reconvene, someone suggested that QUNO would be willing to host a second session. The Quaker representative at the meeting agreed.[148]

An enthusiastic Lawson believed that Canada could take an international leadership position on the landmine issue. His boss, Canadian Foreign Minister Lloyd Axworthy, shared that sentiment. Axworthy, who took office on January 25, was a former political science professor who viewed politics as a way to achieve policy goals, including placing a stronger emphasis on human security, multilateralism, and soft power, and immediately perceived landmines as a top policy priority.[149] He "indicated his interest in a partnership that would link NGO efforts with Canada's ability to champion the issue internationally."[150] It was a partnership that would prove intimately productive over the next two years.

Lawson also had a different view of foreign policymaking. In his action plan, he included NGOs into DFAIT's landmine work. As part of his plan, Lawson started "knocking on NGO doors trying to find out more about NGOs" and meeting with their staffs, including Paul Hannon, special projects officer at Oxfam Canada. He shared with Lawson his recent Rwanda trip experience that was Hannon's personal "trigger on the landmine issue."

> I knew the problems caused by landmines but I never experienced landmines first hand until this trip. They were lethal barriers to development. We checked out areas for re-settlement and no one was living on the land. It was empty. Then, returning through villages we found out that that land was mined. Here we were, middle class white people in Kigali [Rwanda's capital city] for 5–6 days and no one knew landmines were out there. On my trip home to Ottawa all I could think about was being in that landmine field and asking myself "How do Rwandans live with those restrictions on their life?" I decided for Oxfam Canada to get more active when Bob Lawson came knocking to find about more about our work.[151]

Further helping Lawson to propel landmines to the top of Canada's agenda was the November 4th public statement by the longtime Liberal politician André Ouellet in his capacity as minister of foreign affairs (November 4, 1993–January 24, 1996) that Canada should support an immediate APL ban and pledge destruction of the country's mine stockpiles. While shocked by the announcement, Canadian officials were not surprised, as Ouellet supported the U.S. export moratorium resolution at the UNGA and had wanted Canada's Department of National Defense (DND) to destroy its landmine stockpiles. Despite DND's opposition to the destruction request, Ouellet continued to call for Canada's landmine stockpile destruction, including informing Canada's television networks to that effect. When a reporter called Lawson—as DFAIT representative for the landmine portfolio—for comment he was in the middle of preparing for the continued CCW conference negotiations in Geneva in January.

Lawson obtained Ouellet's transcript and then faxed that announcement to the Mines Action Canada (MAC) Co-Chair, Valerie Warmington, whom he had met when she hosted ICRC surgeon Chris Ginnaou, who was outspoken on the need for an immediate ban, for media dissemination.[152] Ouellet's statement

> opened up more possibilities for more assertive action to get the Ministry of Defense [DND] on board. The statement was a classic opportunity to exploit and thus resolve what then appeared to differences in the DND and Ministry of Foreign Affairs' [DFAIT].[153]

As result, the minister's office received congratulatory phone calls on Canada's announcement that it was going to destroy the stockpiles.[154] According to another Canadian DFAIT arms control expert, Mark Gwozdecky, "[T]he Oullete announcement was good for us [DFAIT]. We had a policy then that we could take to others."[155]

On January 26, President Bill Clinton signed into law the Leahy-Evans landmine moratorium legislation as part of the Fiscal 1996 Foreign Operations Bill. It called for a period of one year, beginning three years, later that the United States "shall not use antipersonnel landmines except along internationally recognized national borders or in demilitarized zones within a perimeter marked area that is monitored by military personnel and protected by adequate means to ensure the exclusion of civilians."[156] Although the moratorium did not take effect until January 1999, it once again put the United States with several of its NATO allies in the lead on international efforts to rid the world of APLs. The legislation signaled a significant shift in U.S. policy, but only if the administration was united and active in implementing it.

While the legislation prohibited the use of APLs except under tight conditions, such as marked minefields and along international borders, beginning three years after passage, Leahy's main thrust for the legislation was to set an international example so other governments would enact their own prohibitions.

From the ashes of the futile CCW talks to address the global humanitarian crisis caused by landmines, the ICRC realized that many government delegates believed in the military utility of the weapon, which, in turn, overrode their concerns about its humanitarian effects. Therefore, the ICRC decided to "commission a study of the military use and effectiveness of antipersonnel landmines."[157] It also wanted to provide political cover to governmental policymakers, so the ICRC sought collaboration with military leaders in arguing that the military utility of landmines was minimal. It hosted a meeting for a selection of international military officers in February 1996 to discuss the military utility and effectiveness of APLs in order to help determine whether it was an indispensable weapon of war. It also commissioned a study by them on the actual use and effectiveness of landmines as the ICRC "always felt that the development of international humanitarian law entails a dialogue between military concerns and humanitarian imperatives. In the case of landmines, this dialogue is particularly important since claims concerning the military necessity have always stood as a major obstacle of a total ban."[158]

At the ICRC meeting, the participants examined the actual use of landmines in twenty-six twentieth century conflicts since 1945. They concluded that "no case was found in which the use of antipersonnel mines played a major role in determining the outcome of a conflict." Moreover, even when landmines are "used on a massive scale, they have usually had little or no impact on the outcome of hostilities." In fact, the group concluded that the "effects of antipersonnel mines are very limited and may even be counterproductive." Most importantly, the participants advanced the opinion that even for professional armed forces, balancing humanitarian law against military guidelines in APL use is tremendously challenging and seldom takes place during combat.[159]

After the meeting, the ICRC compiled the discussions and then released it as *Anti-Personnel Landmines: Friend or Foe? A Study of the Military Use and Effectiveness of Anti-personnel Mines*. The report, which became a critical advocacy element in the ICRC's anti-APL campaign, concluded:

> The military utility of AP mines is far outweighed by the appalling humanitarian consequences of their use in actual conflicts. On this basis their prohibition and elimination should be pursued as a matter of utmost urgency by governments and the entire international community.[160]

Meanwhile, on April 3, 1996, the VVAF placed a pro-ban landmine advertisement in the *New York Times* that was an open letter signed by fifteen retired generals and admirals to President Clinton, which urged him to "support a permanent and total international ban on the production, stockpiling, sale and use of this weapon."[161] Among the signatories was American hero Gen. Norman Schwarzkopf (Ret.) who had been commander of the Coalition Forces in the 1991 Gulf War, otherwise known as Operation Desert Storm. The month before he responded to former chairman Frank J. Fahrenkopf, Jr, former chairman of the Republican National Committee (1983–1989), who asked Schwarzkopf to join the VVAF general's letter supporting a ban.

> I do have extensive experience with landmines, having seen hundreds of my own troops killed or maimed by them and having myself been wounded by a landmine detonation. I also am keenly aware of the devastating effects on civilian populations . . . I would be delighted to see AP mines [APL] forever eliminated from warfare. . . . I would be very much opposed to banning antitank landmines, yet we experienced in Vietnam antitank landmines that were easily modified to become APM [APL] by the Vietcong.[162]

The joining of military officers with the ICRC and the ICBL call for a ban added considerable legitimacy to the landmine-ban position and helped to diminish the military-utility argument. Much of the media attention was focused on the stories of landmine victims or the challenges faced by deminers (see photo 3.3). This media framing was a deliberate action on the ICBL's part, as it decided early on in the movement to develop "several traveling photograph exhibits and videos" that graphically portrayed consequences of landmine use.[163] By featuring landmine victims frequently and prominently in their promotional literature and reports, and featuring them in speeches and conferences, the ICBL and ICRC strategies consisted primarily of emotional arguments brought by and on the behalf of victims. There was no real attempt by states opposed to the ban to dispute the humanitarian arguments. Instead, these anti-ban states made strong military and political arguments why landmines should not be banned, while at the same time expressing humanitarian concern for the landmine victims.

Even after the victim and demining angle of the landmine story became worn, the media continued to focus on the unlawfulness of the weapons and the ICBL experts' core arguments supporting a ban. Soon, "one by

Photograph 3.3

Cambodia: Community meeting with landmine survivors and ICBL Ambassador Tun Channareth. (Courtesy of the Cambodia Campaign to Ban Landmines and Cluster Munitions.)

one, major media sources in almost all regions of the world began to endorse the concept of a global ban on AP mines."[164]

By mid-1996, a poll showed that the international public was increasingly united in their belief that APLs were horrific and indiscriminate killers and should be banned. In response to the question "would you personally be in favor or against your country signing the landmine ban treaty," the percentage in favor was overwhelming. Of the twenty-one states surveyed, Japan and the United States scored the lowest in approval at still the relatively high rates of 58 percent and 60 percent, respectfully, while Denmark at 92 percent and Spain at 91 percent scored the highest. Even the citizens of other major power states, such as Russia at 83 percent and India at 82 percent favored their country signing landmine ban treaty.[165]

CHAPTER 4

From Ashes to Success: April 1996–September 1997

APRIL 1996—CCW HOSTAGE TO CONSENSUS

The third and final Convention on Conventional Weapons (CCW) Review session on the Landmines Protocol convened with 51 participating governments from April 22 to May 3 in Geneva at the Palais des Nations. The session's main purpose was to finalize the agreements produced during the first two CCW review sessions (held in Vienna in October 1995 and in Geneva in January 1996). Unknown to all the participants, including the International Campaign to Ban Landmines (ICBL) and International Committee of the Red Cross (ICRC), this conference would signal the end of the CCW as the major international negotiating forum for discussing landmines.[1]

With her opening plenary address, ICBL Coordinator Jody Williams set the urgent tone for the meeting by stating that "[m]ore people have been killed or maimed by landmines since the end of the first session of the Review Conference in Vienna. How many more will it take?"[2] If they had not already done so, government leaders immediately realized that Williams was more formidable than other activists they tried to circumvent and ignore. While recognizing the importance of the CCW Review process in highlighting the landmine problem, she stated that the ICBL remains "discouraged that the likely changes to the CCW are not more far-reaching and immediate."[3]

Williams also continued to coordinate the ICBL's on- and off-site activities to increase pressure on delegates to adopt an APL ban. At the Palais des Nations, ICBL members organized information tables and press conferences for the media. They also placed landmine-victim photos and displays highlighting the mine crisis throughout the Palais's hallways and public places. Iain Guest, a former Geneva-based newspaper correspondent and UNHCR press spokesman in Cambodia, volunteered with the ICBL to organize daily press conferences regarding ICBL activities and conference status reports from an ICBL perspective.

In an April 23 unveiling ceremony of the "The Wall of Remembrance," a memorial to the to the 13,748 landmine victims since the first CCW Review Conference ended in Vienna on October 13, 1996, took place. As a landmine survivor, the author, and Tun Channareth, a Cambodian landmine survivor, asked the somber and quiet group of nearly 100 government delegates, international media, and NGO representatives for a moment of silence in their honor as an electric counter clicked another estimated landmine casualty from 13,834 to 13,835.[4] Besides the counter, the wall also included a large photo display of landmine victims injured between the two conferences from Battambong Province in Cambodia (see photo 4.1).[5]

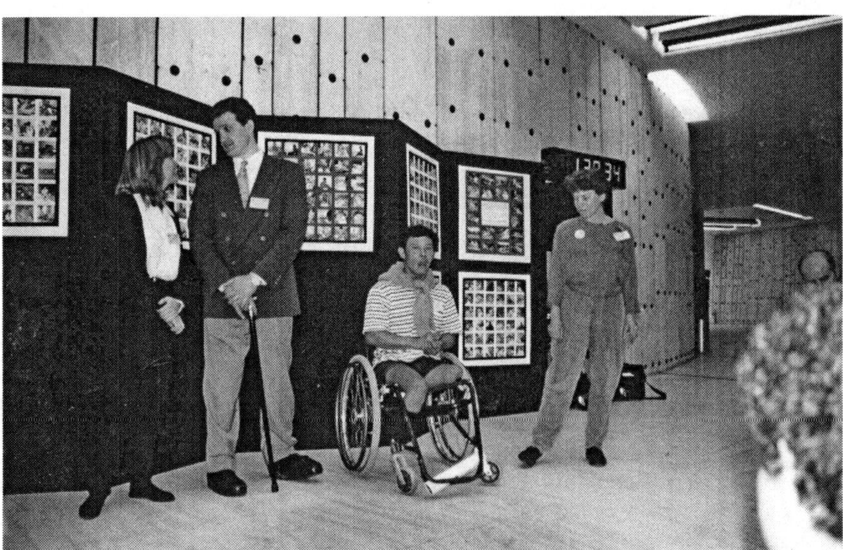

Photograph 4.1

"The Wall of Remembrance," a memorial ceremony. April 23, 1996. Palais des Nations, Geneva. April 23, 1996. Ali Ramsey, Cambodia Campaign to Ban Landmines (L), Ken Rutherford, co-founder, Landmine Survivors Network (LSN), Tun Channareth, Cambodian landmine survivor and member of the Cambodia Campaign to Ban Landmines, and Liz Bernstein, Cambodia Campaign to Ban Landmines. (Courtesy of author.)

The ICBL members' off-site activism was just as intense. Just outside the Palais des Nations fenced compound, Handicap International (HI) led the construction of a five and half ton shoe pyramid in a mock minefield that was previously seen under the Eiffel Tower in Paris (see photo 4.2). The pyramid poignantly symbolized the victims of landmines who would no longer need them.[6] At the entrance gates to the Palais, landmine survivors, many of them in wheelchairs, gave arriving delegates red roses, each tagged with the name of a mine victim. Several delegates refused to accept the flowers and later complained to conference officials that these kinds of public and political displays had no place in diplomatic negotiations.[7]

Most significantly, on April 22, the Quaker United Nations Office (QUNO) hosted a meeting of the ICBL, ICRC, and governmental representatives that supported a ban in their public statements and were on the ICBL's "good guys" list. Though it was an ICBL-sponsored meeting, Steve Goose of Human Rights Watch (HRW) and the coordinator for the U.S. Campaign to Ban Landmines (USCBL) thought it appropriate for the

Photograph 4.2

Today, at the location of the 1995 shoe pyramid in Geneva is a large permanent three-legged chair monument symbolizing the legs lost by landmine survivors. The monument was funded and organized by Handicap International, the NGO responsible for the shoe pyramids. Entitled, The Broken Chair, the chair is 39-feet and stands near the entrance to the UN European Headquarters. (Courtesy Mary Wareham. Used by permission.)

meeting to be held at the QUNO office, "largely because Quakers are known for doing such things in a constructive fashion."[8]

One week after the QUNO meeting and a few days before the CCW session ended, on April 29 Canadian diplomat Robert Lawson hosted a second meeting of the pro-ban group at the Palais des Nations.[9] The agenda for the meeting was developed by the ICBL in consultation with Lawson, who agreed with the broadening dissatisfaction with the minimal advancement made in the Review CCW Convention negotiations. At the meeting, he said that the Canadian government "would be willing, if it was felt to be useful by others, to host an international meeting in Ottawa in the fall [of 1996] to advance the ban agenda."[10] According to QUNO Associate Representative David Atwood, the meeting's participants registered their general support.[11] Lawson then announced that Canada would host an official conference in its capital city, Ottawa, to facilitate a joint strategy for banning APLs and that it would make its invitation public in a few days at the close of the CCW Review Conference.[12]

After two years of preparation and negotiations involving more than 50 countries to develop meaningful controls on the use of APLs, on May 3 the Landmines Protocol was finally amended to prohibit the use of non-detectable mines, long-life (non-self destruct) mines outside marked areas, and self-destruct landmines that do not self-destruct within 30 days at less than a 90 percent effective rate. It also included extending its scope of application to cover both international and internal armed conflicts, by prohibiting the use of non-detectable APLs and their transfer, and by prohibiting the use of non-self destructing APLs outside marked areas.

The amended protocol was the best that could be achieved at the time under consensus rules. The ICBL and ICRC were greatly disappointed with the outcome. According to the ICBL, "governments essentially took a weak document and weakened it further,"[13] while the ICRC called it "weak and overly complex."[14] In his statement near the end of the negotiations, ICRC Vice President Eric Roethlisberger told the delegates that

> the ICRC deeply regrets that, for the first time in a humanitarian law treaty, measures have been adopted which, instead of entirely prohibiting the use of an indiscriminate weapons, both permit its continued use and implicitly promote the use of new models which will have virtually the same effects, at least in the short term.[15]

It was perhaps predictable that efforts to obtain a consensus among more than 50 governments fell far short of what was needed to effectively deal with this humanitarian crisis. According to Johan Molander, president of the Review Conference, "[t]he outcome of the review was in substance far better than could have been expected originally."[16] He suggested that while an eventual ban was desirable, it was not the purpose of the conference to negotiate a ban. Instead, the conference had "the responsibility to adopt rules which will contribute to the goal set by the [United Nations] General Assembly of eventually banning APMs [APLs]."[17]

Both the ICBL and ICRC continued their call—in vain—for the removal of the word *primarily* from the APL definition. Meanwhile, ICRC President Cornelio Sommaruga urged delegates to change the definition:

> [T]he definition of an APM [APL] speaks of a weapon "primarily designed to be exploded by the presence, proximity or contact of a person." If this definition is adopted, any other accomplishments of this Conference could over time be subverted by the confusion and possible abuse which this definition could produce. Efforts to put an end to the humanitarian crisis caused by APMs may well be severely threatened or even totally undermined.[18]

The ICBL and ICRC concerns regarding the retention of the word *primarily* were confirmed when Austria, Canada, Denmark, France, Germany, Ireland, the Netherlands, South Africa, and Sweden declared that the insertion of the word *primarily* was included to separate the definition of anti-vehicle mines set with anti-handling devices from APLs.[19]

As Lawson promised, on the last day of the negotiations, May 3, 1996, he announced that Canada would host a conference of like-minded countries to develop concrete steps toward an international ban.[20] With this announcement, the Canadians moved the APL discussion outside the UN. Thus, the ICBL, ICRC, and the handful of pro-ban governments were particularly pleased with the Canadian initiative, as they were frustrated by the restrictive and traditional diplomatic practices in discussing weapons, especially avoiding its consensus negotiating rules. Within several days, more than 38 countries, including a majority of NATO members, had declared their support for the Canadian initiative to achieve an APL global ban.

Leahy was also very disappointed with the Amended Landmines Protocol and, more significantly, with the U.S. position in not advancing the APL ban. In a letter to U.S. National Security Adviser Anthony Lake, Leahy called the amended protocol a "deplorable failure." He wrote that it does not "deal effectively with this humanitarian crisis . . . It encourages the production and use of a new generation of indiscriminate, APLs . . . [and] it will have little if any impact on this problem in our lifetime. In the next decade alone, the State Department estimated that another 260,000 people will be maimed and killed by mines."[21] Leahy also expressed dissatisfaction with President Clinton, who he thought had a great opportunity as the world leader to make a real difference by announcing an immediate APL ban, as some of America's NATO allies had already done. He further wrote that "such a step would be praised around the world and here at home, and give a tremendous boost to international efforts to stigmatize these inhumane weapons."[22]

According to Bobby Muller, director of the Vietnam Veterans of America Foundation (VVAF) and co-founder of the International Campaign to Ban Landmines (ICBL), President Bill Clinton told him that "I can't afford a breach with the Joint Chiefs" on the anti-personnel landmine (APL) issue, while Lt. Gen. Robert Gard, a retired field commander during the Korean and Vietnam wars and VVAF adviser, said that Vice President Al Gore told him that he "could not break with the Joint Chiefs, politically."[23]

Thus in order to provide Clinton and Gore with the ammunition to overcome expected Pentagon opposition and support the APL ban, Muller spearheaded a VVAF-sponsored April 3 full page *New York Times* letter signed by 15 retired military leaders, including Gen. H. Norman Schwarzkopf, commander of Operation Desert Storm, supporting an APL ban.[24] A few weeks later on April 19, Sen. Patrick Leahy and Secretary of Defense William Perry had breakfast to discuss the administration's developing APL policy, which would be announced the following month. Perry informed Leahy that "the Demilitarized Zone (DMZ) in Korea would be the only exception to supporting a complete United States ban on APLs by the year 1999."[25]

Leahy also immediately supported the Canadian initiative by lobbying for the Clinton administration to participate [and] that "[i]t would be very unfortunate if the U.S. could not actively participate in this encouraging initiative."[26] Instead, Clinton announced a new APL policy on May 16, when he said that U.S. military would immediately cease the use and commence the elimination of non-self-destructing APLs, except for Korea and what was needed for training. In addition, the president directed the secretary of defense to aggressively seek alternatives to APLs.[27] Both steps, Clinton argued, would set the United States on "a concrete plan to a global ban on APMs [APLs]."[28] The latest U.S. APL policy, submitted by the Joint Chiefs of Staff and accepted by Clinton with little debate, made remarkably little progress in the global effort to ban APLs in comparison to the Canadian initiative. The policy's development was based on what a senior defense official said was needed by "the war fighter in place to accomplish the task that we have given him. And we ran excursions using every technique and war-game and modeling that we could do in simulation and we ran it both with landmines and without, and there are thousands of casualties, additional casualties that take place if we do not have anti-personnel landmines in place and available in Korea." Additionally, the proposal endorsed the use of so-called "smart mines" with self-destruct or self-deactivating mechanisms.[29]

The ICBL and USCBL were deeply disappointed in Clinton's failure to implement a meaningful national initiative committing the United States to a timeline for a worldwide APL ban. Clinton's policy now pushed a possible prohibition decades into the future in his administration's belief that interim control measures would significantly alleviate the humanitarian crisis. Leahy was very displeased with the president's policy and expressed his feelings by writing to Secretary of Defense William Perry that he was "not convinced that the administration's new policy now squarely puts the United States on a path toward eliminating landmines and [f]rankly, I feel we lost a great opportunity within our own military and also as a world leader."[30]

Ironically, the Canadians were mildly pleased with Clinton's announcement primarily because it committed to United States to the "eventual elimination" of APLs, which advanced Clinton's previous UNGA speeches. But the Canadians were surprised when U.S. officials soon informed them that they wanted concrete deadlines taken out of the upcoming Ottawa Conference meeting.[31] In particular, Canadian Foreign Minister Axworthy believed that he could still get the United States to participate in the Ottawa process by writing U.S. Secretary of State William Christopher that there was negotiating room for cooperation between the two countries. Based on Christopher's affirmative response, Canadian and U.S. officials met a few times during the summer for bilateral discussions to get the U.S substantially involved.[32]

At one of their Washington, D.C., meetings, the Canadians presented the year 2000 as a deadline to ban APLs. The ICBL and ICRC were unquestionably delighted with them for including the 2000 concrete deadline, while "it was greeted with less enthusiasm by a number of countries, in particular the United States."[33]

The American-Canadian negotiations "quickly focused on whether the Ottawa Declaration would set deadlines for halts in new deployments of mines or for the actual negotiation of a mine ban treaty."[34] The Canadians agreed to the American request to take out the 2000 target deadline for the United States to participate in the October strategy meeting in Ottawa.

Convinced that the United States was still leading the global crusade to solve the APL crisis, Clinton addressed the APL issue at the UN during his September 24 United Nations General Assembly (UNGA) speech. He stated that "we must end the carnage by anti-personnel landmines—the hidden killers that murder and maim more than 25,000 people every year" and renewed his "appeal for the swift negotiation of a worldwide ban on the use, stockpiling, production, and transfer of anti-personnel landmines." In a signal that the global diplomatic community was losing patience with the United States attempts to ban APLs in the future while the Canadians were currently leading an effort, Clinton's remarks raised hackles in the UN. Some diplomats accused him of hypocrisy because his own administration had recently delayed and derailed pro-ban discussions and pressured the Canadians to take all time-deadline references out of the confirmed agenda.[35]

OCTOBER 1996—TRANSFORMATIVE DIPLOMACY: OTTAWA LANDMINE BAN CONFERENCE

On October 4–5 in Ottawa, the Canadian government hosted the "Towards a Global Ban on Anti-Personnel Landmines" conference to discuss an international strategy to achieve an immediate, comprehensive APL ban. The Canadian government's commitment to the ICBL included helping the ICBL to "shape a vision for the conference" and Mine Action Canada (MAC) in ensuring a "Phnom Penh formula" for embedding the ICBL and ICRC in a full range of public activities and as a way "to increase civil-society pressure on state decision-makers."[36]

Although the meeting was not a negotiation, the agenda focused on building momentum in support of a negotiation process as a follow-up line of attack after the frustration of the CCW review. It was designed to catalyze pragmatic steps toward an APL ban and form a collaborative partnership among supportive governments, the ICBL, ICRC, and the UN to generate political will and global action to realize a global APL prohibition. It would also mark the first time that governments declared their support for a ban while convened as a body. According to Mark Gwozdecky, coordinator of the nine action teams in the Canadian Department of Foreign Affairs and International Trade, "many government representatives were embarrassed by questions about their landmine policies and until the CCW died, they could say that they were addressing the humanitarian problem caused by landmines in the CCW. Now there was nowhere to turn because suddenly the CCW is no longer functioning."[37]

In order to pre-empt opposition by governments wanting to prevent a comprehensive APL ban treaty, Canadian diplomats created a "self-selection" process that entailed circulating a "Criteria for Participation," including a rough summary of the eventual Final Declaration that would mention a strong commitment to banning APLs. Gwozdecky was one of the Canadian diplomats who designed and implemented the process. He wanted to have the "negotiation outcome in advance" so he used the declaration as "a screening tool and filter." He said, "Let's draft the declaration in such a way that countries that are landmine ban skeptics could not sign it," and attend as observers, while "those governments that supported the declaration could attend as full participants."[38] The declaration's requirements included supporting an early comprehensive APL ban, UNGA APL resolutions, and regional ban actions.[39]

Back in the United States, the Clinton administration believed that the best strategy for its interests—while staying on the road to achieve an APL ban—was to go through the Conference on Disarmament (CD) in order to capture the major landmine producers.[40] The CD was created by the UN to negotiate arms-control agreements, usually weapons of mass destruction rather than conventional weapons, which is why the UN created the CCW.

The United States continued with its APL strategy to push the CD at the opening day of Ottawa Conference by giving a presentation supporting the CD as the most appropriate forum to discuss APL prohibitions. The United States was also joined by the governments of Australia, Finland, France, and Italy, who all gave interventions in favor of renewing APL negotiations in the CD. As a result, the Canadians feared that that momentum was generating for taking the landmine issue to the CD.[41] They were not caught by surprise, however, as the Canadians were already warned in July by a NGO report produced by the Quaker UN Office (QUNO) in Geneva that governments would try to pursue the CD and that its consensus negotiating format was convoluted and lengthy, usually entailing decades of negotiations to reach agreement. Another concern was that the CD calendar was crowded with already scheduled activities, meaning that APLs could not be taken up until sometime the following year.

During the eve of the final conference day, Axworthy was "increasingly pessimistic" and had a "growing feeling of frustration" with the conference progress. Partly in order to kill the CD as a possible forum to negotiate an APL ban, Axworthy considered the idea for Canada to host a stand-alone pro-ban treaty conference to forge ahead with negotiations. The idea to short-circuit the conventional process came from Ralph Lysyshyn, director-general of Canada's International Security and Arms Control Bureau, who had helped lead the negotiations for the "Open Skies" stand-alone agreement hosted by Canada in 1990.[42] It was a gamble that could have ramifications for other international weapon and humanitarian law negotiations: Axworthy's initiative would bypass the UN, taking the negotiations straight to civil society and the transparent, non-consensus format they favored.

In strategizing on how best to implement his idea, Lysyshyn supported the stand alone ban treaty process because he could see the current negotiations leading nowhere except to the CD.[43] In turn, he successfully sought from his boss Paul Heinbecker, political director in the DFAIT (and former Canadian Ambassador and Permanent Representative to the UN) the political and financial support, including $2 million, and more if necessary that Axworthy required embarking on a stand-alone initiative to negotiate a mine ban treaty.[44]

The following morning, Axworthy also consulted one final time with his arms control team, including Lysyshyn, Gwozdecky, and Jill Sinclair, DFAIT Director for the Non-Proliferation, Arms Control, and Disarmament Division (IDA), about launching the APL ban initiative. Lysyshyn gave Axworthy a long list of negative fallout which would flow from launching such a initiative, such as criticisms that "Canada might also be accused of grandstanding by several of its allies on the landmine issue ... [and] there was also the risk that the initiative would simply fail—dealing Canada and the minister a humiliating policy defeat as well as a potentially devastating blow to the ban agenda."[45] But he also pointed out the positives, such as support from the ICBL, ICRC, UN as well as public opinion. Following this briefing, Axworthy simply replied, "It's the right thing. Let's do it."[46]

On the afternoon of October 5, 90 minutes before the end of the conference, Axworthy invited representatives from ICRC, UN, and ICBL to his office. Away from the conference spotlight's glare, he told them that he was going to announce that Canada would host a ban treaty signing in December 1997, with the major purpose of creating an alternative negotiating track to circumvent the UN bureaucracy and consensus-voting procedures, which they all blamed for holding up a ban agreement.[47]

The Canadians decided to keep the announcement secret from governmental delegations to avoid the risk that speakers would complain that it was not possible, ending the conference on a sour note.[48] The Canadian diplomats planned that after Axworthy's announcement, they would quickly follow with speakers representing the ICBL and ICRC so that no opposing countries could take the floor to oppose the initiative; the conference would immediately be declared closed after the ICRC statement. The ICBL's Williams immediately agreed. Since ICRC President Sommerugia had already left the conference grounds, Peter Herby, ICRC's legal affairs director, reached him by telephone to have him sign a statement of support for the Canada initiative.

In the Ottawa Congress Centre Conference Hall and against a backdrop of diplomatic inertia and nervous ban supporters, Axworthy delivered his speech and issued a call to government delegates at the closing plenary session, telling them to return to Ottawa in fifteen months to sign a comprehensive APL prohibition. A roar rang out among the ICBL members as Axworthy barely finished his statement. By the time it was over, the underdog-loving ICBL members at the conference had drowned Axworthy out of his final words with their loud applause.

By presenting governments with a clear choice—either to completely ban APLs by signing the yet-to-be-drafted treaty or to abstain—the Canadian government pressured governments to act. According to Gwozdecky, a leading Canadian negotiator, the dilemma that governments faced in deciding whether to sign an APL ban treaty was a simple one: "[Y]ou're either in or you're out."[49]

As diplomats puzzled over the proposed details of what could be the biggest conventional weapon prohibition in history, the initial skepticism that greeted its unveiling had only deepened. Some government delegates were horrified at the prospect of putting a negotiating deadline on the line. Others were outraged that Canada, home of multilateral cooperation, would lead a unilateral, non-UN, and non-consensus negotiation, even as the global community was working through the CCW to address the mine issue. According to Gwozdecky, in the announcement aftermath, the Canadians:

> were struggling with the anger of many foreign diplomats because of our call for a ban treaty. There was lots of fluffed up feathers. Some diplomats could not get over personal irritation. Ambassador Inderfuerth from the U.S. was one of the few who got beyond it. Jill [Sinclair—Canada's Ambassador for Mine Action in the Canadian Department of Foreign Affairs and International Trade] worked the phones with personal diplomacy. I would come into work at 7:30 a.m. and she had already been working the phones for hours.[50]

On October 6, the day after the conference closed, civil society members and Canadian government officials met at the conference facilities to plan their strategy for supporting Axworthy's initiative. All were aware that achieving a nearly universal comprehensive APL ban in less than one year against the opposition of countries such as China, the USSR, and the United States would be challenging at best. Therefore, tightly coordinated action among civil society and governments would be required.

The Canadian government's decision for the "the complete integration of the ICBL" in the treaty negotiations was made early in the drafting process.[51] Later, several governmental representatives cited the ICBL presence at the negotiating table as a powerful influence that affected the APL ban policy decisions of their countries.[52] As a result, key civil society members, such as the ICBL and ICRC and pro-ban states led by Canada, created the "Ottawa Process Core Group" that would draft the treaty and encourage international support.

The resulting 15 months of intense diplomatic activity to draft and sign the Mine Ban Treaty (MBT) was called the Ottawa Process. The process was characterized by three innovations. First, the negotiations were held outside the normal UN weapons negotiating forums. Second, they were characterized by a working group of small and mid-size states working together as a like-minded coalition. Third, the NGO-government partnership resulted in a mutually supportive, two-track negotiating process, which Canadian officials developed as part of a "two-track" action plan to move the Ottawa Declaration forward to result in a December 1997 treaty.

The theme of assertive multilateralism would permeate both tracks. *Track I* entailed specific political steps for the treaty's development. *Track II*'s goal was to develop political support for the *Track I* treaty using the ICBL's formula of aggressive and imaginative campaigning activities, events, and stunts. One of the great fears for the process was the huge potential for south-north divide, so the Canadians and other Core Group members decided to take the APL issue to the region as the first step in *Track II*. It was decided that the next ICBL conference would take place in Mozambique, which is on the world's most mine-affected continent.

The Mozambique conference would be the first test in *Track II* and would help generate diplomatic support for the Ottawa Process in Africa, which, to date, had been lacking.

It was also decided that the first *Track I* test would be the Vienna Conference, in order for the Austrian Government to continue drafting a treaty that its delegation brought to Ottawa. It would also host a meeting in Vienna to begin treaty negotiations, while Belgium would host a strategy-planning meeting, in part in recognition of it becoming the first country to ban mines.[53] Finally, the governments would support the ICBL's intensive efforts to develop national campaigns and regional initiatives in support of the ban.

Exploding interest in the ICBL, fueled in part by the Axworthy announcement, had the VVAF's Jody Williams, as the ICBL Coordinator, and Mary Wareham, as the United States Campaign to Ban Landmines (USCBL) Coordinator, scrambling to establish in-country national campaigns, which was an important component of the Core's Group's *Track II* strategy.[54] As the ICBL membership quickly grew, internal coordination among ICBL members continued through its coordinator, Jody Williams. Her regular communications, whether by e-mail, fax, telephone, or face-to-face meetings, provided ICBL members, representing more than 1,000 NGOs from more than 70 countries, with strategic coordination and direction. In this effort, the establishment of regular newsletters and e-mail lists, moreover, was important for building APL-ban transnational alliances and coalitions.

While the ICBL was increasingly relying on e-mail as a major communication avenue among members, many governments, including those in the north, did not have e-mail capability.[55] Even if some governments had e-mail, their Internet systems were limited to internal or inter-governmental correspondence. Some diplomats did not want to be accountable for their written correspondence via e-mail, which could then be disseminated to an activist subscriber network, and several governments discouraged outside e-mail correspondence for political and security reasons.[56] Some diplomats who had e-mail capability simply preferred telephone conversations and fax correspondence. They may have been wary of communicating with NGOs through the Internet and wanted to narrow the range of prospective leaks and minimize their exposure.[57]

Meanwhile, Canadian government officials were able to leverage its Internet assets to promote the Ottawa Process and MBT. According to Gwozdecky, coordinator of the mine action team in the Canadian DFAIT:

> the newly emerging communications technology were instrumental in our efforts. With the click of a button, we were able to send an e-mail to all of our 160 diplomatic missions, with talking points tailored to the specific concerns of the region, along with copies of the draft treaty in all six official UN languages. One e-mail, with 14 different attachments. Before the 1990s, this would not have been possible.[58]

At the UN, the United States continued its efforts to address the global APL crisis through a resolution supporting an eventual APL ban that would introduce interim steps, including the "voluntary adoption of moratoria, either partial or comprehensive, of the transfer, use, production, or stockpiling of these mines."[59] Highlighting, the challenge of banning APL through a consensus forum, a few governmental delegations expressed their disapproval. For example:

- The China representative, Ambassador Sha Zukang, stated that China could not agree with "[t]he proposal to ban all APMs [APLs], an assumption based on an over-exaggeration of humanitarian concerns." [60]
- The Indian representative, Ambassador Arundhati Ghose, stated "that many countries use these mines as weapons of defense along long live borders to keep out enemy forces."[61]
- The Russian representative, Ambassador Grigory V. Berdennkov, also opposed the Ottawa developments. He raised a question about the "costs for frontier guarding . . . particularly in the hot spots where bandit formations infiltrate from the foreign territory virtually every day if APMs [APLs] are banned without adequate substitution? How many people will be killed in the troops that guard those frontiers? Will such a ban serve the purposes of criminal and terrorist persons and groupings?" He concluded by stating that "[t]he formulation of a APM [APL] ban outside and contrary to normal procedures and the mechanism for working out global agreements on aspects of disarmament is not acceptable to us."[62]

On December 10 the U.S. resolution was adopted by the UNGA by 155 governments with no negative votes and only ten abstentions.[63] Since UNGA resolutions are non-binding on members, many governments that opposed an immediate or any APL ban voted in the affirmative. Per its agreement with the United States, Canada withdrew its resolution supporting the Ottawa Process, while the U.S. resolution pulled its original reference to the CD and did not mention the Ottawa Process in order that both Ottawa and non-Ottawa states would support.[64]

By January 1997, ICBL Steering Committee members began using their own APL treaty draft as the basis for discussions with government officials drafting the official version of the treaty. It also shared its drafts with diplomats at the UN mission in New York to help secure binding commitments and introduce stronger APL-ban resolutions that would support the Ottawa Process.

Meanwhile on January 17, the Clinton administration announced that it would pursue an APL ban in the CD rather than joining the Ottawa Process. The administration hoped to have it both ways on APLs—to stigmatize APLs but also keep them available for U.S. forces. U.S. National Security Director Robert Bell stated that the U.S. decision to take the APL issue to the CD as the "best shot" in terms of a global ban—"not just a ban among some countries, but a ban that really reaches the countries that are causing the problem on different continents around the world."[65] Bell later told the USCBL in a conference call that the United States would reconsider its decision if the CD negotiations were "going nowhere."[66]

Leahy said the president's announcement put at risk the goal of achieving a ban before leaving office in four years, and he urged the administration to "become an active participant in the Ottawa Process."[67] While commenting on the seemingly contradictory policy, a disarmament official stated that the administration was split and in "introspective disarray" on the issue.[68]

TRACK ONE OTTAWA PROCESS MEETINGS

Vienna, Austria, February 12–14

The Austrian government hosted the first official Ottawa Process *Track I* meeting February 12–14 in Vienna. The torturously titled "Expert Meeting on Possible Verification Measures for a Convention to Ban Anti-Personnel Landmines" was purposely constructed by the Austrians to allow for maximum governmental participation, including states opposed to an immediate APL ban.

One of the Vienna Conference's goals was to attract both pro-CD and fast-track states, and impinged on any notion that the CD was a viable avenue to discuss the banning of APLs. According to Canadian diplomat Robert Lawson:

> Efforts to "play up" the momentum of the Ottawa Process were motivated, in part at least, by the announcement, in mid-January 1996, that the U.S. intended to seek the negotiation of a ban treaty through the CD. It was clear that some delegations, most notably the U.S., UK and France, were under instructions at the Vienna meeting to express their support for the negotiation of any new landmine instrument within the CD rather through any stand-alone forum. This underscored the wisdom of the Austrian's strategy to stage-manage, as much as possible, the interventions of ban supporters in order to draw the CD supporters into a debate on the Austrian text, as well as to blunt the development of any momentum within the meeting towards the CD option.[69]

The meeting attracted no fewer than 111 governments and many NGOs.[70] The large turnout was a huge boost to the primacy of the fast-track process over the CD and the increasing global media attention to the APL issue. Adding urgency to the Ottawa Process was the continued increase in landmine casualties as reported by the ICRC through its wide global networks of medical facilities in many of the most mine-affected countries.[71] Also propelling media attention to the APL issue was Princess Diana's visit to the minefields and prosthetic clinics of Angola the previous month, promoting her goal of "drawing world attention to this vital, but hitherto largely neglected issue . . . [and to support those] striving in the name of humanity to secure an international ban on these weapons."[72]

The main purpose of the Vienna Conference was to discuss elements of a comprehensive ban treaty based on an Austrian elaborated text, which with ICBL and ICRC input had been developed into 13 articles. The text was drafted by Thomas Hajnoczi, head of the Department of Disarmament in the Austrian Foreign Ministry for Foreign Affairs. He had already drafted an APL-ban treaty a few months earlier that he circulated during the Ottawa Conference. The Hajnoczi draft, in effect, became the key working document leading to the eventual treaty. Jody Williams began referring to Hajnoczi as "the father of the treaty text" for his hard work in drafting the original document.[73] To the surprise of diplomats, only four participating countries (Cuba, Ecuador, Sri Lanka, and South Korea) continued to publicly reserve their right to use APLs as outlined in the CCW Landmines Protocol.

The Ottawa Process supporters considered the Vienna Conference a success because of its high attendance and the draft treaty, which included significant ICRC and ICBL input. A particular ICBL and ICRC contribution was that the revised text eliminated the word "primarily" in the APL definition.[74] They had lobbied strongly to clarify the definition's weakness and that it was of "fundamental importance." The ICRC considered "[t]he subjective judgment as to whether a mine is 'primarily designed' to injure people or may instead be said to have another 'primary' purpose introduced a dangerous ambiguity into the definition central to an effective ban on these weapons."[75] Thus its elimination strengthened the clarity of the APL definition.

Bonn, Germany, April 24–25

The next *Track I* meeting after Vienna, occurred April 24–25 in Bonn, Germany, titled the "International Meeting of Experts on the Possible Verification of a Comprehensive International Treaty Prohibiting Anti-Personnel Landmine." The meeting participants discussed issues of verification and compliance measures based on a German government option paper incorporating various aspects of arms-control treaties, including issues such as information exchange and routine and challenge inspections.

The Bonn meeting attracted 130 countries, or 19 more than in Vienna. This unexpected increase in governmental delegations illustrated that the treaty process was gathering support and that governments perceived the desirability of becoming part of the Ottawa process.

At the meeting, verification was weakened in the treaty draft because some convention negotiators thought that a state-centered verification system for remote parts of the world was unrealistic. A traditional verification system, such as those utilized for weapons of mass destruction (WMD), are not applicable to APLs because of their unique features—small size, weapon of self-defense, and easy to transport. In this approach, therefore, verification needed to be voluntary.This opinion was based on a 1994 Canadian government-commissioned study on ways to verify the CCW Landmines Protocol. The study found that the verification of human rights legal instruments were partially successful because of the involvement of NGOs, as "states are unenthusiastic about filing complaints against other states."[76]

Also, intrusive verification measures were left out in order to attract more states to sign the treaty as a potential counterweight to major-power opposition. ICBL Coordinator Jody Williams supported this decision as a way to get more states to sign. During the conference, she argued that "the verification mechanism should be simple, and not too intrusive, since it might deter potentially supportive countries from signing on."[77]

Kempton Park, South Africa, May 19–21

While not officially categorized as an official *Track One* seminal meeting, the Ottawa Core Process group helped the government of South Africa to host an Organization of Africa Unity (OAU) conference, titled "The First Continental Conference of African Experts on Landmines," held at the World Trade Centre in Kempton Park, South Africa. More than 41 African countries attended, making it one of the better-attended non-annual OAU conferences.

As usual, the ICBL assured a prominent role during the conference proceedings. Williams delivered a keynote speech along with Nobel Peace Prize Laureate Bishop Desmond Tutu, who spoke on behalf of the South African Campaigns to Ban Landmines, and South African Deputy President Thabo Mbeki, who expressed his "sincere appreciation to the NGOs that have for years fought hard to drive this issue to the forefront of world attention."[78]

On the last day of the OAU conference, six ICBL representatives, including the author, accompanied by South African Defense Minister Joe Modise were taken by military transport plane on a three-hour flight covering 900 kilometers to the Alkantpan testing range in the Northern Cape to witness the destruction of more than 5,000 landmines (see photo 4.3).[79] Mechanical problems delayed the return flight for more than five hours, during which time the ICBL representatives and media were hosted at the local military officers club. It was at the club where Modise said that South Africa's decision to ban landmines was greatly influenced by the VVAF's's full-page advertisement in the *New York Times*, which was an open letter to President Clinton signed by fifteen retired generals,

Photograph 4.3

Witnessing the destruction of more than 5,000 landmines at the Alkantpan testing range in the Northern Cape, South Africa, as part of South Africa's commitment to banning APLs and on the occasion of the "First Continental Conference of African Experts on Landmines," held in Kempton Park, South Africa. (Courtesy of author.)

including General Norman Schwarzkopf, the U.S. commander in the Gulf War.[80] At the end of the conference, the African delegates unanimously agreed to ban APLs on the continent as a first step in declaring Africa a mine-free zone.[81] By the end of the meeting, 25 African governments had committed themselves to signing the treaty.

According to Canadian diplomat Robert Lawson, the U.S. representatives at the conference tried to derail African support for the Ottawa Process, but generated the opposite reaction:

> In the wake of an agreement on language that would urge all African states to participate in the Ottawa Process, a frustrated U.S. delegation intervened to urge all states to reject the Ottawa Process and instead support efforts within the CD. Not only was it highly inappropriate for a non-African state to directly intervene in a solely African discussion, it was also viewed as an essentially hostile attack on the authority of the South African chair, Ambassador Selibi. With the exception of Egypt, not a single African delegation supported the U.S. intervention. In the end, consensus minus one (Egypt) was achieved behind the OAU's full support for the Ottawa Process.[82]

Brussels, Belgium, June 24–27

The Belgian government hosted the third official *Track One* meeting June 24–27 to continue drafting the treaty. Soaring public support had turned the steady migration by governments to join the Ottawa Process into a stampede, as evidenced by 161 governments, and 125 NGOs from 45 countries participating in Brussels. It helped build momentum toward an APL ban, with 97 states signing the Brussels Declaration, which affirmed the goal of finishing negotiations and signing a landmine ban treaty by December 1997. The declaration was drafted and widely circulated before the conference for suggestions regarding form but not substance, and as a result, participating states were principally obliged to affirm their ban commitment in Brussels.

As usual, the ICBL maintained a high profile during the meeting, starting with a well-covered media event of a landmine survivor bicycle trip from Paris to Brussels. Several ICBL representatives and landmine survivors wore effigies of international political leaders such as Boris Yeltsin and Bill Clinton, who had refused to support the ban. To enter the conference facilities, diplomats had to walk across a minefield carpet laid by Handicap International (HI) that boomed every time a landmine was 'detonated'. In the meeting, Williams spoke at the opening plenary, where she asserted that the ICBL "wants a simple, comprehensive ban treaty with no reservations, no exceptions and no loopholes." That was to be a mantra for the remainder of the Ottawa Process.[83]

The ICBL members also monitored the negotiations in order to hold states accountable to previous commitments and lobby others in stronger statements. As an example of campaigners' innovative use of the Internet for lobbying purposes during the Brussels Conference, the New Zealand Campaign to Ban Landmines (CALM) notified campaigners back in New Zealand of Australia's statement supporting the CD as the proper avenue to ban APLs and reneging on a promise to sign the Brussels declaration. One New Zealand campaigner, also serving as a spokesperson for the Women's International League of Peace and Freedom, notified her counterpart in Australia, who then wrote letters to Australia's prime minister. That same day, the *Sydney Morning Herald* published an editorial titled "Australia's Hypocrisy on Landmines," which, in turn was circulated via the internet by CALM.[84]

TRACK TWO OTTAWA PROCESS MEETINGS

Maputo, Mozambique, February 25–28

The first *Track Two* meeting of the Ottawa Process took place as the fourth NGO meeting from February 25–28, 1997, in Maputo, Mozambique, where some 450 participants from more than 70 NGOs and 60 countries attended.[85] In August 1996, the ICBL sent Liz Bernstein to begin conference planning and to help strengthen national campaign capacity of Africa national landmine-ban campaigns. Building on strong ban organizations in South Africa and Mozambique, the ICBL helped develop and launch additional national campaigns in Angola, Somalia, Zambia, and Zimbabwe.

On February 26, the conference's second day, Mozambique's foreign minister announced that Mozambique would immediately ban the use, production, and trade of APLs. This announcement came one week after the South African Defense Minister Joe Modise announced that South Africa would immediately implement a comprehensive APL ban.

Because Mozambique and South Africa were mine-infested countries themselves, the symbolism was not lost among African governments and NGOs. Immediately after their announcements, a cascade of other African governments announced that they would also ban APLs and officially support the Ottawa Process. In addition to encouraging other African states to join the treaty, South Africa's ban-APL position was significant for two other reasons. First, it was the leading arms and APL producer in Africa. Second, the South Africa military and its allies had used APLs during the Apartheid-era in regional conflicts, thus helping southern Africa become the most mine-infested region in the world.[86]

The South African government's decision was brought about in part by pressure from the South African Campaign to Ban Landmines (SACBL), a coalition of more than 100 South African NGOs. This racially diverse coalition, coupled with the coming to power of Nelson Mandela and the first country's democratically elected government in 1994, allowed "unprecedented access to senior political and bureaucratic officials" that "greatly facilitated the eventual symbiosis of governmental and nongovernmental activities and policy positions."[87] Since the SACBL started with the joining together of humanitarian NGOs and student associations in 1993, there were many common bonds and friendships between SACBL members and governmental officials, including Nelson Mandela, because they were "historical partners" in the anti-Apartheid struggle.[88] For example, Nobel Peace Prize Laureate Archbishop Desmond Tutu helped the SACBL's launch on July 24, 1995 with the words "this is a moral crusade just as our struggle against the madness of apartheid was a moral crusade."[89]

The overwhelming and sudden participation by African governments in the Ottawa Process was not surprising, as these states were the ones most grievously affected by APLs: Their nationals constituted most of the victims, and their soil hosted the world's most emplaced APLs. Since southern states contained the most deployed landmines and suffered the most landmine victims, their support was especially needed in order for the ICBL message to be taken seriously. For example, one key failure for the CCW had been the lack of participation by African mine-affected countries.

While there had been initial resistance among a few African states to banning APLs since they are cheap and retain military utility, the inclusion of demining and victim assistance into the ICBL's campaign platform helped alleviate their concerns about banning APLs. In the final Maputo conference statement, the ICBL asked "the international community to increase resources for mine clearance and assistance to survivors."[90] As a further incentive to persuade African governments to join the Ottawa Process, the statement asserted that assistance should be given "especially in those countries and regions that have banned landmines."[91]

The ICBL also planned more *Track Two* meetings apart from the governmental treaty drafting conferences, so that the campaign could be expanded to more NGOs and more governments might join the Ottawa Process. These meetings were planned and organized by national campaigns or NGOs from each host country with the major purpose to generate political will for the landmine ban in the host countries and/or region. Following the Maputo Conference, ICBL member NGOs held regional meetings in:

Tokyo, Japan, March 6–7

The "Tokyo Conference on Anti-Personnel Landmines" included participants from 27 countries and ten international organizations, including the ICRC. Because of the Japanese government's caution toward and avoidance of the Ottawa Process, ICBL members were only allowed to attend the opening session, and the mine-ban discussion was officially limited but "impossible to avoid."[92] The following day, the ICBL and its Japanese members organized its own Tokyo landmine conference, which was attended by more than 200 organizations.

Sweden, May 23–25

The Swedish ICBL Conference "Baltics to the Balkans" was attended by 75 representatives from eighteen states. While the conference was held in a non-mine-affected country, its purpose was to generate support from and for the mine-affected Balkans.

Australia, July 14–17

The ICBL organized an APL conference in Sydney where 22 governments and 27 NGOs from the region participated in order to mobilize support for the Ottawa Process around Asia and the Pacific. Participating countries included Afghanistan, Australia, Bangladesh, Fiji, Myanmar, Nepal, New Zealand, Philippines, Sri Lanka, Thailand, and Vietnam.

Ashgabat, Turkmenistan, June 10–12

This ICBL conference, titled the "Ashgabat Central Asia Regional Conference on a Global Ban on Anti-Personnel Mines," was hosted by the Turkmenistan government with support from the Canadian Government. The main purpose was to inform Central Asia government officials about the APL issue and encourage support for the treaty. The final declaration was weaker for its support of the Ottawa Process than most other regional conferences by merely agreeing that the APL problem needed urgent attention.[93]

San'a, Yemen, November 3–4

ICBL member, the Swedish-based Radda Barnen, held a seminar on landmines in San'a in order to address the lack of response by the Middle East region to the Ottawa Process. Only three regional countries, Jordan, Qatar, and Yemen, had declared their support for the Ottawa Process, making it the least-represented region in it. Several government delegations gave statements explaining why they could not support the Ottawa Process. For example, the Egyptian and Iranian ambassadors stated that the proper venue to discuss APLs was the CD; Lebanon stated that it would be unable to sign because of the Israeli occupation; and the Sudanese ambassador said his country could not sign because of ongoing insurgencies.

Concurrently, the ICRC also hosted and planned its own regional meetings with the same *Track II* objective—laying the political groundwork for government to participate in the Ottawa Process and ban APLs. These meetings included:

Addis Ababa, Ethiopia, February 23–24

The ICRC hosted an APL seminar in Addis Ababa, which became the first of four such meetings to be held for African countries. The purpose of these seminars "was to increase support for a ban or greater restriction on the use of mines, encourage ratification of Protocol II to the 1980 CCW and promote participation in the forthcoming 1980 CCW Review Conference."[94]

Zimbabwe, April 21–23

ICRC co-hosted with the Organization of African Unity (OAU) a regional seminar "Anti-Personnel Mines: What Future for Southern Africa?" in which military and foreign ministry officials from all 12 members (Angola, Botswana, Lesotho, Malawi, Mauritius, Mozambique, Namibia, South Africa, Swaziland, Tanzania, Zambia, and Zimbabwe) of the Southern Africa Development Community (SADC) participated. The meeting was opened by Nobel Laureate Archbishop Desmond Tutu, who called for an APL ban. The governments agreed in its final declaration that they would all sign the APL ban treaty and declared the southern African region a mine-free zone.

Manila, Philippines, July 20–23

The ICRC invited military experts from 18 Asian countries to consider the utility of APLs and to counter standard military arguments that they were necessary tools of warfare and to mobilize support for the ban among Asian governments.

Managua, Nicaragua, May 28–29

The ICRC sponsored a regional seminar that was attended by all six Central American countries and Mexico. The participants agreed to create the world's first official mine-free zone and signaled their support for a comprehensive mine ban. Capitalizing on the ICRC Managua momentum, Canadian and Mexican officials worked closely on an Organization of American States (OAS) general assembly resolution that was adopted on June 7, 1996, and called on its members to adopt "as goals the global elimination of anti-personnel land mines and the constitution of the Western Hemisphere as an Anti-Personnel Land Mine-Free Zone."[95] Because of U.S. pressure, the OAS was unable to adopt similar language to support an APL ban in its general assembly.[96]

In Washington, D.C., meanwhile, the relentless Leahy continued his efforts to get the United States to change its APL policy and join the Ottawa Process. At a well-attended June 12 press conference outside the Capitol building, Leahy and Sen. Chuck Hagel, a Nebraska Republican, introduced the Landmine Elimination Act, which urged Clinton to participate in the Ottawa Process (see photo 4.4). The act's key point called for a ban on all U.S. APLs beginning January 1, 2000, with an exemption for the Korean Peninsula. This would nearly bring U.S. policy into compliance with the proposed Ottawa Treaty, cease U.S. resistance to the Ottawa Process, and re-assert its leadership role on the APL issue.

The Leahy-Hagel legislation was co-sponsored by a bipartisan group of 56 senators, including several conservatives and all six Senate Vietnam veterans. As chief co-sponsor of this bill, Hagel brought military and political credibility to the legislation because he was a landmine survivor from the Vietnam War. And, as a Republican, he added a high-profile bipartisan appeal to Leahy's efforts.

A major Leahy strategy was to influence the media to build public support, with the aim of getting the administration to participate

Photograph 4.4

On June 12, 1997, Senators Patrick Leahy and Chuck Hagel introduced legislation to ban new deployments of anti-personnel mines by the United States, except in Korea, beginning January 1, 2000. Congressmen Lane Evans and Jack Quinn introduced identical legislation in the House. Leahy news conference. (Office of Senator Patrick Leahy. Used by permission.)

internationally, specifically in the Ottawa Process.[97] Leahy's staff also cultivated the media to educate them about the landmine crisis and to amplify the issue. Leading Leahy's office efforts, Tim Rieser spent hours on the phone speaking to the media, which resulted in seminal articles, such as John Ryle's *New Yorker* and Donavan Webster's *New York Times* articles. As a result, members of Congress started to hear from constituents. Leahy's political effectiveness was demonstrated in July 1996, when Motorola announced that it would immediately cease selling components intended for inclusion in APLs. The announcement followed *60 Minutes* report that recorded Cambodian fighters opening a Chinese APL, revealing a Motorola electronic chip.

Not all senators were supportive of the Leahy-Hagel legislation, and they let their views be known on Capitol Hill. Senator Jesse Helms sent a "Dear Colleague" letter to senators stating his concern that while "Leahy's landmine legislation will not do one thing to solve this problem . . .

Our young troops in the field will pay the price for this legislation." He continued to write that of the 100 million landmines in more than 70 countries "the United States is not responsible for the emplacement of a single one of those mines—not one."[98] When the United States does use landmines, Helms wrote

> it uses highly sophisticated munitions which are set to disarm in 4 hours, 48 hours, or 15 days (as the case may be). These mines deactivate within the specified time frame with 99.9 percent reliability. Only one out every ten thousand mines does not disarm within the allotted time frame. And guess what happens to that mine? Within 90 days the battery runs down and the mine becomes inert—this with a reliability rate of 99.9999 percent. This is why the military calls these munitions "smart mines."[99]

The Pentagon also reacted quickly in opposing the act by taking its case to Capitol Hill. John Salikashvili, chairman of the Joint Chiefs of Staff, wrote Sen. Strom Thurmond, Chairman of the Armed Services Committee, that U.S. troops require the protection of anti-personnel landmines and that the Senate should consider this fact before unilaterally banning them."[100] The U.S. Army chief of staff, Dennis J. Reimer, also wrote to Thurmond, arguing that the legislation "unfairly penalizes" U.S. soldiers by removing "an important force multiplier and force protection capability for which there is, at present, no viable alternative."[101]

Meanwhile, in brutal violation of the administration's word, solemnly and repeatedly given that it would not impede the Ottawa Process and reconsider it if there was not markedly progress in the CD, the United States had sent a delegation to Brussels to encourage governmental delegations to break away from the Ottawa Process.[102] The U.S. delegation was effectively and literally outside the meeting. It did not join the conference multilateral negotiations but remained at their nearby hotel hosting bilateral meetings with delegations that were shuttled back and forth in vehicles mostly paid for by the United States. Leaving and returning delegates were briefed and debriefed by ICBL representatives as they went and returned from the Americans' hotel in order to encourage the delegates to adhere to their APL ban positions.

The Clinton administration realized that by mid-summer, its APL policy was cooked. It is not clear from the records, and one gathers the impression that they did not quite know themselves. Well-meaning though they were, they were gripped by utter confusion and a paralyzing sense of futility. For example, the administration's strategy to take the APL issue to the CD collapsed in Brussels as its CD members failed to reach an agreement to address APLs. The CD Special Coordinator on Landmines, the Australian Permanent Representative, John Campbell, characterized the APL discussions in the CD as "talks about talks" and recommended a few months later, on August 15 that further discussion on APLs in the CD were hopeless until the results of the Oslo Conference—to take place in September—were known.

Attempts to get landmines on the CD agenda had failed because several delegations were preoccupied with nuclear weapons and not interested in putting the APL issue on the agenda at the expense of other issues. In addition, particular delegations, such as Mexico, felt that addressing landmines in the CD would undermine the Ottawa process. The Mexican delegate argued that the global landmine crisis demanded urgent action and said that the "swiftness is not this conference's main virtue."[103] Mexico's opposition to placing the mine-ban issue on the CD agenda was also due in part to its concern that nuclear powers would use the mine debate to divert attention from nuclear disarmament.[104]

Once committed to the CD as the sole avenue addressing landmines, the governments of Bosnia, Czech Republic, Hungary, Italy, Spain, and the United Kingdom (UK) joined the Ottawa Process during late spring. In the UK's case, opposition to the ban disappeared relatively soon after the May 1 landslide victory of Tony Blair's Labour Party over the unpopular John Major's Conservative government.[105] The Labour Party had made banning APLs one of its campaign platform goals. Upon taking office in May, the Blair government did announce a ban but with significant reservations, including the "the right to use mines in exceptional circumstances."[106] This directly contravened the Ottawa Process's goal of allowing no exceptions for APL use. But even though it was in the Labour Party campaign platform, it took Princess Diana's lobbying to encourage Blair to follow through on his party's ban APL campaign pledge.

The APL issue in the UK had quickly gathered attention with Princess Diana's involvement a few months earlier when she visited Angolan minefields and prosthetics clinics, and called on the UK's government to ban APLs. At the time of her statement, the UK's APL position was in support of the legality and continued use of APLs. Her remarks created a buzz within the Majors' Conservative government and led some to discuss a response in favor of retaining APLs. One governmental official called Princess Diana a "loose cannon."[107] Responding to past Conservative Party criticism about her involvement into what was then perceived to be a security issue, she said, "I am not a political figure. I'd like to reiterate now, my interests are humanitarian. That is why I felt drawn to this human tragedy. That is why I wanted to play my part in working towards a worldwide ban on these weapons."[108] Blair's newly appointed international development secretary, Clare Short, stated that "[w]e need a worldwide ban and the more the Princess can do to bring that about, the better.... The Princess has drawn the world's attention to this problem."[109]

Princess Diana gave her first public speech on landmines at London's Royal Geographical Society (RGS) on June 12 at a seminar co-sponsored by the Mines Advisory Group (MAG) and Landmine Survivors Network (LSN). They designed the seminar to provide her a platform to address the landmine issue, challenge the widely-held perception that the eradication of landmines is an insurmountable task and present a case for an international response based on the real needs of mine affected communities.[110] Princess Diana's involvement helped MAG and LSN transform the landmine debate from a military to a humanitarian issue in many people's minds, including those of many diplomats.[111]

As Princess Diana sat in the lecture theatre's front row, the seminar began with a slide show comprised huge black and white images of the horrific devastation caused by landmines taken by MAG photographer Sean Sutton and set to the atmospheric and quite haunting soundtrack of "Refugee Oud." Sutton designed the show to remind everyone of what this was all about—"to set the tone."[112] The author remembers that there was complete silence at the end and everyone was ready to talk about how we should tackle this deadly legacy of war.

After opening presentations, the seminar participants broke for tea and refreshments and to tour Sutton's photo exhibition in the RGS foyer. As Sutton guided Princess Diana around his exhibit, she was disarmed with conversation about her two boys as Sutton said that he also has two boys. She was genuinely moved by the images and particularly taken by the images from Lao showing how people utilized the remnants of war in daily life. One image they spoke about was a picture of a boy looking out of a house window and above him there is a row of mortar bombs that were placed there to act as weights to hold the roof down during seasonal winds (see photo 4.5). According to Sutton, Princess Diana "found this very extraordinary and we discussed how indicative the image was of the level of contamination there must be in the country."[113]

The public heat on the Clinton administration to join the Oslo negations increased when on August 12, 1997, the *New York Times* published an editorial calling for President Clinton to override the Pentagon's "narrow and mistaken advice" and ban APLs.[114] Later in the day, Pentagon spokesman Kenneth Bacon was asked about the *New York Times* position. Bacon replied that the United States was working "toward a worldwide ban on antipersonnel landmines" through the CD but to date is not "subscribed to the Ottawa Conference—or the Ottawa Process, as it's called—because it is not comprehensive and global."[115]

One week later, the APL issue still would not leave Clinton alone even while he was vacationing on Martha's Vineyard. He felt pressured to issue a statement on August 18, and he decided the United States would finally take part in the Ottawa Process.[116] However, Clinton's announcement was problematic for some Ottawa Core Group members and the ICBL because he did not necessarily say that the United States would sign the treaty but that it would work toward a treaty that achieves U.S.

Photograph 4.5

Bombs on roof. Villagers use unexploded mortar bombs and rockets as ballast to help hold down thatched roofs during seasonal winds. Savannaket Lao. Princess Diana was particularly taken with this picture of a boy looking out of a house window and above him there is a row of mortar bombs that were placed there to act as weights to hold the roof down during seasonal winds. "She found this very extraordinary and we discussed how indicative the image was of the level of contamination there must be in the country" recalls Sutton. (Courtesy Sean Sutton/Mines Advisory Group (MAG). Used by permission).

humanitarian goals while protecting its national security interests. Reading between the lines, Clinton wanted to participate in the Oslo negotiations, but only with non-negotiable amendments that would burden its diplomats sent to the Oslo conference.

Two days after Clinton's announcement, Secretary of State Madeleine Albright sent a letter to foreign ministers stating definitely the U.S. requirements for its signature to the ban APL that required five interlocking demands:

1. Non-time bound exception for Korea for both self-destruct and dumb mines;[117]
2. Exception for munitions in anti-tank systems, which included the Gator and Volcano, which were a mix of self-destructing APLs and anti-vehicle mines;
3. Delay the treaty's effective date with an optional deferral period or for entry-into-force provision requiring 60 ratifications, including those of the permanent five, and at least 75 percent of the historic producers and users of APLs;
4. Increase verification measures; and
5. Do away with the no exception clause on use during war.[118]

Albright also expressed her hope that the United States could count on the Ottawa Process Core Group's support for a mutually acceptable Mine

Ban Treaty (MBT) text "agreed upon in accordance with the positions outlined above" and reminding the minister's that "[t]he treaty would be much stronger and more effective with the United States as a signatory."[119] She presented this position to the Core Group members at an August 22 meeting at the U.S. Embassy Mission in Geneva.[120]

In anticipation of U.S. diplomatic pressure to change the draft treaty to fit its demands and "to respond strongly and unambiguously to the U.S. [United States] immediately before it has time to try to consolidate support for its attempt to gut the treaty," the ICBL's Williams and Steve Goose, who also served as chairman of the U.S. Campaign to Ban Landmines (USCBL) Steering Committee, sent a letter to core group countries expressing the ICBL and USCBL's "extreme concern" about the U.S. demands and its participation in the Oslo negotiations.[121] They wrote that it "is abundantly clear that the United States has not in any substantial way changed its policy" and that the only reason for its decision to participate in the Ottawa Process was that it considered "the cost of non-participation to be too high."[122] They urged the Core Group governments in their meeting with the U.S. delegation "to send the unmistakable message ... that this is going to remain a ban treaty—as such, it must contain no geographic exceptions, no exceptions for any APLs (even those artificially renamed as submunitions in mixed anti-tank mine systems), no reservations and no loopholes."[123]

The USCBL's leader Steve Goose had to deal with a few USCBL members that wanted to characterize the U.S. announcement that it would be going to Oslo as a victory. Goose believed that if they played the announcement as the victory as some of the media labeled it, that it would be harder to move the U.S. position on the exceptions. Also, despite the public expressions of support for the U.S. participation in Oslo, many of the Core Group countries were secretly concerned that the U.S. presence in Oslo would pose serious dangers for achieving a comprehensive ban. They informed Goose that they were "appalled and frightened" by the U.S. participation and demands, and therefore were imploring the ICBL and USCBL "to go after the United States as hard as possible."[124]

The most important meeting of the Ottawa Process and the global movement to ban APL would take place at the September treaty drafting conference in Oslo, Norway. It was to be the last official *Track One* meeting for governments that signed the Brussels declaration. It was also to be the ICBL's most important moment to get governments to adhere to a comprehensive APL ban and not allow them to create linguistic wiggle room. As most of the world readied for the conference, the United States made a dramatic announcement that it would participate for the first time in the Ottawa Process, but with significant reservations, which, in turn, would lead to tension-filled days and nights during the Oslo meeting.

CHAPTER 5

The Road to Ottawa: Rallying the World—September 1997

[T]he receipt of the Nobel Peace Prize is recognition of the accomplishment of this Campaign. It is recognition of the fact that NGOs have worked in close cooperation with governments for the first time on an arms-control issue, with the United Nations, with the International Committee of the Red Cross. Together, we have set a precedent. Together, we have changed history.

Statement by Jody Williams, ICBL coordinator, Nobel Lecture, Oslo, Norway, December 10, 1997

SEPTEMBER 1997—OSLO NEGOTIATING CONFERENCE

On September 2–19, 121 nations that had endorsed the Brussels Declaration met in Oslo, Norway, to finalize and negotiate a comprehensive Mine Ban Treaty (MBT).[1] At the opening there were 90 governments registered and 32 observer states, representatives of the International Campaign to Ban Landmines (ICBL), International Committee of the Red Cross (ICRC), and UN agencies. Ambassador Jacob Selibi from South Africa was well-prepared to serve as the conference president. He was South Africa's ambassador to the UN in Geneva and he had African National Congress (ANC) credentials that would help continue to galvanize the important Africa support.[2] Mark Gwozdecky, coordinator of the Mine Action Team in the Canadian Department of Foreign Affairs and International Trade, had suggested that Selibi would be a good option to chair the Oslo conference. The Canadians were aware that the Ottawa process was driven by Western countries and Gwozdecky knew Selibi "was unimpeachable, not white, not from the North, from a landmine-affected region and an exceptional diplomat that could get the job done in three weeks [the Oslo Conference was scheduled for three weeks, an extremely tight time-frame for a weapons negotiating conference]".[3]

The Oslo Conference came on the heels of an emotional week of outpouring for the death of Diana, Princess of Wales, who since her January trip to Angola had quickly addressed herself to supporting the global movement to ban landmines. She later wrote:

> I am extremely grateful that I have been given the opportunity to help, in some way, to highlight the horror of these dreadful weapons. I have received many, many letters of support from all over the world and with this encouragement, I shall carry on fighting this cause, striving for a worldwide ban and for continued support for the victims, those who care for them and their families and also for those demining land.[4]

Princess Diana was killed in a car wreck in Paris on August 31, just a few days before the conference was scheduled to begin. Her September 6th funeral in London was beamed by the media around the world, while more than 7 million people lined the downtown London funeral procession route. The international attention and shock generated by her death galvanized an international public and media into focusing on the landmine issue, specifically on the Oslo Conference that started the week between her accident and funeral. One leading international newspaper ran an editorial the first week of the Oslo Conference that called upon states for "the eradication of land mines and help for their victims" as the best way to remember her life.[5]

The last working week of Princess Diana's life had been in Bosnia meeting landmine survivors from August 8–10.[6] Her hosts American landmine survivors Jerry White and the author of this book, co-founders of the Landmine Survivors Network (LSN), which was a member of the U.S. Campaign to Ban Landmines (USCBL) and ICBL. Her high-profile tour of the war-torn country brought global media attention and public support to ban landmines and ensure the inclusion of victim assistance provisions in any MBT agreement. She also helped LSN reach out to people who might not normally listen to what it had to say about bringing hope and a sense of personal values to landmine victims and their families. At the time, no one was more photographed or attracted more media attention than Princess Diana so it was quite straightforward for her to be very successful in drawing attention to the landmine issue spawned by the reporters that covered and chased her. While she did not like the public coverage, Princess Diana knew that it could produce attention to worthwhile causes, such as banning landmines and aiding their victims. When asked by the author, "Why did you decided to join us in Bosnia," she replied, "The reporters and photographers have made my life horrible, so I would like to make their life horrible by taking them to places they normally otherwise would not visit and covering issues they normally otherwise would not cover."[7]

During her three-day Bosnia visit, she visited the homes of five landmine survivor families in Sarajevo, Tuzla and the northern countryside, and dined with 12 military veteran landmine victims and their wives at the Hotel Bristol in Tuzla. In witnessing these visits, the author noted that Princess Diana touched their stumps, clasped their hands, and brought some hope to an otherwise hopeless situation each time, every time. In one particular case, she held hands with a woman who had just lost her husband only a few months before and now put in the unfamiliar position of providing for their two daughters and his mother without an income. In another case, Princess Diana listened to two boys, a Bosnian Muslim and Serbian Orthodox Christian, injured by mines on opposite sides of the inter-ethnic boundary line (see photo 5.1).

Photograph 5.1

From August 8–10, 1997, Princess Diana visited Bosnia with LSN Co-Founders, Ken Rutherford and Jerry White, to meet landmine survivors. Her high-profile tour of the war-torn country brought global media attention and public support to the issue of landmines. After the death of Princess Diana, LSN became the only American-based charity to receive support from the Diana, Princess of Wales Memorial Fund. (Courtesy of author.)

Two days after returning to London from Bosnia, she wrote wonderful individual thank you notes to White and the author.

I hope that you felt that all your hard work was worthwhile in raising awareness of the plight of survivors and helping to ensure that they are not forgotten in the framework of negotiations for a ban on anti-personnel landmines. I could not help but be intensely moved by the needless and senseless injuries of the victims I met and, no less so, by the sensitive care and support they receive from their families. You should be justifiably proud of the wonderful work you are doing to bring hope and a sense of personal values to those who have suffered so much at the hands of these terrible weapons.[8]

At the first session of the conference, Norwegian Foreign Minister Bjoern Tore Godal told the audience, "We shall spare no effort . . . to achieve the goals she set for herself."[9] In a newspaper interview, Sen. Leahy opined, "Because of what she did and because of her death, the whole world is watching what we do here."[10] United Kingdom (UK) Foreign Secretary Robin Cook said that the treaty's "achievement is due in part to the work of Diana, Princess of Wales, who did so much to focus the attention of the world on the horrific effects of anti-personnel landmines [APLs]."[11]

Canadian diplomat Lawson wrote, "Diana's support for the ban agenda was significant on a number of levels. As an international celebrity, her association with the ban agenda provided instant global media reach for its normative demands. As a 'Royal' to whom millions looked for standards of 'proper' behavior, she was extremely well placed to 'teach' the public about the landmine issue."[12] Williams and Goose later noted that Princess Di's death "certainly increased the media attention to the process unfolding" and "put the issue before the world public as few other events had on this issue."[13]

On September 3, UN Secretary General Kofi Annan addressed the conference by insisting that it must make APLs "a weapon of the past and a symbol of shame." Most significantly, he said "[t]hat the treaty will serve not only as a complement but also an inspiration for greater and swifter progress in the Conference on Disarmament's (CD) own deliberations toward a total ban on land-mines."[14] His attendance and statement were important because the Ottawa Process circumvented the UN's CD, where negotiations were stalled, but included UN Security Council permanent countries, such as China and Russia, not present in Oslo.

The Oslo Conference's Rules of Procedure were agreed without debate, which was significant because the rules allowed for decisions to be adopted with only a two-thirds majority, in contrast to the consensus rules for the CD and CCW, which, as evidenced from those processes, a single country could hold up agreement. According to the ICRC's Legal Division Representative Peter Herby, "this is where Selibi was so strong. He said 'stand aside to make up your mind as we've seen and heard your objections, but you convinced no one to vote for it so let the overwhelming numbers say so.'"[15]

There was a fear among Ottawa Process supporters of the potential for crippling amendments from governments already committed to the ban. For example, the United Kingdom wanted no demining in the Falkland Islands because there were few people threatened by them there, and France for the right to use landmines when stationing troops overseas.

The United States posed the main threat for spearheading dramatic changes to weaken the comprehensive prohibitions listed in the draft treaty. Its delegation came to the Oslo negotiations with a series of requests that they wanted incorporated into the treaty. In addition, Sen. Jesse Helms sent two staffers to Oslo to tell the American delegation that even if the delegates agreed to the treaty, he would lead an effort to oppose and not ratify it.[16] The American demands in Oslo were presented in a take-it-or–leave-it package consisting of five interlocking components:

1. An exception for landmine use in Korea;[17]
2. Deferral of the treaty's enter-into-force date, specifically a permanent nine-year deferral for entry into force of the treaty's provisions;
3. Changes in the definition of an APL with the purpose to exempt and protect American AT (anti-tank) systems that included APLs embedded in these systems, which had recently been categorized as sub-munitions, and thus captured by draft text;[18]
4. More intensive verification measures; for example, there are no explicit measures to monitor compliance in Articles 4, 5 and 7;
5. Withdrawal clause from the treaty in cases of national emergency: the U.S. wanted written into the treaty that a state party could withdrawal if it is the victim of aggressors.

Meanwhile, the ICBL organized a parallel forum attended by more than 225 representatives from more than 130 NGOs that produced an action plan for entry into force by the year 2000.[19] By the end of its forum, the ICBL had developed a detailed action plan for the three months leading up to the treaty signing in Ottawa in December.[20] To ensure that states abided by their commitments, ICBL members met with national delegations in Oslo and also used e-mail to communicate with national ban-landmine campaigns back in their countries, directing them to contact and lobby their governments about critical issues and policies discussed at the treaty negotiations. These campaigns, in turn, provided updates to the ICBL activists in Oslo regarding their governments' positions.

Symbols were also important during the conference proceedings. Outside the Oslo government negotiating hall, one ICBL NGO, Norwegian People's Aid (NPA), provided public de-mining demonstrations to highlight for the media and government delegates the difficulty of taking landmines out of the ground. These activities and ICBL's communication network proved extremely useful in holding states accountable to their previous landmine policy commitments. For example, the Australian national campaign intensely lobbied their government in Canberra after being informed by ICBL activists in Oslo that they understood that its country's delegate was attempting to weaken the prohibition language.

The Conference as a whole through the rules of procedure adopted gave ICBL members official observer status, which included the right to participate and access all the meetings during the negotiations. According to Goose, a key ICBL leader, "There's never been an instance where, in negotiations on a treaty dealing with arms control or even international law issues, NGOs have been allowed inside the room, allowed to make interventions the same as any government."[21] During these important negotiations, ICBL members coordinated among themselves to respond to government policies and conference statements.

Two major ICBL interventions concerned anti-handling devices for anti-vehicle and anti-tank mines, and landmines that could be retained for training purposes by states party to the convention.[22] Confronted with the prospect of a semantic discussion over booby traps, the ICBL, ICRC and their pro-ban government supporters "wisely opted for distinctions based on the capability of weapons rather than textbook definitions."[23]

As they came to terms with Clinton's disastrous last-minute decision to influence the Oslo negotiations with red-line items for others to accept, it was striking how calmly many reacted and strongly opposed the U.S. demands. Governments, the ICBL, and ICRC all opposed these requests, including the Korea exemption. A Korea exemption in the treaty, for example, they argued, would open a Pandora's Box of other related exceptions by inviting countries to carve out their own exemptions, and that this would set back efforts for an international ban.

Now that its core supporters, the UK and France, had abandoned the United States, many of its other political allies lost faith in the U.S. position.[24] Canadian representative Jill Sinclair said, "I'm sure the American delegation is feeling a bit lonely."[25] A Dutch diplomat observed that conference delegations "should not be deaf to reality, but if we go on a slippery slope of exclusions and loopholes, we have to ask what we are even doing here," while a Norwegian diplomat stated that his delegation "looks forward to hectic days and nights of debate with the U.S. delegation, but we cannot yield on a total and absolute ban."[26] When nearly universal opposition to the red-line items came to light, twenty-five congressional representatives wrote President Clinton:

> the United States should not be engaged in issuing threats and ultimatums at its first appearance in a process that has been going on for many months. The U.S. should be signaling its support for and seeking ways and means to strengthen the consensus that exists within a coalition of more than 100 nations on banning

antipersonnel land mines, rather than on ways to breed dissension . . . We hope that you will bear these concerns and consideration in mind and issue a new set of instructions for U.S. negotiators in Oslo, Norway—ones that would allow for the full participation of the United States and for the U.S. to join the more than 100 nations prepared to sign an international treaty to ban antipersonnel land mines.[27]

Leahy and Hagel also wrote President Clinton that the U.S. proposals would permit any military to continue using mines, and thus were not acceptable to "those who have worked long and hard for a treaty that does nothing less than ban these weapons."[28]

Not gaining traction on its five red line demands after the first week of negotiations, the U.S. delegation reformulated its demands in order to join the treaty. In doing so, it stripped away some of its original demands in an attempt to shape a landmine agreement allowing members to claim a prohibition and get the United States on board. On September 16, the U.S. delegation submitted its changed demands, most significantly dropping the Korea exception, and made one final push by slightly revising three of the five original demands and resubmitting them as a take-it-or-leave-it offer for U.S. signature: (1) re-categorize the APLs in the U.S. AT systems as something other than APLs; (2) withdrawal from the treaty in case of armed conflict; and (3) an option for a state party to delay treaty implementation for nine years.

As the American delegation tried to rebuild its strained relationships among its NATO allies, the ICBL stepped in vigorously, offering support to the participants in order to keep the U.S. requests from being accepted. The ICBL saw the last-minute U.S. decision to participate in the conference as provocative and accused the U.S. of trying to weaken the treaty. Its tone against the U.S. demands intensified as the three-week conference raced to a close, with the Canadian government seemingly marshaling extensive diplomatic energy in order to bring the United States into the process, which the ICBL and some pro-ban governments believed could undermine the comprehensive prohibitions in the final treaty as the U.S. would push for its exemptions. In anticipation of a possible weakening of the treaty, Jody Williams stated that these "proposals are not really new at all" because "[t]hey are a repackaging of previous U.S. demands" that "are actually worse than earlier U.S. amendments, causing more harm to the treaty than before."[29]

At one point in the treaty negotiations, Axworthy considered allowing some of the U.S. concerns to be heard and possibly include in the treaty to induce the United States to sign. During the second week of negotiations, the U.S. delegation requested a 24-hour postponement for further consultations, which entailed President Clinton, Secretary of State Madeleine Albright, and National Security Adviser Sandy Berger making telephone calls to other governments.[30] According to Mark Gwozdecky, who was coordinator of the Mine Action Team in the Canadian Department of Foreign Affairs and International Trade and back in Ottawa, since "Monday was an election day in Norway, and Axworthy said since the Oslo Conference was a three-week conference and this was the beginning of the third week, "why not give the Americans a chance to come on board."[31] Axworthy and Gwozdecky got on the phone with the Americans and explained to them where they thought the redlines were and where the negotiating room might be. Axworthy, Gwozdecky, Lawson, Sinclair, and other Canadian officials facilitated these efforts in order to bring the United States on board.

Lawson was concerned that his "nightmare scenario with the Americans was coming true." He always thought that they would stay out of the negotiations until the very end, as many of his American counterparts "were under a gag order on the Ottawa Process," and then would "throw their weight around in Oslo." Even though he knew that "the Americans could not move people in Oslo, the Americans thought they could."[32]

Both the granting of the delay request and the Canadian involvement attracted ICBL and ICRC considerable criticism and skepticism about the reputed agreement between Axworthy and Canada's effort to bring the United States into the MBT. To the chagrin of Conference Chair Selibi, ICBL members and most participating governments, Axworthy's attempts to bring the United States into the fold postponed the conference ending by a day. Axworthy in Ottawa and the Canadian delegation in Oslo found themselves taking a lonely stand, defending the proposed extra 24 hours for the Americans while critics from both governments and NGOs lined up against it.

Despite its best intensive efforts to cajole concessions, the U.S. delegation failed in achieving any of its demands. Intuitively, it is exceptional that all of the U.S. demands were fended off. On the other hand, the other delegations simply did not consider U.S. demands reasonable. The Core Group of Ottawa Process governments, along with the ICBL and ICRC, argued that anything less than a ban would result in a complex set of legalistic rules that any nation could interpret to its own ends. The clear goal of a comprehensive ban also would affect how the treaty was implemented.[33] In opposing the U.S. attempt to create exceptions, the NGO experts found key support in Leahy, who also argued that holding states to different standards would defeat the stigmatization force that a comprehensive treaty could deliver. He said "an effective international agreement that is based on stigmatizing a weapon cannot have different standards for different nations."[34]

A clear goal was critical to the treaty's success because some legal concepts may have very different interpretations and meanings in other cultures and languages. When the prohibition is clear and concise, governments and armed forces personnel can better understand its meaning and intent; they are more likely to affect behavior change and, therefore, are more likely to be perceived as legitimate international law. In contrast, unclear terminology makes it difficult to understand what is right and wrong, which makes it easier to justify noncompliance.[35]

After the delay, Clinton announced that the United States could not sign the treaty and recalled the U.S. delegation from Oslo. The next day, the remaining delegations adopted the MBT and the conference was formally closed a few ticks past noon on September 18. As frenzied supporters spilled into the Oslo Conference hallway to celebrate the adoption of the MBT, most diplomats stood and applauded.

While the Oslo Conference center halls echoed with joyous applause at the treaty's achievement, there was similar elation in the Pentagon's corridors that Clinton did not instruct the U.S. delegation to sign. In fact, Clinton stated that the American delegation "went the extra mile and beyond to sign this treaty . . . [b]ut there is a line that I simply cannot cross, and that line is the safety and security of our men and women in uniform."[36] Most especially pleased with the Clinton's decision were the Joint Chiefs of Staff, who thought: "It was courageous. We know there were pressures on him. He made the right decision for the right reason. All the chiefs are grateful."[37]

The only Republican member of Clinton's Cabinet, Secretary of Defense, William Cohen provided a straightforward explanation on why the United States did not support the MBT: "I do not believe that our mixed systems, in which we use self-destructing anti-personnel submunitions to protect anti-vehicular mines, are the problem—the problem is with the words of the Convention [MBT] itself. A principle reason we cannot sign the Convention is that it includes an unnecessarily restrictive definition of anti-tamper devices permitted in the Ottawa treaty."[38] He reacted angrily to accusations that the United States tried to weaken the treaty: "[T]he mass media's coverage of the recent talks in Oslo on land mines could easily leave the impression that the United States is largely responsible for this humanitarian tragedy, or at least stands in the way of international efforts to stop the dying and maiming. Such an impression is simply wrong."[39]

Commenting later on these events, Cohen said that U.S. armed forces required APLs for Korea.[40] Meanwhile, Clinton asserted that the American arguments "were rejected, partly because the Landmine Conference [the Oslo Conference] was determined to pass the strongest possible treaty in the wake of the death of its most famous champion, Princess Diana, and partly because some people at the conference just wanted to embarrass the United States or bully us into signing the treaty as it was."[41] He recollected that the U.S. position boiled down simply to two changes—despite his original instructions to the U.S. delegation going to Oslo as previously discussed—that the United States wanted:

The first was an adequate transition period that would have provided us the time we need to develop alternatives to anti-personnel landmines. The second was protection of our 'mixed' systems containing anti-tank mines protected by anti-personnel submunitions. Unfortunately, these changes were not made.[42]

Another, possibly more practical, explanation for the U.S. decision not to get its amendments to the MBT approved was that they joined the negotiating process too late to break the package that had already developed since the first Ottawa Process meeting in Vienna seven months earlier. At the time, the Americans may have underestimated the power of multilateralism and overestimated its unilateral power to make a difference at the negotiations.

Immediately after the Oslo conference, the indefatigable Leahy continued his relentless lobbying to get Clinton to support the MBT. On the Senate floor, he expressed his deep disappointment with the U.S. decision not to support the MBT: He stated that the "treaty ends the 20th century, the bloodiest in history, in a way in which the world can be justly proud. It is our gift to the next century. The United States should be part of it."[43] From the Senate floor, Leahy continued addressing the administrations concerns regarding banning APMs and Korea:

Last week, the Secretary of Defense wrote in the *Washington Post* that 'millions' of lives could be lost if the United States signed the treaty, because North Korea might interpret our signing as a loss of resolve and start a war because of it. Not only is that about as far-fetched as any dire Pentagon prediction I have heard yet —and that includes its assessment of a Red Army that was fit to conquer the world and turned out to be unable to capture Chechnya—it ignores the conclusion of every serious Pentagon analyst that a North Korean invasion would be destroyed, with or without landmines, before it can traverse the 50 miles down narrow, pre-targeted mountain passes to Seoul.[44]

In further lobbying, Leahy wrote to Clinton to say that he believed the Korean issue was solvable in order for the United States to participate in the MBT while addressing the Pentagon's concerns.

The problem, as presented, was that certain types of US (AT) mines use APLs to prevent tampering and, therefore, were banned by the treaty. The Pentagon wanted to be able to place these "mixed" mines, for example, on the North Korean side of the demilitarized zone (DMZ) to delay a North Korean tank assault by approximately 30 minutes. There are informed Pentagon officials who say that alternative technology and tactics already exist to accomplish this mission without APLs. Whether adapting or developing alternative technology, we are convinced this problem can be solved if we decided to solve it and are committed to do whatever we can to ensure the resources are available to do so.[45]

A few months after Oslo, during meetings with Canadian Prime Minister Jean Chrétien in Vancouver, British Columbia, Clinton defended his decision not to sign by blaming others. He said it "is a question of how the treaty was worded and the unwillingness of some people to entertain any change in the wording of it. I believe I was the first world leader at the United Nations to call for a total ban on land-mine production and deployment."[46] He reinforced his blame on other people:

> We implored the people there [in Oslo] to give us the exceptions we needed, recognizing that in the Korean peninsula, we have never had indiscriminate use of land mines that have put civilians, children at risk, and that we had the unusual situation of having a huge North Korean army there, just a few miles from Seoul. And no way to stop the movement there without leaving the existing minefields there. But the people who were at Oslo decided they would not try to accommodate us, for whatever reason.[47]

OCTOBER 1997—NOBEL PEACE PRIZE

After the Oslo Conference success and resulting accolades, the ICBL's already-strengthened prestige in the international community was ennobled on October 10, 1997, by the Norwegian Nobel Committee's announcement that the Nobel Peace Prize was being awarded to the "ICBL and to the campaign's coordinator Jody Williams for their work for the banning and clearing of anti-personnel mines."[48]That night, the formerly obscure American human rights activist rocketed to fame in the world of politics by being named co-laureate of the 1997 Nobel Peace Prize. Williams was the personality most recognizable for the ICBL, as she had traveled internationally, essentially nonstop, campaigning for a ban since 1995. She had proved to be an agile coordinator and effective leader by building a campaign that was suffused in thousands of organizational and personal relationships that at times were complicated by acrimony and weighted by the profound emotional baggage of humanitarian suffering in most of the world.

In announcing the award, the committee recognized the NGO coalition that the ICBL and Williams had brought together and leveraged into a "broad wave of popular commitment in an unprecedented way." The committee also said of the ICBL: "As a model for similar processes in the future, it could prove of decisive importance to the international effort for disarmament and peace."[49] The committee factored in two variables in its consideration of awarding the Peace Prize to the ICBL. First, there was the success of bringing the utopian idea of a ban to the international political arena and turning it into a legal reality with remarkable speed. Second, the ICBL model of networking worldwide among a range of actors to achieve the treaty provided a new model of diplomatic efforts of governments and NGOs working together.[50]

The award of the Nobel Peace Prize, arguably the most distinguished global political honor, provided the ICBL and Williams with added international prestige and power to pressure governments to support the MBT. Japan, which had been a strong opponent of the MBT, announced after the Nobel award statement that it would conduct a review of Japanese APL policy in the hope of signing the ban in Ottawa in December. According to Canadian government official Robert Lawson:

> An indication of the impact that the Prize had on state decision-making is provided by the unexpected Japanese decision to reverse its support for U.S. landmine policy during the fall of 1997. Japan's Foreign Minister Keizo Obuchi, explicitly referred to the Nobel Prize as a new factor in his decision to review Japanese landmine policy with a view to signing the Mine Ban Treaty. Not only would Japan sign the Ban Treaty in Ottawa, but it would also place the mine ban issue at the centre of its Peace Appeal for the Nagano Winter Olympics.[51]

DECEMBER 1997—OTTAWA MINE BAN TREATY SIGNING CONFERENCE

Three months later, in early December in Ottawa, a celebratory mood characterized the Government Conference Centre in Ottawa, where more than 2,600 participants, including more than 1,848 government delegates, 500 media members, and 350 ICBL members attended.[52] The diverse delegate profile illustrated the truly international network that developed to ban APLs (see Table 5.1). The festive party atmosphere had been fostered by several comments announcing support for the ban in the days leading

Table 5.1

Profile of National Delegations[a]

Number of States Signing	**125**
Number of Observing Delegations	27
Number of Delegates	1848
National Governments	817
NGO	538
Other	493
Number of Delegations	433
National Governments	180
NGO	221
Other	32

[a]Conference Aggregate Report, December 4, 1997.
Source: Conference Aggregate Report, December 4, 1997

up to the convention, and the participation of previously disinterested states, such as Israel, Jordan and Syria, in the proceedings.[53]

On a frigid morning on December 3, the hottest place to be in the world was at the Government Conference Centre. The draw inside the towering hall was not a rock concert or sporting competition, but the signing of the MBT, the most comprehensive conventional weapons prohibition, which eliminated a whole category of weapons. The MBT was unprecedented in scope for a conventional weapons agreement: It obligated state parties to destroy APL stockpiles within four years of entry into force and APLs in the ground within 10 years. It also called on state parties to cooperate and provide assistance for landmine clearance and mine victims, and had good transparency and verification measures. Perhaps the most extraordinary feature with reference to the treaty-signing ceremony was the final result: 122 signatories, which was 35 more states than participated in Oslo, where 87 countries signed the declaration.

The day opened with speeches by Canadian Prime Minister Chrétien, who recognized the work of Williams, and UN Secretary-General Kofi Annan, who highlighted the ICBL's power in mobilizing public opinion and governments. Annan specifically addressed civil society members with the words: "You have led the global grass-roots movement that carried us all to this place and time."[54] Williams, in her remarks, recounted a chronological perspective of the ICBL's history and influence, and ended her address with a call for everyone to join in and become a superpower, as the conference hall audience rose to its feet and gave her a standing ovation.[55]

After the opening speeches, the treaty was opened for signatures. First, Canada signed and then Norway and South Africa signed in front of the diplomatic audience. The signing process continued in separate rooms throughout the Government Conference Centre. The Canadians also organized a parallel forum that was open to NGOs, Government officials and others. The forum participants discussed issues and future strategies dealing with legal issues, non-state actors, and resources for mine action and regional action plans. ICBL members also developed an action plan to secure the forty ratifications needed for the MBT to enter into force. Other important goals were promoting universalization of the MBT, working cooperatively with governments to monitor implementation and compliance with the agreement, and increasing international resources for victim assistance and de-mining programs.[56]

Having NGOs at the table during the treaty-negotiation process was cited by governmental representatives as a "powerful force" in influencing policy decisions.[57]

Furthermore, many governmental decision- and policymakers learned to become team players with each other, the ICBL, and the ICRC. Some of these diplomats felt more kinship with the ban coalition forces than their own governments.[58] In a survey conducted the day after the official treaty signing, a majority of governmental officials participating in the treaty negotiations felt that "the role of NGOs throughout the process was invaluable and atypical with respect to the high degree of NGO and government cooperation."[59] One of the leading Canadian government negotiators, Robert Lawson, opined that the ICBL members were critical to the success of achieving the MBT because they were especially helpful "in bringing the issue from the field to foreign capitals."[60]

Lawson also pointed out that the treaty reflects how NGOs can rapidly organize to address and solve issues, and that, coupled with "the new tools of the Information Age," they are tremendously important in any state's diplomatic tool kit.[61] Axworthy commented that these technologies allowed for information collection and dissemination in an issue area once monopolized by states, namely security, and that it allowed information from far-away places to be brought to the public and their governments.[62] The ICBL and ICRC provided faster and higher-quality information than governments were able to produce, analyze, and address. According to Axworthy, the ICBL became indispensable to this process in that it could provide informational power that states could not ignore.[63]

Because of the U.S. contribution to humanitarian demining, Clinton was surprised that the United States could be labeled as a non-contributor to solving the global mine crisis. He believed that American mines were not causing the problems, especially as the United States was the world's leading supporter of demining operations and funding. At the Ottawa conference, the United States was represented by Ambassador Karl F. Inderfurth, who was instrumental in moving the UN through U.S.-sponsored resolutions toward a ban. Now he was designated special representative to the president and secretary of state for global humanitarian demining and spoke of the administration's "De-mining 2010 Initiative" designed to "end the plague of landmines posing threats to civilians."[64]

However, it was generally agreed that Clinton would not oppose the Pentagon because he believed there was some merit to the Pentagon's point of view that they would be giving up many of their anti-tank (AT) mines. Moreover, Clinton needed the Department of Defense to support his policy of extending operations in Bosnia, expanding NATO, and closing military bases. According to Vietnam of Veterans of American Foundation (VVAF) Executive Director and ICBL co-founder, Bobby Muller, the United States did not sign because of fear that it would set a precedent that civil society pressure could influence other weapons programs.[65]

One week after the treaty signing, on December 10, 1997, the ICBL and Williams received the Nobel Peace Prize in Oslo. On the occasion of the award, Professor Francis Sejersted, chairman of the Norwegian Nobel

Committee, noted that the ICBL "bears promise that goes beyond" landmines by appearing "to have established a pattern for how to realize political aims at the global level." [66] Williams was only the 10th woman to be among the 87 Peace Prize laureates, and the first American in 11 years to receive the award. Accepting the prize on behalf of the ICBL were Rae McGrath, founder of the Mines Advisory Group (MAG), and Tun Channareth, a Cambodian landmine survivor who had figured prominently in speaking at landmine conferences and events around the world.

After the treaty signing, the two ICBL co-founders, VVAF and Medico International (MI), resigned from the ICBL steering committee. VVAF said that it wanted to focus its "efforts to bringing the U.S. aboard the Ottawa treaty [MBT]," which it believed that the ICBL leadership did not feel was terribly important.[67] A few months later, MI Director Thomas Gebauer informed the ICBL that MI was resigning from the steering committee to focus more on its victim-assistance activities. Gebauer stated that MI, which was also a member of the ICBL Steering Committee, was not informed of the Nobel Peace Prize nomination letter until "months after it was sent out."[68] The most significant change in the ICBL's structure was the resignation of Jody Williams as ICBL coordinator and the hiring of Liz Bernstein, who was instrumental in helping to launch the Cambodia Campaign to Ban Landmines and coordinating many of the ICBL meetings, and Susan Walker, who had spent years working with landmine victims on the Cambodian-Thai border working for HI, to be coordinators.

In the months after the United States refused to sign the MBT, Leahy was in quandary as to his next policy steps in order to get the United States on board. If he introduced legislation that reflected the MBT treaty, he would immediately lose nearly half of his 60 Senator sponsors, including many Democrats, because they would find out that it would take away most of the U.S. military's AT mines, because they were packaged with APLs. Therefore, he decided not to introduce his legislation because it would be more useful and credible as a threat to nudge the American APL position toward a prohibition. Leahy's problem in getting the United States to join the Ottawa process was that the American AT mines were manufactured in a way that made the problem confusing. His concern was that if he made a statement supporting the MBT, then another senator would read a general's letter stating that the actual results would be a loss of AT mines, then another senator would make an amendment to make exceptions for AT mines.

Leahy refocused his advocacy efforts to encourage the Clinton administration to follow through on its commitments to search for alternatives for APLs in the mixed systems with the goal of putting the United States in a position to sign the MBT. He wrote Cohen that "if we can drive a robot around the surface of Mars from a distance of 50 million miles, we can find another way to protect our anti-tank mines from tampering for the 30 minutes that such devices are able to deter enemy soldiers."[69] Secretary of Defense Cohen assured the administration that the military was continuing its development of alternatives. If successful, Clinton said, "It would put us in a position to sign the Ottawa Convention [MBT] as soon as we have also developed alternatives for our anti-personnel landmines in Korea."[70]

CHAPTER 6

The Uncompleted Journey

We must ban their use! We must ban their production! We must destroy those that are stockpiled!

UN Secretary General Boutros Boutros-Ghali, September 1995[1]

Once satisfactory alternatives are fielded, the [U.S.] military will be fully prepared for a total ban on APL [anti-personnel mines].

John M. Shalikashvili, chairman of the Joint Chiefs of Staff, February 6, 1997[2]

No other issue in recent times has mobilized such a broad and diverse coalition of countries, governments and non-governmental organizations [NGOs]. Much of this momentum has been the result of the tremendous efforts made by NGOs to advance the cause to ban APM [APLs]. Their commitment and dedication have contributed to the emergence of a truly global partnership.

Canadian Foreign Minister Lloyd Axworthy, February 1997[3]

HUMANITARIAN DIPLOMACY

Since the Mine Ban Treaty (MBT) entered into force on March 1, 1999, more than 155 governments have ratified it. The fastest multilateral global arms-control treaty to enter into force in the twentieth century, the MBT marks the first time in history that a conventional weapon that has been used by almost every fighting force in the world has been taken out of military arsenals.

Through the opening of anti-personnel landmines (APLs) debate to humanitarian issues, such as noncombatant casualties, mine victim assistance and mine clearing, the International Campaign to Ban Landmines (ICBL) and International Committee for the Red Cross (ICRC) were allowed significant access to traditional government foreign- and military-policy decision-making actors and their negotiating forums, such as the UN General Assembly and the UN Convention on Conventional Weapons (CCW), and, ultimately, the Canadian created MBT negotiating process, otherwise known as the Ottawa Process. According to Robert Lawson, a key Canadian Government official leading the MBT negotiations, the ICBL was different than the usual NGO coalition that tended to be solely composed of disarmament groups, but the ICBL members "were NGOs that had post-war reconstruction experience and great diversity."[4] Meanwhile, a New Zealand diplomat at the time believed that some NGOs "had expertise in more than simply post-conflict reconstruction: some had particular knowledge and experience in reporting on field situations, while others brought to the mix skills useful in lobbying and otherwise influencing policy process."[5] NGOs were therefore able to inject themselves into the global landmine public policymaking process. They transformed the APL debate from a security to humanitarian issue, which, in turn, expanded the scope of diplomatic conflict about APL policy, thereby helping these nontraditional weapons-policy actors to increase the visibility of the issue to the international public and, in turn, involving them more actively in policy discourse.

The ultimate effect extends far beyond the MBT, boding well for a healthy global civil society, as was exemplified by the awarding of the 1997 Nobel Peace Prize to the ICBL and its coordinator, Jody Williams (see photo 6.1). The Norwegian Nobel Committee stated that the ICBL mediated "a broad wave of popular commitment in an unprecedented way" and that "[a]s a model for similar processes in the future, it could prove of decisive importance to the international effort for disarmament and peace."[6]

By converting the APL issue from a strictly military concern to a humanitarian one, the ICBL and later the ICRC gave themselves the diplomatic space to play important expert roles in disseminating information to the media, policymakers, and the public. While governments were wrestling with the unclear balance of military demands and humanitarian standards, the ICBL and ICRC successfully argued that a complete prohibition on APLs was the only political and practical way to eliminate the harm they cause to civilian populations and the environment.

Another ongoing transformation that helped spur the global APL ban movement was the strengthening relationship between various UN agencies, such as the UN Children's Fund (UNICEF), and NGOs on security issues. The UN members themselves were bounded by its own consensus voting rules at their own behest in the UN negotiating forums of the Convention on Conventional Weapons (CCW) and Conference on Disarmament (CD). Yet the UN secretary-general (UNSG), Boutros-Ghali, stepped in to support the APL-ban negotiations through the Ottawa Process, a non-UN sponsored negotiating track. His pro-ban statements early

Photograph 6.1

Jody Williams, ICBL Ambassador, 3rd Meeting of the States Parties to the Mine Ban Treaty, Managua, Nicaragua. September 18–21, 2001. (Courtesy International Campaign to Ban Landmines. Used by permission.)

in the global process helped to add a sense of legitimacy and urgency to the ICBL and ICRC call for a ban.

The support of UNICEF and the UNSG's support for the global APL-ban movement points to a broader implication in international politics: NGOs are taking on an increased role at and within the UN to assist, lobby, and support governments on a range of global security issues at a higher and deeper role than previously had been the case. The ICBL and ICRC pressure on governments to achieve the MBT also indirectly encouraged the UN to reorganize itself to better address the APL issue from a humanitarian perspective. Even though APLs affect a range of economic and social issues, such as commerce, environment, health, and security, the UN was initially unable to coordinate among its various agencies to address the APL issue without tremendous internal bureaucratic challenges. Regarding APL, one UN official admitted that "there has been too much overlap, which has led to duplication of functions and some confusion in our dealings with donors and with NGOs."[7]

Facilitated by ICBL and ICRC advocacy, UN agencies eventually began working more closely with each other and NGOs to address the humanitarian problems caused by APL use. These collaborative relationships were reinforced by UN Undersecretary–General Yasushi Akashi, who commented that "[t]he land-mine issue has been unique in the way it has brought together the various departments within the United Nations—the Department of Political Affairs on the process towards a ban; the Department of Peacekeeping Operations in its mine-clearing role not just for the peacekeepers but to allow early access for humanitarian workers; and, of course, the Department of Humanitarian Affairs as the focal point within the United Nations for all landmine-related activities."[8] UNSG Boutros-Ghali's successor, Kofi Annan, later alluded to the UN's internal organizational problems in addressing APLs, when he commented that as part of his reform process, he had "merged all the landmine functions in the department of peacekeeping operations as part of my reform process."[9]

In addition to lobbying governments and the UN, the ICBL, and ICRC assisted Canada and other pro-ban governments with MBT drafting and with delivering public support for the ban through information and analytical reports. Canadian Foreign Minister Lloyd Axworthy recognized the importance of the civil society in helping to create the regime when he stated at the Ottawa October 1996 Conference that the NGOs "are largely responsible for our being here today. The same effective arguments you used to get us here must now be put to work to get foreign ministers here to sign the treaty."[10]

According to one ICBL representative active in the process, the civil society presence:

> strengthened those states seeking to resist attempts to weaken the draft ban treaty; it helped to prevent the reversion to traditional forms of diplomatic negotiating practice; it provided a visible point of public accountability for the national delegations; it was a reference point for expertise and information on key elements in the text.[11]

The use of human-rights arguments in banning APLs follows a line of recent expansion of international NGO human-rights activities from the early 1990s to economic and social rights. This is partially a result of developing states being increasingly focused on social and economic rights, which also helped create a North-South ban-APL coalition atypical for arms control and disarmament treaties. Moreover, including previously universally agreed-to norms, such as human rights, also helped to ensure that the APL issue would receive sustained attention, unlike more complex international issues.[12]

Not only were the ICBL founding members effective at coordinating its members and recruiting new NGOs to the campaign, they also mirrored the wide range of problems caused by APLs around the world (see Table 6.1).

Through advocacy and research, the ICRC and members of the ICBL helped marshal expert military opinion to counter military arguments against the APL ban. By incorporating innovative research and analysis into their publications, the ICRC and ICBL members were better able to

Table 6.1

Founding ICBL Members and their Expertise Areas

ICBL Founding Member	Landmine Expertise Area	Landmine Infested State Area	Home State
Handicap International (HI)	Physical Rehabilitation	Cambodia, Vietnam, Mozambique	France
Human Rights Watch (HRW)	Human Rights	Cambodia	USA
Medico International (MI)	Physical Rehabilitation	Angola, El Salvador	Germany
Mines Advisory Group (MAG)	Demining	Afghanistan, Cambodia, Kurdistan	United Kingdom
Physicians for Human Rights (PHR)	Medical Support and Human Rights	Bosnia, Cambodia	USA
Vietnam Veterans of America Foundation (VVAF)	Physical Rehabilitation	Angola, Cambodia, Vietnam, El Salvador	USA

mobilize opinion that defeated military arguments for retaining APLs. Several ICRC and ICBL member publications became seminal publications in the APL debate as they provided important new landmine information and analysis (see Table 6.2).

Publications of the ICBL and ICRC reinforced its global networking effectiveness by inspiring governments and the UN to take more assertive actions toward an APL ban. This argument is confirmed and strengthened by Lawson, who helped spearhead the Canadian leadership on the landmine issue:

> I think the ICRC 1996 study was absolutely critical to the core military utility versus humanitarian impact of AP mines "debate" and swinging many important military experts on side. This study was certainly widely used during the Ottawa Process regional conferences over the course of 1997 and we saw first-hand its impact on government officials, many of which argued that it had the practical effect of giving them evidence-based "cover" when it came to taking a decision re the treaty—a decision that often saw foreign affairs departments, initially at least, on the other side of the issue from defence departments. Also, the data from our December 1997 survey of participants at the Ottawa signing ceremony, suggests that many respondents felt that a key reason why their government decided to sign the Ottawa Treaty was because they clearly understood the humanitarian argument

Table 6.2
Seminal NGO and ICRC Research Publications

Date and Report	NGO(s) or ICRC	Expertise/New Information
1991—The Coward's War	HI, HRW, MAG, PHR	First study on the humanitarian impact of APLs on a specific country—Cambodia.
1993—Deadly Legacy	HRW and PHR	First survey of mine exporters and users, and detailed legal arguments why APLs should be banned.
1995—After the Guns Fall Silent	VVAF	First global assessment of the social and economic impact of antipersonnel weapons, especially APLs, on developing nations that have been torn apart by war.
1996—Anti-personnel Landmines: Friend or Foe? "A Study of the military use and effectiveness of anti-personnel landmines"	ICRC	Report conducted and endorsed by military officers from fifty-five countries concluding that the military utility of APLs is more limited than previously believed.
1997—Landmine Producers and Exporters	HRW	First detailed account of names of APL exporters and producers in the United States.

behind the treaty. With the exception of the US state department, I think that most of the important and widely read studies on the landmine issue were actually generated by the NGO community. In other words they were agile and effective in filling an information void and so when governments starting looking for policy evidence, they tended to use the NGO information/studies. I think this underscores the importance of this 'evidence' in moving government's and the UN forward on the issue.[13]

This effort was underpinned by ICBL's tenacious and successful recruiting efforts that broadened its membership base, increased its credibility and, just as importantly, brought diverse NGOs from many countries into the APL-ban movement. The ICBL dramatically increased its membership and geographical representation every year from its founding in 1992, when six NGOs joined together, until the MBT signing in December 1997. (See Table 6.3.)

Since the APL issue affected many sectors of society (e.g., doctors caring for survivors, international humanitarian lawyers concerned with indiscriminate weapons development, and workers concerned with rehabilitating post-conflict societies), it was important to incorporate that energy into a single message. The challenge for the ICBL leadership in

Table 6.3

Progressive Expansion of the ICBL

Date and Conference Location	# of NGOs & Countries (if available)
May 1993, London[a]	40–70 NGOs
March 16/17, 1995, Rome[b]	250 NGOs
June 1995, Cambodia[c]	350 NGOs from more than 20 countries.
October 13, 1995, Vienna[d]	350 NGOs from 25 countries
April 22, 1996, Geneva[e]	450 NGOs
October 1996, Ottawa[f]	650 NGOs from more than 36 countries
June 24, 1997, Brussels[g]	1,000 NGOs from 50 countries
October 1997, Ottawa[h]	1,093 NGOs from more than 63 countries
March 1999, MBT Entry into Force[i]	1,300 NGOs from more than 80 countries

[a]a Statement by Jody Williams, VVAF, Chair of the ICBL, at the Plenary Session of "International Conference: The Socio-Economic Impact of Landmines: Towards an International Ban." June 2, 1995.

[b]ICBL Landmines Campaign Rome Meeting Summary Points, March 16/17, 1995.

[c]Statement by Jody Williams, VVAF, Chair of the ICBL, at the Plenary Session of "International Conference: The Socio-Economic Impact of Landmines: Towards an International Ban." June 2, 1995.

[d]Statement by Carl von Essen, Closing Plenary Speech, on behalf of the ICBL, CCW Review Conference, Vienna, October 13, 1995.

[e]Statement by Jody Williams, VVAF, representing the ICBL to the Opening Plenary Session, Review Conference of the CCW, Geneva, Switzerland, April 22, 1996.

[f]Statement of Chris Moon, ICBL Presentation to the Opening Session of the Ottawa Conference, October 3, 1996.

[g]Statement by Jody Williams, Coordinator, International Campaign to Ban Landmines, to the Brussels Conference on Antipersonnel landmines, June 24, 1997.

[h]ICBL, "Organizations Working to Ban Landmines," December 1997 Listing.

[i]Statement by Susan Walker, ICBL Co-Coordinator, at the "Ceremony to mark Entry into Force of the Mine Ban Convention" held at the United Nations, Geneva, Switzerland, March 1, 1999.

recruiting NGOs to the ICBL was placing their various interests on "very fertile ground for development of a broad-based coalition."[14]

A wider membership helped alleviate the effects of special interest group problems that would lead to serving narrow interests, such as overcoming the division between northern and southern NGOs. It also made the campaign less dependent on individual donors. Lastly, it allowed the ICBL to assure pro-ban governments that it would assist in monitoring the convention once it entered into force.

The spreading of the APL issue from NGO APL experts to NGO non-expert parties signified that the message was being heard. The incorporation of non-APL experts, such as religious organizations, professional associations and civic-minded grassroots groups, showed how the APL issue had entered into contemporary international discourse and politics. This broader base of support, moreover, gave the ICBL a stronger sense of legitimacy, both in the public eye and to government policy makers.

DOES THE MINE BAN TREATY MATTER?

One of the two key strategic-planning successes for the ICBL and ICRC advocacy effort was their focus on a *clear goal*—an APL ban. A ban was also the easiest method to accomplish their objective rather than debating further restrictions regarding their use. They believed that merely focusing on managing APL use—such as allowing certain types of APLs and prohibiting others, or determining conditions when landmines could be used—would be too vague to achieve and difficult to enforce. More importantly, they believed that the only realistic solution was the complete prohibition of APLs.

The second ICBL and ICRC strategy was to keep the issue simple by focusing on only APLs and the humanitarian effects of their use. In doing so, they were able to confine the movement and negotiations to APLs to the exclusion of other victim-activated weapons, such as anti-tank landmines, sea mines, unexploded cluster bombs, and similar forms of ordinance. Focusing on a single weapon also helped the ICBL and ICRC to transform the debate from the military utility of APLs to their humanitarian consequences. The simple issue characteristics helped them to educate other NGOs and the public about the consequences of APL use, which also helped broaden and expand the movement (see photo 6.2).

By combining the strategies—*focusing on a clear goal* and *simple issue*—the ICBL and ICRC leaders could achieve the ban, while the NGO members with less expertise could explain very simply the APL issue. In other words, they probably would not have been as effective if their strategy had concerned a complex issue with a multitude of goals.

Meanwhile, the governments of major countries refused to give up APLs. While most smaller and mid-size states support the MBT, major

Photograph 6.2

Mines Advisory Group (MAG) community liaison staff present a mine and UXO risk education session with children from Magwi primary school. Sudan 2007. (Courtesy Sean Sutton/Mines Advisory Group (MAG). Used by permission.)

powers, such as China, India, Pakistan, Russia, and the United States, did not sign because it was perceived not to be in their interest to do so (see Table 6.4).

What is so important about the characteristics of the international movement to ban landmines is that it has changed state behavior, even among the major-state non-signatories, in an area traditionally at the heart of state sovereignty: military methods and weapons. Some MBT critics and political observers, however, may question the MBT 's effectiveness because the major states, which are the world's largest APL producers and users, did not sign.

Even though these major countries did not sign, the MBT, ICRC, and NGO pressure encouraged them to unilaterally implement certain APL policy changes. Even as they continued to state their opposition to the MBT, China, India, Pakistan, Russia, and the United States have instituted unilateral APL policy changes that closely reflect the MBT's objectives (see Table 6.4). In other words, while the major states did not sign the MBT, they did change their APL policies.

What is especially noteworthy is that the United States is the world's single largest financial supporter of landmine clearance and victim assistance programs. Since the global movement to ban landmines was

Table 6.4

Major Non-Signatory States Changing Landmine Policies Since ICBL Founding in 1991

Major State	Treaty Position	Change in Landmine Policy Since ICBL Founding
China	Non-Signatory	Unilateral landmine export moratorium.[a]
India	Non-Signatory	Support for ban on all landmine transfers.[b]
Pakistan	Non-Signatory	In light of humanitarian concerns, Pakistan observes "high standard of regulating use."[c]
Russia	Non-Signatory	Unilateral landmine export moratorium.[d]
United States	Non-Signatory	1. Unilateral landmine export moratorium.[e] 2. Cap on landmine stockpiles.[f] 3. Cessation of landmine use in 2006 if "suitable alternatives to APLs and mixed munitions" are identified and fielded.[g]

[a]"The Issue of Anti-Personnel Landmines," China National Defense White Paper, op. cit.
[b]"India Calls for Int'l Consensus on Banning Landmines," Xinhua English Newswire, November, 15, 1998.
[c]BBC Worldwide Monitoring Source, Radio Pakistan external service, March 17, 1999.
[d]"Yeltsin affirms support for ban on mines," Reuters, October 29, 1997, http://www2/nando.net/newsroom/ntn/world/102097/world6_468_norrames.htm; "Landmines: A media round-up," British Broadcasting Service, December 2, 1997, http://news.bbc.co.uk:80/hi/english/world/monitoring/newsid_36000/36510.stm.
[e]"Suspension of Transfers of Anti-Personnel Mines," U.S. National Defense Authorization Act for Fiscal Year 1993, U.S. Federal Register, Volume 57, p. 228, November 25, 1992.
[f]Statement by the Press Secretary, The White House, May 16, 1997.
[g]President Clinton letter to Marissa A. Vitagliano, August 31, 1998.

officially launched in 1993, the U.S. government has led all international donors in providing a total of more than $1.5 billion to clear landmines and unexploded ordnance and treat accident victims.[15] For example, in 2009, the U.S. Department of State continued its global leadership role in addressing the needs of landmine victims and mine clearance operations by granting $130 million in aid to 32 countries, while in 2008 it provided $123.1 million in assistance to 35 countries (see Figure 6.1).[16]

The MBT is unique in another way: The ICBL members play an important part in the treaty's implementation, such as promoting compliance through its *Landmine Monitor Report* initiative. It was created in June 1988 after discussion among a few Government diplomats and ICBL leaders determining that there was a need "to track and report on state parties' compliance and the humanitarian response more generally to the landmine crisis."[17] State Parties and ICBL members now use the *Landmine Monitor* to

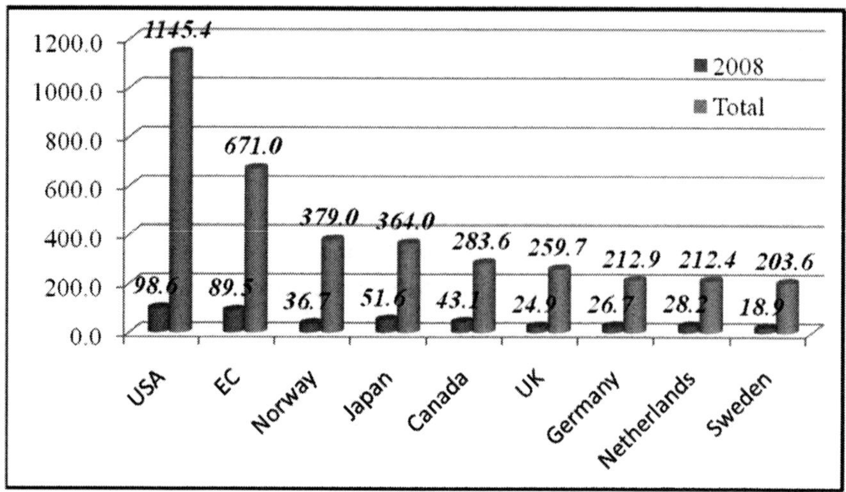

Figure 6.1

International Mine Action Funding (USD in millions). Total funding amounts are from 1992 to 2008 and all figures include funds considered "Additional R&D Funding." International Campaign to Ban Landmines. *Landmine Monitor Report 2009: Toward a Mine-Free World*. Ottawa: Mines Action Canada, 2009.

monitor government statements and actions in public and other forums, such as the regular MBT states parties meetings. These meetings are held in accordance with MBT Article 11 calling for state parties to

> meet regularly in order to consider any matter with regard to the application or implementation of this Convention, including: (1) The operation and status of this Convention; (2) Matters arising from the reports submitted under the provisions of this Convention; (3) International cooperation and assistance in accordance with Article 6; (4) The development of technologies to clear anti-personnel mines; (5) Submissions of States Parties under Article 8; (6) Decisions relating to submissions of States Parties as provided for in Article 5.

The ICBL also helped establish interim meetings in Geneva to discuss issues of importance to the success of the MBT between broader annual meetings. At these meetings, the governments come together and discuss problems of MBT implementation. They discuss questions such as: Are they destroying the stockpiles in time? Are there violations? Are they dealing with the mine victims? Are they dealing with the mine clearance in an appropriate fashion? Where is the weak link in universalization?

The ICBL's *Landmine Monitor*, which is typically more than a thousand-plus-pages with specific reports, country by country, provides a basis for

ICBL members to use the bully pulpit to stigmatize violators.[18] Its research also "finds its way into official reports, declarations and plans of action, as well as statements and reporting by individual states parties, and has become an accepted, if tacit, part of the official Mine Ban Convention [MBT] landscape."[19]

The *Landmine Monitor* initiative has had an immediate effect on state behavior, especially among signatories. For example:

- The *1999 Landmine Monitor Report* detected violations by state signatories Angola, Guinea-Bissau, and Senegal. These states were especially targeted by the ICBL for criticism at the opening of the First Meeting of State Parties to the MBT in Maputo, Mozambique, on May 3, 1999.[20] Senegal immediately denied use; while Angola said its APL usewas discriminate because it was using them to protect security targets during the civil war.
- The *2000 Landmine Monitor Report* highlighted actual violations by state signatory Angola and possible violations by state signatories Burundi and Sudan (see photo 6.3).[21]
- The ICBL also encouraged the European Union (EU) to follow through on its members' obligations for demining assistance. Subsequently, a March 14, 2000, EU announcement reinforced budgetary support for European demining programs and noted that this action was due in part to NGO pressure highlighting weaknesses in the EU's approach.[22] European Commission

Photograph 6.3

Alberto was planting cassava when he found this landmine. Angola. 2004. (Courtesy Sean Sutton/Mines Advisory Group (MAG). Used by permission.)

> Commissioner Chris Patten stated that the *Landmine Monitor's* mention of EU contributions to alleviating the effects of APLs is the beginning of "redressing the perception held worldwide of the Community's mild engagement in the fight against landmines" and furthermore implied that the mention in the *Landmine Monitor Report* helped promote EU action on landmines because "visibility implies accountability."[23]

What the ICBL, ICRC, and Canada and other small and mid-size governments helped achieve is much more than the MBT. They built a partnership model that is a powerful example of what the general public can do when people work together and with their governments to express their views. Some experience arms control observers feared that major powers outside the MBT would make it meaningless and, actually, propel the landmine crisis since a few of them, such as China, are among the world's largest APL producers. But these worries have not been borne out. The MBT's principal accomplishment, though, is the fact that most of the world (more than 155 countries and increasing) is unswerving to the idea that APLs should never be used, produced, stockpiled or transported, thus moral momentum, which, in turn, sways the APL behavior of non-signatories too, including China and the United States.

This book's findings are significant for larger concerns in international affairs. It sheds light on a few conditions under which NGOs can affect state behavior in an area traditionally at the heart of state sovereignty—security and weapons. Meanwhile, the international legal community should be interested in the book's findings because it provides a process model for current and future NGO-state collaborative efforts to alleviate the negative effects of certain weapons, especially those with a dubious military utility (see photo 6.4). Since the ban-APL norm originated from the NGO and not the governmental level, and not with the world's major powers, the rise of the APL-ban norm may help explain why particular issues take off. This point leads us to probe further and ask if the emergence of the APL-ban issue says something more general about international law and relations.

This book also suggests that NGOs can be productive players in the evolving arms-control agenda by identifying weapons or other security practices that are contrary to humanitarian principles. For example, NGOs can help target weapons currently in development in order to reduce political opposition and lower implementation costs. Perhaps there should also be a clearer obligation for governments to review their weapons currently on-line. NGOs can be integral to this process by identifying these weapons and placing and controlling the issue on the international political agenda. Finally, the ICBL and ICRC role in placing the APL issue on the international political agenda and controlling it once it got there suggests ways that international society

Photograph 6.4

"The Price of Water." A young boy walks through a contaminated mine field to fill his canisters with water. Identity unknown, Svay Rieng province, Cambodia 2008. (© Wade C. Roberts, Ph.D. Used with permission.)

can address uncontrolled weapons proliferation and use in a timely and unified manner. As night follows day, another international global NGO coalition, Cluster Munitions Coalition (CMC), with the ICRC and small and mid-size governments as partners, applied the ban-APL advocacy, diplomatic and networking strategies concept to cluster munitions, resulting in the 2008 Cluster Munitions Convention (CMC), which is a comprehensive prohibition on the export, production, and use of cluster munitions with strong obligations for victim assistance and clearance.

Notes

PREFACE

1. Lugh is located on the Juba River in the Gedo region, near the Ethiopian and Kenyan borders.

2. The loan funds came from a monetization project funded by the U.S. government to convert surplus American food aid into Somali currency. The loans were used to help Somalis recover from war and starvation by supporting indigenously inspired economic projects.

3. Tamara Morgan, trauma Nurse, African Medical and Research Foundation, E-mail correspondence with author, July 3, 2010.

4. Joe Moran, air pilot, African Medical and Research Foundation, conversation with author, Dublin, Ireland. May 28, 2008.

5. Joe Moran, air pilot, African Medical and Research Foundation, as quoted in television documentary *Landmines: A Princess Legacy,* produced by British Broadcasting Corporation (BBC) Bristol. 1998.

6. Unless noted, all references to landmines or mines refer to anti-personnel landmines (APLs) and not other forms of landmines, such as anti-tank mines, anti-vehicle mines, and sea mines.

7. Officially known as the Ottawa Convention on the Prohibition of the Use, Stockpiling, Production, and Transfer of Anti-Personnel Mines and on Their Destruction.

8. Boutros Boutros-Ghali, "Forward," in Kevin M. Cahill, ed., *Clearing the Fields: Solutions to the Global Land Mine Crisis* (Council of Foreign Relations: New York, 1995) 1. Patrick Blagden, "The Use of Mines and the Impact of Technology," in Ibid., 115.

9. Kevin M. Cahill, "Introduction," in Ibid., 1.

CHAPTER 1

1. Statement of Canadian Prime Minister, Jean Chretien, at the Signing Conference for the Mine Ban Treaty, December 3, 1977.

2. International Campaign to Ban Landmines, "Report on Activities: Review Conference on the Convention on Conventional Weapons" held in Vienna, Austria. 106.

3. As of May 23, 2010 there are 156 *States Parties.*

4. International Campaign to Ban Landmines "Report on Activities: Review Conference on the Convention on Conventional Weapons." 106. Most multilateral disarmament agreements have taken years rather than months to attain. The Chemical Weapons Convention (CWC), for example, took more than twenty-four years to negotiate once it was placed on the international political agenda. Kenneth R. Rutherford, "The Hague and Ottawa Conventions: A Model for Future Weapon Ban Regimes?" *Nonproliferation Review,* Spring-Summer 1999, Volume 6, Number 3, 43–44.

5. The International Campaign to Ban Landmines consists of over 1,400 arms control, development, environmental, humanitarian, human rights, medical and religious NGOs representing some 70 countries.

6. A notable example is John Borrie, *Unacceptable Harm: A History of How the Treaty to Ban Cluster Munitions Was Won* (United Nations Institute for Disarmament Research: Geneva, Switzerland, 2009). Borrie explains how the Convention on Cluster Munitions (CCM) was achieved through the "Oslo Process," a partnership of NGOs, mid-size states, and international agencies similar to the Ottawa Process that resulted in the MBT.

7. While some of the biggest states, such as the United States, China, India, and Russia did not join the MBT, they unilaterally altered their behavior due to the stigmatizing effect of the norm against landmine use. This is discussed later in the chapter and book. See Table 1.2 later in this chapter.

8. Col. Dennis Barlow (U.S. Army Ret.), conversation with author on June 29, 2010. Besides serving as the Director of Humanitarian Policy in the Office of the Secretary of Defense (September 1994–November 1995) and the first leader of the Humanitarian Demining Task Force in the Pentagon (November 1995–August 1996), he also helped spearhead humanitarian efforts by leading some of the world's first coordinated civil-military actions with nongovernmental organizations and the United Nations in Panama, Saudi Arabia, Iraq, Kurdistan, and Haiti. After retiring from the U.S. Army, Barlow established the Mine Action Information Center (MAIC) and Center for International Stabilization (CISR) at James Madison University (JMU), Harrisonburg, Virginia, because he thought "that mine clearance and victim assistance was a perfect complement to effective U.S. nation building, COIN, and civic action missions." Col. Dennis Barlow (U.S. Army Ret.), e-mail correspondence with author July 1, 2010.

9. For a comparison of the issues and strategies in the movements to ban landmines and to restrict the use of Small Arms and Light Weapons see Stefan Brem and Kenneth R. Rutherford "The Landmine Ban and the Debate on Small Arms and Light Weapons: Walking Together or Divided Agenda?" *Security Dialogue.* Volume 32, Number 2, June 2001, 169–186. In the small arms and light weapons case and arms trade cases, "there are some very large states supportive of the work on

these issues, even if they may not be so keen on some specific elements of substance." For this and other insights, I would like to thank John Borrie, who led the "The Road from Oslo: Analysis of Negotiations to Address the Humanitarian Effects of Cluster Munitions" project for the United Nations Institute for Disarmament Research (UNIDIR). He is also co-founder Disarmament Insight, and prior to joining UNIDIR, worked for the Mines-Arms Unit of the International Committee for the Red Cross and was Deputy Head of Mission for Disarmament in Geneva with the New Zealand Government between 1999 and 2000. John Borrie, Senior Researcher & Project Manager, UNIDIR, e-mail correspondence with author, June 2, 2010.

10. It was further strengthened in the 1977 Additional Protocol I to the 1949 Geneva Conventions, which in Article 51, Paragraph 2 protects noncombatants, of whom the civilian population is the largest group, against direct attack unrelated to a legitimate military objective. Another restriction under international law concerns proportionality, which was also listed in Protocol I. Article 35, paragraphs 1 and 2, require belligerents to weigh the expected military utility of a particular weapon against the humanitarian costs. Essentially, the law bars attacks that may cause more harm to noncombatants than is needed to fulfill the military objective. A noncombatant will, however, forfeit his protection if he participates in hostilities.

11. David Smith, *Sherman's March to the Sea 1964: From Atlanta to Savannah* (London: Osprey Publishing, 2007) 76.

12. As quoted in the Official release by the German Government, published in the *Kreuz-Zeitung*, November 11, 1918. http://wwi.lib.byu.edu/index.php/The_Allies%27_Armistice_Demands. from the WWI Document Archive residing on the server at the library of Brigham Young University. Accessed June 7, 2010.

13. Based on the 1954 discussions, the ICRC wrote the *1955 Draft Rules for the Protection of the Civilian Population from the Dangers of Indiscriminate Warfare of Indiscriminate* that considered "delay-action" weapons, including "delay-action mines, which are used by armies during land operations," and bombs and mines that are deployed by air and "have a delayed action in the sense that they explode after a given lapse of time or when they are touched." The ICRC wrote that land mines "raises great difficulties and the ICRC study of the subject is not sufficiently advanced to enable it to propose a rule concerning it" and "proposes to continue its study of the question."Louis Maresca & Stuart Maslen, eds., *The Banning of Anti-Personnel Landmines: The Legal Contribution of the International Committee of the Red Cross 1955–1999* (Cambridge University Press: Cambridge, United Kingdom 2000) 17–18.

14. International Committee for the Red Cross, "Landmines Must Be Stopped," ICRC 1998, 16. This figure was useful in illustrating the large magnitude of the human cost of mines.

15. Statement by Elizabeth Dole, President, American Red Cross, "Statement by Elizabeth Dole on The Use of Antipersonnel Landmines." Press statement issued by the American Red Cross, April 21, 1993.

16. *Hidden Killers 1998: The Global Landmine Crisis*, U.S. Department of State Bureau of Political-Military Affairs, 9; *Hidden Killer 1993: The Global Problem with Uncleared Landmines* (U.S. Department of State, Washington, D.C., July 1993), 2.

17. Tim Friend, "Millions of land mines hinder Afghan recovery: 2-decade legacy hurts workforce, farmland," *USA Today*, November 28, 2001. 1A and 10A.

18. In Additional Protocol I, Article 55, governments are required to take care in warfare to protect the natural environment, while Additional Protocol I, Article 1, makes warfare illegal if it is "intended or may be expected to cause damage to the natural environment and thereby to prejudice the health or survival of the population." Roberts and Williams, 491.

19. United Nations Environment Programme, *A Rapid Assessment of the Impacts of the Iraq-Kuwait Conflict on Territorial Ecosystems*, 1991 quoted in UNICEF in *The Global Landmine Crisis*, 30.

20. Anne Goldfeld, "Killers in the Earth," *Washington Post*, July 9, 1996, C1.

21. *Afghanistan: The Development of Indigenous Mine Action Capabilities*, A study prepared by Robert Eaton, Chris Horwood, and Norah Niland, (Lessons Learned Unit, United Nations Department of Humanitarian Affairs, United Nations, publication date not provided) 5 and *Mine Action Programme for Afghanistan: Workplan 1999*, United Nations Office for the Coordination of Humanitarian Assistance to Afghanistan (UNOCHA), Mine Action Center for Afghanistan, publication date not provide) 12.

22. Shawn Roberts and Jody Williams, *After the Guns Fall Silent: The Enduring Legacy of Landmines* (Oxfam, 1995), 13.

23. Kevin M. Cahill, "Introduction," in Cahill, 1.

24. Gregory K. Hartman, *Weapons That Wait: Mine Warfare in the U.S. Navy*, (Naval Institute Press: Annapolis, Maryland, 1979) 15.

25. Jody Williams, *Brief Assessment and Chrononlogy of the Movement to Ban Landmines*, Vietnam Veterans of Amreican Foundation document. Not Dated.

26. Hartman, 14.

27. Statement of Mark Gwozdecky, Co-ordinator of the Mine Action Team in the Canadian Department of Foreign Affairs and International Trade, at the Ottawa Process Forum, Ottawa, Canada, December 5, 1997. Mark Gwozdecky, Co-coordinator of the Mine Action Team in the Canadian Department of Foreign Affairs and International Trade e-mail correspondence with author, June 7, 2010.

28. Ibid.

29. John Borrie, former New Zealand Government diplomat for disarmament and arms control issues, e-mail correspondence with author, June 2, 2010.

30. The Convention on Conventional Weapons is officially known as the 1980 United Nations Convention on Prohibitions or Restrictions on the Use of Certain Conventional Weapons which may be Deemed to be Excessively Injurious or to have Indiscriminate Effects. It was created to codify and develop "specific rules on the use of weapons, either by totally prohibiting the use of certain weapons, or by regulating their use." *Report to the International Committee of the Red Cross for the Review Conference of the CCW, International Committee of the Red Cross*, February 1994, 127. The Landmines Protocol attached to the CCW as Protocol II is officially known as the Protocol on Prohibitions or Restrictions on the Use of Mines, Booby Traps and Other Devices. The two other Protocols were Non-detectable Fragments (Protocol I) and Prohibitions or Restrictions on the Use of Incendiary Weapons (Protocol III). The CCW Review held in Vienna in September 1996 adopted Protocol IV that called for restrictions on the use of laser weapons. The four protocols are regulated by the provisions of the Weapons Convention. This essay will address only the Landmines Protocol. U.N.G.A. Document A/C.1/48/L.42.

31. Richard Price, "Reversing the Gun Sights: Transnational Civil Society Targets Land Mines," *International Organization* 52 (Summer 1998): 623.

32. Statement by Jurg Lauber, Diplomatic Adviser, Switzerland Ministry of Foreign Affairs, at the Ottawa Process Forum, Ottawa, Canada, December 5, 1997.

33. David C. Atwood, Associate Representative, Disarmament and Peace, Friends World Committee and Consultation, Quaker United Nations Office, Geneva, "Banning Landmines: Observations on the Role of Civil Society," Paper prepared for the volume *Peace Politics of Civil Society*, June 1998, 7.

34. Jody Williams, Interview, KSMU Radio, Southwest Missouri State University, February 21, 2001.

35. Patrick Blagden, "The Use of Mines and the Impact of Technology," in Cahill, 113.

36. John Borrie correctly points out that "[a]lthough when the Ottawa process gathered steam, the U.S. and others began to push a proposal for work on landmines in the Conference on Disarmament!" e-mail correspondence with author, June 2, 2010. At the time, Borrie was a New Zealand diplomat working disarmament and other arms control issues.

37. Stuart Maslan goes into this period in exceptional detail in *Mine Ban Treaty* as part of *Oxford University Commentaries on Arms Control Treaties Series* (Oxford, UK: Oxford University Press, 2004).

38. *The United Nations Disarmament Yearbook*, The United Nations Disarmament Yearbook (Department of Disarmament Affairs; New York, 1997) 105–106.

39. Final Report, Review CCW Conference, p. 11, U.N. Document CCW/ CONF. (/16 1 (Part I) (1996).

40. Statement by Steve Goose, Human Rights Watch, to the Regional Conference on Landmines, Budapest, Hungary, March 27, 1998. Report: Regional Conference on Landmines, International Campaign to Ban Landmines, Budapest, Hungary, March 26–28, 1998, 52.

41. Ibid., 52.

42. *The United Nations Disarmament Yearbook* 106.

43. Statement by UN Secretary-General Boutros Boutros-Ghali to the Review Conference of States Parties to the Convention on Prohibitions or Restrictions on the Use of Certain Conventional Weapons Which May Be Deemed to Be Excessively Injurious or to Have Indiscriminate Effects, Vienna, Austria, September 1995.

44. At the September 1997 Oslo final treaty drafting conference, Annan said "[i]t gives me great pleasure to address you meeting at this vital point in *our efforts* to achieve a world-wide ban on anti-personnel mines" [emphasis by the author]. Statement by UN Secretary-General Kofi Annan, at the Diplomatic Conference on Landmines, Oslo, Norway, September 3, 1997.

45. Statement by Kofi Annan, United Nations Secretary-General, to the Signing Ceremony of the Anti-Personnel Mines Convention, December 3, 1997.

46. Neo-realists explain the MBT as epiphenomenal, since international norms do not have independent effects on state behavior. For example, a prominent neo-realist, John Mearshimer, argues that states do not follow international norms if the latter do not serve the former's self-interests.John Mearshimer, "The False Promise of Institutions," in Michael E. Brown, Sean M. Lynn Jones, and Steven Miller, eds., *The Perils of Anarchy: Contemporary Realism and International Security*

(Cambridge: The MIT Press, 1995) 334. In a peer-reviewed article, I previously wrote that "Since neo-realists believe anarchy remains constant, and the units of an anarchic system are functionally undifferentiated, they focus on material capabilities as the most identifiable characteristics of the states, rather than sociological influences such as norms. Therefore, according to neo-realist principles, those states banning landmines do so because they perceive some relative gains to be made in prohibiting landmine use. The written compact is a means to ensure their own survival, and signing and ratifying a treaty is merely an easy way for states to help achieve their goal of survival. The neo-realist assumption is that norms do not impinge on state actions, so therefore neo-realists need not address international norms. The existence of an international norm simply reflects the interests of these states adhering to it. Similarly, neo-realism considers NGOs as a non-factor in international relations. Although some NSAs [non-state actors] have some capabilities of states, neo-realists believe that NGOs need the support and at least acquiescence of the principal states concerned with the matters at hand; otherwise, NGOs are powerless." Kenneth R. Rutherford, "A Theoretical Examination of Disarming States: NGOs and Anti-Personnel Landmines," *Journal of International Politics*. Vol. 37, Number 4, December 2000, 457–477; Kenneth Waltz argues that international relations theories that deny "the central importance of states" can be discounted as inaccurate reflections of international relations until "non-state actors develop to the point of rivaling or surpassing the great powers, not just a few minor ones." Furthermore, "When the crunch time comes, states remake the rules by which other actors operate . . . one may be struck by the ability of weak states to impede the operation of strong MNCs [multi-national corporations] and NGOs and by the attention the latter pay to the wishes of the former." Kenneth N. Waltz, *Theory of International Politics* (New York: McGraw-Hill, 1979) 95.

47. Waltz, *Theory of International Politics*, 73 and 94.

48. Kenneth N. Waltz, "The Origins of War in Neo-Realist Theory," in Richard K. Betts, *Conflict After the Cold War: Arguments on Causes of Peace* (Boston: Allyn and Bacon, 1994), 92–95.

49. Ibid., 94.

50. Waltz, *Theory of International Politics*, 184–185.

51. For this observation, I would like to thank Kerry Brinkert, Director of the MBT's Implementation Support Unit (ISU). Kerry Brinkert e-mail correspondence with author, June 16, 2010. Housed in the Geneva International Center for Humanitarian Demining (GICHD) in Geneva, the ISU was created 2001 based on an agreement of MBT States Parties with the purpose to further enhance the MBT's operation and implementation.

52. International Campaign to Ban Landmines, *Landmine Monitor 1999*, Human Rights Watch, New York, 2000. 5.

53. Rosalyn Higgins, *Problems and Process: International Law and How We Use It* (Oxford: Oxford University Press, 1995), 252.

54. The following three books primarily focus on mine development and warfare and, as such, are also outside this particular topic area, which provides an in-depth analysis of the global movement's rise. Mike Croll has written two landmine books—*The History of Landmines* and *Landmines in War and Peace: From Their Origin to Present Day*—which provide a wide ranging description of the development of

APL use and efforts to clear them. Similarly, Norman E. Youngblood's *The Development of Mine Warfare: A Most Murderous and Barbarous Conduct: War, Technology, and History* traces the history of mine warfare development, while also includes a significant discussion of sea mines. Two other noteworthy landmine books which are highlighted in the following chapter are *After the Guns Fall Silent*, by Shawn Roberts and Jody Roberts, that focuses on the socio-economic devastation caused by landmines, and *Landmines: A Deadly Legacy*, co-produced by The Arms Project of Human Rights Watch and Physicians for Human Rights, which centers on the devastation caused by landmines by examining their social and medical consequences, global production and trade, and international laws governing their use. Finally, another book to consider is Mathew Bolton's *Foreign Aid and Landmine Clearance: Governance, Politics and Security in Afghanistan, Bosnia and Sudan* that explores the politics behind the allocation and implementation of foreign aid by the United States and Norway for demining in Afghanistan, Bosnia, and Sudan.

CHAPTER 2

1. Shawn Roberts and Jody Williams, *After the Guns Fall Silent: The Enduring Legacy of Landmines* (Oxfam, 1995) 3.
2. The U.S. military manual is *The Conduct of Armed Conflict and Air Operations*, U.S. Department of the Air Force, Pamphlet Number 110-31, 1976. Paragraphs 6-6d, quoted in Lt. Col. Burris M. Carnahan, "The Law of Land Mine Warfare: Protocol II to The United Nations Convention on Certain Conventional Weapons," *Military Law Review*, Summer, 1984, 73.
3. Ibid., 27.
4. Louis Maresca & Stuart Maslen, eds., *The Banning of Anti-Personnel Landmines: The Legal Contribution of the International Committee of the Red Cross 1955–1999* (Cambridge University Press: Cambridge, United Kingdom 2000) xvii.
5. Robert Lawson, Deputy Director, Canadian Mine Action Team, Conversation with Author, Irvine, California. May 8, 2000.
6. Martin Pinder, Senior Organisation and Methods Officer, *Landmines and UNHCR persons of concern*, a draft discussion paper on possible UNHCR study, prepared for the Liaison Unit, Southern Africa Operations, UNHCR Geneva, June 10, 1997 3.
7. Of the 9,300 UNCHR documents produced between 1994 and June 10, 1997, only two documents addressed landmines. In addition, there were no landmine NGOs listed in the UNHCR directory nor budget codes for landmine related expenditures as of 1997. Ibid.
8. According to Jan Eliasson, who served as the first UN Undersecretary-General for Humanitarian Affairs, the most common reason given by the nearly 1.5 million Afghani refugees in Pakistan for delaying their return to Afghanistan is "the danger of land mines" as quoted in Jan Eliasson, "An International Approach Toward Humanitarian Assistance and Economic Development of Countries Affected by Land Mines," in Kevin M. Cahill, ed., *Clearing the Fields: Solutions to the Global Land Mine Crisis* (Council of Foreign Relations: New York, 1995) 174.

9. Dr. Robin Gray, Surgical Coordinator, ICRC, *Humanitarian Consequences of Mine Usage*, report presented to the ICRC Symposium on Anti-Personnel Landmines, April 1993 as reprinted in Maresca & Maslen, 148.

10. Ibid., 148.

11. Sharif Baaser, Program Specialist, Mine Action and Small Arms Child Protection, Programme Division UNICEF, Presentation at the Mine Action Program Manager Course organized by the Center for International Stabilization and Recovery at James Madison University June 1, 2010 and e-mail correspondence with author, June 21, 2010.

12. Rae McGrath, *Landmines: Legacy of Conflict: A manual for development workers* (Oxfam: United Kingdom, 1994), 2.

13. Jody Williams, ICBL Ambassador, Interview, KSMU Radio Interview, Southwest Missouri State University, Springfield, Missouri. February 21, 2001.

14. Letter from Lou McGrath, MAG Executive Director, welcoming visitors to the MAG website: www.mag.uk.org.

15. Rae McGrath, *The Reality of the Present Use of Mines by Military Forces*, report presented to the ICRC Symposium on Anti-Personnel Landmines, April 1993 as reprinted in Maresca and Maslen, 138. A karez is a water management system used to provide a reliable supply of water to human settlements. They are especially found in the Southern Afghanistan provinces of Kandahar, Uruzgan, Nimroz, and Hilmand.

16. J. Rautio, Paavolainen, "Afghan War Wounded: Experience with 200 Cases," *Journal of Trauma* (1988): 523–25, quoted in Chris Giannour, M.D., and J. Jack Geiger, M.D., "The Medical Lessons of Land Mine Injuries," in Kevin M. Cahill, ed., *Clearing the Fields: Solutions to the Global Land Mine Crisis* (Council of Foreign Relations: New York, 1995) 115.

17. D. Johnson, J. Crum, and S. Lumjiak, "Medical Consequences of the Various Weapons Systems Used in Combat in Thailand," *Military Medicine* 146 (1981): 632–34, quoted in Giannou and Geiger, in Ibid., 115.

18. Robin M. Coupland and Remi Russbach, "Injuries from Anti-Personal Mines: What Is Being Done?", *Medicine and Global Survival*, Volume 1, Number 1, March 1994, 18–22;

19. Sue J. Jeffrey, The ICRC Medical Division, Geneva, Switzerland "Antipersonnel mines: who are the victims?" *Journal of Accident & Emergency Medicine* 1996 September; 13(5): 343–346.

20. Robin M. Coupland and Adriaan Korver, "Injuries from antipersonnel landmines: the experience of the International Committee of the Red Cross," *British Medical Journal*, December 14, 1991, 1509–1512; The Arms Project/Human Rights Watch and Physicians for Human Rights, *Landmines: A Deadly Legacy*, October 1993, 117–140.

21. International Committee for the Red Cross, *Landmines Must Be Stopped: The Worldwide Epidemic of Landmine Injuries: The ICRC's health oriented approach*, September 1995. 5.

22. Ibid., 6.

23. B. Eshaya-Chauvin and R.M. Coupland, "Transfusion Requirements for the Management of War Injured: The Experience of the International Committee of the

Red Cross," *British Journal of Anesthesia* 68 (1992): 221–223 quoted Giannou and Geiger, in Cahill, p. 140.

24. J. Rautio, Paavolainen, "Afghan War Wounded: Experience with 200 Cases," *Journal of Trauma* (1988): 523–525, quoted in Chris Giannour, M.D., and J. Jack Geiger, M.D., "The Medical Lessons of Land Mine Injuries," in Cahill, 115, and D. Johnson, J. Crum, and S. Lumjiak, "Medical Consequences of the Various Weapons Systems Used in Combat in Thailand," *Military Medicine* 146 (1981): 632–634, quoted in Giannou and Geiger, in Cahill, 115.

25. L.N. Bisenkov and N.A. Tynyakkin, "Osobennosti okazaniya khirugicheskoy pomoshchi postradavshim s minnovsryvnymi raneniyami v armii respubliki Afghanistan" [Providing special surgical care to land mine casualties in the army of the Republic of Afghanistan], *Voenno-medisinkiy zhurnal (VMZ), Military medical journal,* January 1992, 22, as referenced in Lester W. Grau and William A. Jorgensen, "Guerrilla Warfare and Land Mine Casualties Remain Inseparable," *US Army Medical Department Journal*, Foreign Military Studies Office Publications, October-December, 1998.

26. Neil Andersson, Cesar Palha de Sousa, Sergio Paredes, "Social Cost of land mines in four countries: Afghanistan, Bosnia, Cambodia and Mozambique," *British Medical Journal*, Volume 311, September 16, 1995, 718.

27. Ibid., 718. A similar conclusion was found in another study of mine victims in affected areas in Mozambique that the number of mine victims was low before 1982 "but increased rapidly afterwards, remaining high until 1993." Alberto Ascherio, Robin Biellik, Andy Epstein, Gail Snetro, Steve Gloyd, Barbara Ayotte, Paul R. Epstein, "Deaths and injuries caused by land mines in Mozambique," *The Lancet*, September 16, 1995. 723.

28. Robin M. Coupland and Hans O. Samnegaard, "Effect of type and transfer of conventional weapons on civilian injuries: retrospective analysis of prospective data from Red Cross hospital," *British Medical Journal*, Volume 319, August 14, 1999, pp. 410–411.

29. Ibid., 410–411.

30. Sean Sutton, photographer, Mines Advisory Group (MAG), conversation with author. North Atlantic on the Queen Mary II. May 4, 2007. Sutton was the first photographer to be employed full time to cover the landmine issue. Many of his photographs are used by NGOs, the United Nations, and governments to promote support for landmine clearance operations, risk education programs, and victim assistance projects. A few of them appear in this book with his permission. Sutton first documented the landmine issue in 1989 in Burma and began working with MAG full time in 1997. He had previously worked with MAG in the field in Lao, Cambodia, and Angola and with Halo Trust in Angola and Afghanistan.

31. Letter from Peter D. Bell, President, CARE to Anthony Lake, Assistant to the President for National Security Affairs, May 3, 1996.

32. According to a 1996 UN landmine report on Cambodia, "[t]he UN first became involved in supporting humanitarian mine action initiatives in Afghanistan in 1988 within the context of UNOCHA, the UN programme for the Coordination of Humanitarian Assistance. The UN Department of Humanitarian Affairs (UNDHA) was designated UN focal point for landmines in December 1994; thus, the UN did not have personnel focused exclusively on the problem of

landmines as a humanitarian issue before the end of 1995. *Cambodia: The Development of Indigenous Mine Action Capacities*, A study prepared by Robert Eaton, Chris Horwood, and Norah Niland, (Lessons Learned Unit, United Nations Department of Humanitarian Affairs, United Nations, publication date not provided), p. 1.

33. Robert J. Lawson, *Ban Landmines: The Social Construction of the International Ban on Anti-Personnel Landmines 1991–2001*, Master Thesis, Carleton University, Ottawa, Canada, April 2002, 114.

34. Charles P. Wallace, "Land Mines Take Toll on Cambodian Peace," *Los Angeles Times*, December 14, 1991, p. A4.

35. Gray, 147.

36. Ratana Khun, Chief of Secretariat for the Public Cambodian Mine Action Center, letter to author, June 1, 2010.

37. Gerhard Bornmann, UNHCR Demining Officer, *Programme For Protection Against Explosive Land Mines*, in connection with the tasks of UNHCR, March 1993, p. 4.

38. International Committee for the Red Cross, *Landmines Must Be Stopped: The Worldwide Epidemic of Landmine Injuries: The ICRC's Health Oriented Approach*, September 1995, p. 3. In an ICRC study of weapon injuries based on admissions to the ICRC Mongkol Borei (Cambodia) hospital from January 1991—after the peace treaty took effect—to February 1995, the findings showed that of the 863 weapon related injuries, 317 were due to mines and more than half (110) were civilians. David R. Meddings and Stephaine M. O'Connor, "Circumstances around weapon injury in Cambodia after departure of a peacekeeping force: prospective cohort study," *British Medical Journal*, Volume 319, August 14, 1999, pp. 412–413.

39. Joel R. Charny and Anne Goldfeld, "Cambodia: Don't look away." *New York Times*. May 10, 1990.

40. Asia Watch and Physicians for Human Rights, *The Coward's War*, (Human Rights Watch and Physicians for Human Rights: New York, 1991). The report was written by Rae McGrath, Eric Stover, human rights activist and consultant to HRW and PHR, and Dr. James C. Colby, a Red Cross consultant and an orthopedic surgeon who was asked by PHR to join the study of the landmine problem because of his public health background.

41. Ibid.,102–103.

42. Ibid., 2.

43. Ibid., 2.

44. *Landmines in Cambodia*, 35.

45. As quoted in Jim Colby, "One Doctor's Crusade," Physicians for Human Rights, *Record*, Volume XI, Number 1, April 1998, p. 6.

46. Eric Stover and Dan Charles, "The Killing minefields of Cambodia," *New Scientist*, October 19, 1991, p. 27. A 1998–1999 study found that while Cambodia's populations had grown to 10 million people, "at least 24,410 survived mine injuries" and more than "14,500 have died as a result of landmines. International Campaign to Ban Landmines. *Landmine Monitor Report 1999: Toward a Mine-Free World*. Washington DC: Human Rights Watch. 1999. 405.

47. James C. Colby, MD, MPH, FACS, "Medical Complications of Antipersonnel Land Mines," Volume 81, Number 8, *Bulletin of the American College of Surgeons*. August 1996, p. 9. The two statistics cited here and in the previous reference are close but not identical. The sources give slightly different calculations.

48. *The Coward's War*, 102.

49. Ibid., 102.

50. "A Working Chronology of the International Movement to Ban Anti-Personnel (AP) Mines," published by the Centre for Negotiation and Dispute Resolution, The Norman Paterson School of International Affairs, Carleton University, Ottawa, Canada, 10.

51. Anne E. Goldfeld, M.D., Testimony before the Asia Pacific Sub-Committee of the House Foreign Affairs Committee, April 10, 1991. Goldfeld also made the call for a ban on landmines in a January 8, 1991, press conference at the Bangkok Foreign Correspondents Club a few months before. Anne Goldfeld, e-mail correspondence with author, June 30, 2010. The conference occurred at the end of the delegation visit of the Women's Commission for Refugee Women and Children to Cambodia, which witnessed "[t]he inhumane practice of laying land mines should be immediately stope [*sic*]" and the horrifying effects wrought by APLs on the women and children refugees. "Cambodia—On the Brink of Peace," report from a delegation of The Women's Commission for Refugee Women and Children delegation visit to Cambodia, January 1–8, 1991.

52. Ibid.

53. Anne Goldfeld, "The Dying Fields: New Horror in Cambodia," *New York Times*. June 4, 1991.

54. Anne Goldfeld, "A Weapon We Can Live Without," *Boston Globe*, September 22, 1996.

55. Anne Goldfeld, e-mail correspondence with author, July 1, 2010.

56. Anne Goldfeld end of tour report sent to Karen Elshazly, Director of International Programs, American Refugee Committee and Bob Medrala, American Refugee Committee Country Director, Thailand. July 14, 1990. The following year, Dr. Goldfeld became the first American to testify before Congress calling for a comprehensive ban on landmines.

57. Anne Goldfeld, e-mail correspondence with author, July 1, 2010.

58. Quoted in *Ban Landmines: The Ottawa Process and the International Movement to Ban Landmines*, a compact disc produced by the Canadian Department of Foreign Affairs and International Trade, 1998.

59. Walker subsequently carried that leg to "to every meeting, every conference, to the Oslo treaty negotiations and signing of the Convention in Ottawa, to the Nobel Peace Prize ceremonies and to every landmines related event for years after, until it was stolen at the CCW in 2001." Susan Walker e-mail to selected ICBL members, including the author, June 2, 2005.

60. Ibid.

61. In 1981, Muller had helped lead the first American veteran delegation to Vietnam since the end of that war. Three years later, he returned to the region and visited Cambodia to tour rehabilitative facilities, which sparked his interest in forming an American veteran charity that would help the victims of landmines. As a Marine veteran paralyzed in combat in Vietnam, he was appalled and outraged at the effects of landmines on the local population.

62. Quoted in Susan Reed and Andrea Pawllyna, "A Marine's Reparation: Thanks to a Vietnam vet, Cambodian amputees have new legs and jobs," *People*, December 11, 1995, 103. Mueller's resultant feelings for the disabled remained

with him throughout the campaign as he started to broaden VVAF's prosthetic work to other mine-infested countries, especially Angola and Vietnam.

63. Statement of Thomas Gebauer, Medico International, "On the way from a legal prohibition to an effective abolition of mines: Remarks on Integrating Mine Action," at the Oslo Landmines NGO Forum, Oslo, Norway, September 7–10, 1997.

64. Jody Williams, "Brief Assessment and Chronology of the Movement to Ban Landmines," Vietnam Veterans of America Foundation, undated documents, [not dated], 1.

65. Comments by Bobby Muller, Vietnam Veterans of America Foundation, "Record of the 6 October 1992 meeting of the founding members of the ICBL," 6.

66. Jody Williams, Interview, KSMU Radio, Southwest Missouri State University, Springfield, Missouri. February 21, 2001.

67. Ibid.

68. Jody Willams, "Thoughts/Questions on Land Mines Campaign," Memorandum to Bobby Muller, VVA, November 25, 1991 as referenced in Lawson, 94.

69. Interview with Jody Williams, February 13, 2002 as quoted in Ibid., 95.

70. Louise Doswald-Beck, ICRC Legal Advisor, as quoted in the "US Group Meeting on Landmines" meeting minutes, Vietnam Veterans of America Foundation, Washington, D.C., September 26, 1994.

71. Statement of Cornelio Sammaruga, ICRC President, "International Strategy Conference Towards a Global Ban on Anti-personnel Mines," Ottawa, Canada, October 4, 1996 as reprinted in Maresca & Maslen, 474; Cornelio Sommaruga, President of the ICRC, as quoted in "Why Red Cross Opposes a Partial Ban on Land Mines," *Christian Science Monitor*, September 27, 1995, p. 6.

72. Jody Williams memo "Response to draft of talking points," April 9, 1992. Document retrieved in the official records of the International Campaign to Ban Landmines at Library and Archives Canada. Ottawa, Canada. Accessed by author on August 13, 2009.

73. Philippe Chabasse, "The French Campaign" in Maxwell A. Cameron, Robert J. Lawson, and Brian W. Tomlin, eds., *To Walk Without Fear: The Global Movement to Ban Landmines* (Oxford University Press: Toronto, 1998), 60.

74. Handicap International, "Antipersonnel landmines: For the banning of massacres of civilians in time of peace—Facts and chronologies (2nd Edition), not dated, 58.

75. "A Working Chronology of the International Movement to Ban Anti-Personnel (AP) Mines," 1. Weil, Nobel Peace Prize laureate Elie Wiesel and former UN Secretary-General Perez de Cuellar were among the first to sign.

76. Tim Carstairs, "Letter to Jody Williams," Handicap International, June 19, 1992 as referenced and quoted in Lawson, 94.

77. Ibid., 60.

78. Letter from Jody Williams, Coordinator, Landmines Campaign, to Senator Patrick Leahy, July 30, 1992.

79. Boutros Boutros-Ghali. *An Agenda for Peace* A/47/277 (1992).

80. Williams secured commitments from, among others, Aryeh Neier, Human Rights Watch; Bishop Walter Sullivan, Diocese of Richmond; Ambassador Charles Flowerree; and Rae McGrath of MAG.

81. Record of the October 6 meeting of the founding members of the ICBL, 2. As referenced and sourced in Lawson, 98.

82. "Report of the Final Plenary Session," NGO Conference on Antipersonnel Mines, London, May 26, 1993, pp. 4 and 5.

83. *Ban Landmines: The Ottawa Process and the International Movement to Ban Landmines*, a compact disc produced by the Canadian Department of Foreign Affairs and International Trade, 1998.

84. Muller would pour in over $5 million over the next five years to help achieve the 1997 Mine Ban Treaty (MBT). James Bandler, "Laureate in a minefield," *The Boston Globe Magazine*, June 7, 1998, p. 28.

85. As quoted in Philip C. Winslow, "The Case Against Landmines," *Red Cross, Red Crescent*, Issue 2, 1997, p. 11.

86. "Portfolio Synopsis: Patrick J. Leahy War Victims Fund," USAID Document, October 1997, p. 1.

87. Congressman Lane Evans (D-IL) led the moratorium efforts on the House side. As a former Marine and Vietnam Veteran, his background was the perfect complement to the legislation and he and Leahy worked together for years in encouraging the United States to ban landmines and support victim assistance programming.

88. Letter from Peter J. Davies, President and CEO, InterAction, to Sen. Patrick Leahy, August 7, 1992. The organizations included Africare, American Friends Service Committee, American Refugee Committee, Bread for the World, CARE, International Medical Corps, Oxfam America, U.S. Committee for Refugees, and World Vision.

89. U.S. Federal Register, Volume 57, 228, November 25, 1992; "Suspension of Transfers of Anti-Personnel Mines" (regulations implementing the Landmine Moratorium Act); U.S. National Defense Authorization Act for Fiscal Year 1993, Publication No. 102-484, sec. 1365 (The Landmines Moratorium Act). Since that time he has proposed additional amendments to control landmines. The following year the Senate passed (100-0) a three-year extension, which is now permanent.

90. Jody Williams and Stephen Goose, "The International Campaign to Ban Landmines," in Cameron, et al., 23–24.

91. Sen. Patrick Leahy letters to Senators Hank Brown, John Kerry, and Thomas Daschle, November 30, 1992.

92. For example, after returning from trip to Vietnam to resolve the MIA/POW issue, Sen. Thomas Daschle wrote Leahy that during his trip he "was deeply saddened at the sight of countless civilians of all ages who were missing limbs or were otherwise disabled by antipersonnel landmines . . . I share your concern for those innocent victims, and I was proud to be a cosponsor of your legislation to impose a one-year moratorium on the sale, export or transfer of antipersonnel landmines." Letter from Sen. Thomas Daschle to Sen. Patrick Leahy, December 9, 1992.

93. Letter from Sen. Patrick Leahy to Handicap International, January 28, 1993. The CCW's revision could be determined only by those states that are party to it as its Article 8 states that "New protocols can be adopted at a new conference, which is to be convened either if a majority of states parties so agree, or upon the request of a single state party if there has been no new conference for the past ten years."

94. Handicap International, 59.

95. Ibid, p. 59.

96. Prepared statement of Bobby Muller, May 13, 1994. Executive Director, Vietnam Veterans of American Foundation. Subcommittee of the Committee on Appropriations, U.S. Senate, May 13, 1994. Senate Hearing "The Global Landmine Crisis." Washington, D.C., 103–666 Report.

97. Handicap International, 59.

98. Chabasse, 62.

99. "A Working Chronology of the International Movement to Ban Anti-Personnel (AP) Mines," 2.

100. Letter from Douglas Hogg, Foreign and Commonwealth Office, Minister of State, United Kingdom, to Chris Mullen, MP, House of Commons, United Kingdom, January 22, 1993.

101. "Introduction" to the Report on the ICRC Symposium on Anti-Personnel Mines held in Montreux, Switzerland, April 21–23, 1993, p. 1.

102. Gray, 146.

103. Dr. Robin M. Coupland, FRCS, and Remi Russbach, MD, 14.

104. Ibid., 20.

105. "Summary of United Nations Demining," *Symposium on Anti-personnel Mines*, Montreux 21–23, April 1993, (Geneva, ICRC) 117. The U.S. Department of State estimates that there are 80–110 million APL mines in 64 countries. U.S. Department of State,*Hidden Killers: The Global Landmine Crisis*, 1994 Report to the U.S. Congress on the Problem with Uncleared Landmines and the U.S. Strategy for Debiting and Control (Department of State Publication 10225), December 1994, p. v.

106. "Summary of United Nations Demining," Preparatory Report by Patrick M. Blagden, United Nations Demining Expert, *Montreux Symposium on Anti-Personnel Mines Report*, International Committee of the Red Cross, Montreux, Switzerland, April 21–23, 1993, p. 117. Patrick Blagden, "The Use of Mines and the Impact of Technology," in Cahill, 114.

107. Ibid., 114–115.

108. Ibid., 115.

109. Donovan Webster, "One Leg, One Life at a Time" *New York Times*, January 23, 1994, p. 29.

110. Ibid., 29.

111. The symposium call for more research was immediately picked up by ICBL Steering Committee members and the ICRC, each of which was soon to produce seminal publications to be released in the next two-and-a-half years and that would help educate governments and influence the negotiations. These publications included *Deadly Legacy* by the Human Rights Watch-Arms Project, *After the Guns Fall Silent* by VVAF, and *Anti-personal Landmines: Friend or Foe? A study of the military use and effectiveness of antipersonnel mines* by the ICRC. As a result, the ICRC continued exploring legal avenues to curtailing the mine crisis. The first ICRC publication on antipersonnel landmines was released in May 1993 called *Mines: A Perverse Use of Technology.* It called for greater controls on mine use rather than a ban, albeit highlighting the indiscriminate use of mines and their humanitarian effects. It also suggested that self-destructing and self-neutralizing mechanisms should be explored to incorporate into mines to ensure shorter-duration

mines and that the Landmines Protocol should apply to internal conflicts. Meanwhile, after the Montreux Symposium, Jody Williams held discussions with a number of organizations in order to coordinate "the production of a socio-economic report to investigate the long-term costs to society of the widespread use of landmines" that was to lead to Shawn Roberts' and Jody Williams' book *After the Guns Fall Silent* published by the Vietnam Veterans of America Foundation (VVAF) in 1995.

112. *Hidden Killers: The Global Problem with Uncleared Landmines*. A Report to the U.S. Congress on the Problem with Uncleared Landmines and the U.S. Strategy for Deming and Landmine Control, Department of State publication, Bureau of Political-Military Affairs. July 1993, p. 3.

113. Interagency Working Group Participants include National Security Council, White House Office of Science and Technology Policy, Deputy Assistant Secretary of State for Policy and Missions and representatives from the Bureau of Political-Military Affairs, Bureau of Population, Refugees, and Migration, and the regional bureaus, Deputy Assistant Secretary of Defense for Policy and Missions, Office of Special Operations and Low-Intensity Conflict, and representatives form the Office of the Undersecretary of Defense for Acquisition and Technology, Office of the Assistant Secretary of Defense for international Security Affairs, and the Defense Security Assistance Agency; the Joint Chiefs of Staffs, Agency for International Development, Information Agency, and Central Intelligence Agency.

114. For example, during the previous ten years the administration approved only ten licenses for the commercial export of antipersonnel landmines with a total value of $980,000, and the sale under the Foreign Military Sales program of 109,120 antipersonnel landmines. Letter from Senator Leahy and thirty-four Senators to Senate Colleagues, July 22, 1993.

115. One example is the United Kingdom's "Ranger, which can fire 1296 mines in one minute." Lt. Col. C.E.E. Sloan, RE, *Mine Warfare on Land* (Brassey's Defense Publishers, 1986), 38 quoted in Shawn Roberts and Jody Williams, *After the Guns Fall Silent: The Enduring Legacy of Landmines*, Vietnam Veterans of America Foundation (Washington, D.C.: 1995) 7. Another example would be the Italian SO-AT system, which allows a helicopter to drop 2,496 landmines. Alder, "Modern Land Mine Warfare," *Armada International*, 6 (1980), quoted in Carnahan, 79. This is contrast to minefield laying "only a few years ago, it might have required up to eight hours work by a full company of troops" quoted in Ibid., 79.

116. Peter J. Ekberg, "Remotely Delivered Land Mines and International Law," *Columbia Journal of Transnational Law*, Volume 33, number 1, 1995, 151; Carnahan, 74.

117. Steve Askin and Stephen Goose, "The Market for Anti-Personnel Landmines—A Global Survey, *Jane's Intelligence Review*, September 1994, pp. 425 and 430. The United States started exporting its scatterable systems in 1985. Ibid.

118. Statement of Captain Michael Doubleday, U.S. Defense Department at Defense Department regular briefing, August 19, 1997.

119. "China prototypes minelayer system," *Jane's Defence Weekly*, July 3, 1993, p. 24.

120. Letter from Toby Watson, President and Chief Executive Officer of Alliant Techsystems to Sen. Patrick Leahy, June 11, 1993.

121. Ibid.

122. Letters from C. M. Welch, Chairman Executive Committee, Mohawk Electrical Systems, Inc. to Sen. Patrick Leahy, August 12, 1993, and September 8, 1993.

123. The export was valued at $2,250. Terry Davis, PM/DTC, Bureau of Politico-Military Affairs, Office of Defense Trade Controls, Department of State. This would be around $790 per mine, which seems expensive for a weapon that is usually described as being cheap. These particular mines are technologically more complex than the stand alone APL.

124. These sales were to Belize, Columbia, Denmark, Ecuador, El Salvador, Greece, Korea, Kuwait, Lebanon, Morocco, Netherlands, New Zealand, Peru, Saudi Arabia, Thailand, Turkey, and the United Kingdom. Foreign Military Sales of Anti-Personnel Land Mines for the Period FYI 1982–1993 as of June 11, 1993. Fax from Peter Ipsen, DSAA/LPD to Tim Rieser, SACFO. June 14, 1993.

125. Stephen Goose, Washington Director, The Arms Project of Human Rights Watch, Statement before the Senate Appropriations Subcommittee on Foreign Operations, June 15, 1993.

126. NGO Conference on Antipersonnel Mines, *Report of the Final Plenary Session*, London, May 26, 1993, p. 3.

127. Ibid., 4.

128. Ibid., 3 and 4.

129. Ibid., 1.

130. Ibid., 2.

131. Ibid., 2.

132. Report of Rae McGrath, Director, MAG, "The Reality of the Present Use of Mines by Military Forces," Report on the ICRC Symposium on Anti-Personnel Mines held in Montreux, Switzerland, April 21–23, 1993, 12.

133. Rae McGrath, Mines Advisory Group, "Safe Mines" and Sub-Munitions," January 1994, 2 as reprinted in *Handicap International, To ban slaughtering in peace time: Facts and chronologies*, September 22, 1995.

134. "A Joint Call to Ban Antipersonnel Landmines," Meeting Statement, October 2, 1992, in *Ban Landmines: The Ottawa Process and the International Movement to Ban Landmines*, a compact disc produced by the Canadian Department of Foreign Affairs and International Trade, 1998.

135. Interview with Stephen Lewis, February 27, 2002, as quoted in Lawson, 117.

136. UNICEF, "Letter to Stuart Maslen, VVAF from Bilge Ogun-Bassani, Deputy Director UNICEF Geneva, August 16, 1993, as referenced in Ibid., 117.

137. Letter from Madeleine Albright, U.S. Ambassador to the UN, to Sen. Patrick J. Leahy, October 6, 1993.

138. Ibid.

139. Besides Albright and Inderfurth, other trip members included an Army Lt. Col and National Security Council staff member Mike Sheehan, who later became the UN Assistant Secretary General of Mission Support and James Rubin, *Assistant Secretary of State for Public Affairs*, who later married Christiane Amanpour, CNN's chief international correspondent from 1992 through 2010. Ambassador Karl Inderfurth interview with author, Washington, D.C., May 15, 2001.

140. Ambassador Karl Inderfurth interview with author, Washington, D.C., May 15, 2001.

141. Ambassador Karl Inderfurth, e-mail to author, June 19, 2010.

142. Ambassador Karl Inderfurth interview with author, Washington, D.C., May 15, 2001; Ambassador Karl Inderfurth, e-mail to author, June 19, 2010.

143. Letter from Sen. Patrick Leahy to Ambassador Madeleine Albright, October 25, 1993.

144. Statement of Sen. Patrick Leahy to the United Nations General Assembly's First Committee on Disarmament and International Security, November 30, 1993.

145. HRW also announced the creation of a new division, the Arms Project, which would research the relationship of weapons to international law. Its first project would be to compile the available information on landmines into a single report to highlight the humanitarian harm caused by mines.

146. Malcolm W. Browne, "Land Mines Called a World Menace," *New York Times*, November 15, 1993, p. A9.

147. Telegram "landmine export moratorium demarche," from Department of State to U.S. missions in landmine producing countries. December 7, 1993.

148. An often-forgotten but important fact about the CCW is that the protocol also establishes, for the first time, a modest role for the UN in its Article Seven concerning the enforcement of the law of armed conflict. This article holds tremendous implications for the evolution of the landmine issues and the UN and NGO roles in it. It states that "wherever the parties to a conflict are required to notify the other side locations of landmines and booby traps, they are required to give this information to the secretary-general of the UN, presumably so he can insure that it is properly dismissed for the protection of the civilian populations." Put otherwise, the Protocol gave the secretary-general flexibility to use the information as he wanted in order to facilitate UN and other humanitarian operations, and "a role in the enforcement of humanitarian law that, as one military legal expert comments may ultimately have effects far outside the field of mine warfare.", Article seven, paragraphs 3(a) (ii) (iii), of Protocol II to the CCW as quoted in Carnahan, 93–94.

149. Williams and Goose, 28.

150. Williams, 2.

151. Letter from Sen. Patrick Leahy to President William J. Clinton, December 23, 1993.

152. Ironically, one of the main government opponents to the landmines protocol was Libya, who in the first few months after the CCW's signing became the first state to introduce a UNGA resolution calling for landmine victim assistance on December 5, 1980. Libya wanted colonial powers that fought in WWII on its soil to de-mine the millions of mines deployed during that conflict that "they had implanted in former colonies, and to compensate anyone injured by such mines." Carnahan, 88.

153. Sen. Patrick Leahy, letter to the *New York Times*, January 13, 1994.

154. Letter from President Bill Clinton to Sen. Patrick Leahy, February 22, 1994.

155. Letter from Madeleine Albright, U.S. Ambassador to the UN, to Senator Patrick Leahy, January 21, 1994.

156. Christopher C. Joyner, "UN General Assembly Resolutions and International Law: Rethinking the Contemporary Dynamics of Norm-Creation," *California Western International Law Journal* 11 (Summer 1989), 448.

157. Rosalyn Higgins, *The Development of International Law Through the Political Organs of the United Nations* 3 (1963) 2. Quoted in Ibid., 459.

158. Joyner, 459.

159. Canadian Government of Foreign Affairs and International Trade, "Canada in the World: Government Statement, Communications Group, 1995, 48–49, quoted in Maxwell A. Cameron, "Democratization of Foreign Policy: The Ottawa Process as a Model," in Cameron, et al, 433; Valerie Warmington and Celina Tuttle, "The Canadian Campaign," in Cameron, et al., 49.

160. MAC is a coalition of over 100 Canadian NGOs committed to banning landmines.

161. Warmington and Tuttle, 49.

162. MAC instituted a toll-free telephone number that people could call for information, recruited Canadian celebrities such as singer Bruce Cockburn to the cause, instituted a letter writing campaign to government officials, and gave landmine victims an opportunity to present personal testimonies Ibid., 54. As some members in the government, especially the foreign ministry, became more open to the idea of a ban, they invited MAC representatives to join the Canadian CCW negotiating teams in 1995 and 1996.

163. Ibid.

164. Colin King "Legislation and the Landmine," Jane's Intelligence Review, Special Report No. 16, November, 1997, 4.

CHAPTER 3

1. Donovan Webster, "It's the Little Bombs That Kill You," *The New York Times*, January 23, 1994, pp. 27–32.

2. I would like to thank COL Dennis Barlow (U.S. Army Ret.) for stressing the bi-partisan support for Sen. Leahy's landmine legislation as an important factor in U.S. leadership on the landmine issues. Conversation with COL. Dennis Barlow (U.S. Army Ret.), June 29, 2010. Barlow was the Director of Humanitarian Policy in the Office of the Secretary of Defense and the first leader of the Humanitarian Demining Task Force in the Pentagon. He also established the Mine Action Information Center and Center for International Stabilization at James Madison University, Harrisonburg, Virginia.

3. Senator Leahy's Paris Statement in November 1993 was the first salvo in the impending battle. It made the case for restrictions "up to and including a total ban" on landmines.

4. Landmine production by the American weapons industry does not generate the large monetary sales that its other weapon products generate. Mines are inexpensive, and competition is intense, especially in conventional mines, so scenarios for lofty profits are limited. In 1994, the estimate of the combined mine production was below $100 million per year, a small amount in the estimated $20 billion annual global arms trade. The Arms Project/Human Rights Watch and Physicians for Human Rights, *Landmines: A Deadly Legacy*, October 1993, 57.

5. Senator Ben Nighthorse Campbell letter to author, June 20, 1994.

6. Self-destruct mines blow up, while a self-neutralizing mechanism has a battery that will die out and thus the mine self-neutralizes if the self-destruct does not function.

7. For example, Sen. Patrick Leahy had written to Secretary of State Warren Christopher that, in his view, "a central purpose of the meetings should be a thorough discussion of what actions would be necessary to stop the killing and maiming of civilians by landmines. This should involve full consideration of all the options, up to and including a total ban on these weapons." Letter from Sen. Patrick Leahy to Secretary of State Warren Christopher, February 25, 1994.

8. Stephen D. Biddle, Julia L. Klare, and Jaeson Rosenfield, *The Military Utility for Landmines: Implications for Arms Control*, Institute for Defense Analyses, June 1994, IDA Document D-1559, p. 5. Highlighting the complex nature of measuring military utility, the USCBL chair, Steve Goose, expressed a contrasting opinion by stating that the report "[i]n its own language . . . cast doubt on the army's assumptions and assertion that landmines are essential. They say that in many scenarios, landmines are of marginal utility." Steve Goose, Arms Project, HRW-Washington, as quoted at "U.S. Group Meeting on Landmines" meeting minutes, Vietnam Veterans of America Foundation, Washington, D.C., September 26, 1994.

9. Final Report of the Governmental Experts, Article 49, CCW/CONF.I/GE/23. Many NGO representatives were present at the first meeting, while Steve Goose and Jody Williams were the only NGO representatives attending the second meeting, and they all boycotted the final two in protest over their lack of access. Steve Goose e-mail correspondence with author, July 5, 2010. Therefore, many individuals with some of the most practical field experience with landmines were not allowed to participate. Don Hubert, *The Landmine Ban: A Case Study in Humanitarian Advocacy: Occasional Paper #42* (Providence, Rhode Island: Thomas J. Watson Jr. Institute for International Studies, 2000), pp. 13 and 76.

10. Several days before the first experts session convened, the ICBL requested that the meeting of experts permit participation by NGOs "with demonstrated experience" and to establish a broad agenda "with consideration of the fullest range of options" to address "[t]he appalling deterioration of the global landmine crises in the ten years since the Landmine Protocol went into effect." Letter from Jody Williams, coordinator, ICBL and Vietnam Veterans of American Foundation; Kenneth Anderson, director, Arms Project of Human Rights Watch; and Stephen Goose, Washington director, Arms Project of Human Rights Watch, to Mr. Sohrab Kheradi, secretary of the Review Conference and deputy director, Mr. Sohrab Kheradi, Deputy Director of the United Nations Centre for Disarmament Affairs, February 22, 1994.

11. Letter from Sen. Patrick Leahy to Ambassador Karl F. Inderfurth, deputy U.S. representative to the UN, October 26, 1993. The ICBL did, however, influence the discussions in two ways. First, it distributed copies to the governmental experts of the recently released *Deadly Legacy,* which included key arguments for a ban and detailed case studies of the humanitarian harm caused by landmines. Second, Jody Williams requested that the expert group discusses a number of priority issues, including: a comprehensive mine ban; extension of the protocol to cover all circumstances; clear landmine definition; encompassing verification regime to include legal enforcement and fact-finding inspections; and user responsibility for mine clearance. Letter from Jody Williams, et al. to Sohrab Kheradi, 1994.

12. Molander had served as assistant undersecretary for legal affairs of the Swedish Ministry for Foreign Affairs. After the CCW Review process was

completed, he served in various capacities at Swedish missions abroad and held a number of international appointments, including ambassador to Russia and Finland.

13. Louis Maresca and Stuart Maslen, eds., *The Banning of Anti-Personnel Landmines: The Legal Contribution of the International Committee of the Red Cross 1955–1999* (Cambridge University Press: Cambridge, United Kingdom 2000) 275. The ICRC also reported that based on "several expert reports" that "[a]t the current rate of mine clearance . . . it is estimated that it would take 4,300 years to clear that single country of landmines." Report of the ICRC for the Review Conference of the 1980 United Nations Convention on Prohibitions or Restrictions on the Use of Certain Conventional Weapons which may be Deemed to be Excessively Injurious or to Have Indiscriminate Effects, March 1994 as referenced in Ibid., 299.

14. United Nations secretary-general report to the United Nations General Assembly, "Moratorium on the export of antipersonnel land-mines," A/49/275, July 27, 1994.

15. The ICRC report and analysis was especially important because the ICBL continued to remain in the hallways rather than in the negotiating room. Because of continued objections by China, the ICBL and other NGOs were excluded from the negotiations. In an attempt to address the ICBL's concerns, Molander would provide daily briefings on the negotiations. Other information was provided by friendly diplomats. After the second experts meeting, the ICBL wrote to Molander to thank him for keeping them informed during the negotiations but added that "unless and until our meaningful participation can be secured our mere presence in the building does not constitute sufficient contribution to the process to warrant our being here. We are concerned lest we give the appearance, by remaining outside of the meeting of the Group, of contributing to a process where our voice is not being heard." ICBL, "Letter to Johan Molander, chairman, Expert Group, Preparatory to the Review Conference of the 1980 Conference of the 1980 Conventional Weapons Convention," May 19, 1994. Since an exception for ICBL participation was not forthcoming, the ICBL boycotted the two subsequent GGE meetings. HRW's Kenneth Anderson and a key author of *Deadly Legacy* argued that ICBL non-participation was not a serious setback because the GGE discussions are going "in the direction of only the most cosmetic changes in the Landmines Protocol; it appears to me initially that we should begin publically attacking the meetings as disastrous repeat of the meetings in the 1970s that produced the current mess." Kenneth Anderson, "Memorandum to Kenneth Roth, HRW," May 19, 1994.

16. The GGE established four working groups, including a Technical Military Experts Group on Definitions, and another working group on mine prohibition, marking, and clearance. The discussions extending the scope and application of the landmines protocol failed to reach a recommendation for two reasons: First, many of the mine-affected states, such as Afghanistan, Angola, Cambodia, and Mozambique, did not participate in the discussions as they were not State Parties to the Protocol. Second, China, India, Mexico, and Pakistan all opposed extending the scope to internal conflicts because they feared interference in their internal affairs, especially when coupled with intensive verification measures that other states were requesting.

17. Carl von Essen, *Sweden's Landmine Defence*, Radda Barnen: Swedish Save the Children, Stockholm, Sweden, March 1996, p. 16. At the October 1995 CCW Meeting, Sweden withdrew its proposal. In previous meetings, Mexico had stated its support for a ban but never submitted a formal proposal.

18. At this final GGE session, Australia, New Zealand, and Sweden delegations included NGO representatives as part of their delegations. Earlier the U.S. delegation invited Steve Goose from Human Rights Watch and an ICBL leader to serve with them, but he declined. Steve Goose e-mail correspondence with author, July 5, 2010. According to Williams, he declined "to join the delegation as their terms were too restrictive." It was important, Williams continued, that NGOs are participating at the upcoming CCW Review Conference in September and October "[a]s separate entities and not part of government delegations, so we are free to speak and lobby our own position." Jody Williams e-mail "Cambodia Campaign" to Coalition Peace and Reconciliation, which is a Cambodian-based organization focusing on a multi-religious movement for active non-violence as a means of political, social, and economic transformation. January 6, 1995. Document retrieved in the official records of the International Campaign to Ban Landmines at Library and Archives Canada. Ottawa, Canada. Accessed by author on August 13, 2009. Steve Goose, Human Rights Watch Arms Project, USCBL meeting summary, "U.S. Campaign to Ban Landmines Meeting," December 13, 1995, p. 3.

19. Article 2, Paragraph 3, Protocol on Prohibitions or Restrictions on the Use of Mines, Booby-Traps and Other Devices. Amended May 3, 1996.

20. In March, Belgian and Irish NGOs launched national campaigns against landmines. The prestigious Council of Foreign Relations hosted an April 24 seminar in which the secretary-general of the United Nations and former U.S. Secretary of State Cyrus Vance publicly joined the call for a landmine ban. Also, in April, the Arms Project of HRW released, *Landmines in Mozambique*, a study which documented "how this [landmine] tragedy came about and it's terrible, ongoing consequences for the Mozambican people." Human Rights Watch Arms Project, *Landmines in Mozambique* (Human Rights Watch: New York, March 1994) 1; In May UNICEF published *Anti-Personnel Land-Mines: A Scourge on Children*, arguing that it is "unconscionable that the humanitarian objections to antipersonnel landmines should be disputed" and that the use of antipersonnel landmines violated many of the core provisions of the Convention on the Rights of the Child. UNICEF, *Anti-Personnel Land-Mines: A Scourge on Children (UNICEF House, New York, 1994)* 4; Also in May 1994, *War of the Mines: Cambodia, Landmines and the Impoverishment of a Nation*, authored by Paul Davies with photographs by Nic Dunlop, was released. Dunlop's photography and Davies's chronicle of the landmine devastation highlighted the humanitarian problems and challenges caused by mines. At the book's beginning, there is a statement supporting a landmine ban that is endorsed from forty-seven NGOs and two UN agencies working in Cambodia. Paul Davies with photographs by Nic Dunlop, *War of the Mines: Cambodia, Landmines and the Impoverishment of a Nation* (Pluto Press: London, 1994), xv.

21. Statement of Robert O. Muller, VVAF, Keynote presentation "The International Campaign to Ban Landmines: Where Do We Go from Here?" at the Second NGO Conference on Landmines, Report of Proceedings, Geneva, May 9–11, 1994, p. 9.

22. *Hidden Killers: The Global Problem with Uncleared Landmines* (U.S. Department of State, Washington, D.C., July 1993), 2.

23. Report of Working Group 3: Promoting the Ban: Countering the Opposition," at the Second NGO Conference on Landmines, Report of Proceedings, Geneva, May 9–11, 1994, p. 114.

24. As quoted in "International Campaign Advances Call to Ban Landmines, Says Landmine Protocol Is a Failure," International Campaign to Ban Landmines, Press release, May 11, 1994.

25. Statement of ICRC Representative, ICRC legal department, "International Committee of the Red Cross: The Review Process of the 1980 Convention," at the Second NGO Conference on Landmines, Report of Proceedings, Geneva, May 9–11, 1994, p. 90.

26. Statement of Philippe Chabasse, HI, "The French Campaign," at the Second NGO Conference on Landmines, Report of Proceedings, Geneva, May 9–11, 1994, p. 39.

27. The action plan helped the ICBL members coordinate international activities and lobbying, and coordinate future events and conferences. According to Jody Williams, the action plan and its dissemination to ICBL members became the "single most critical element" to the ICBL's success in eventually achieving the landmine ban. Statement of Jody Williams, ICBL ambassador, at the USCBL grass-roots meetings associated with the 2,000 presidential primaries in Iowa, Des Moines, Iowa, January 8, 2000.

28. *The Global Landmine Crisis*, Hearing Before a Subcommittee of the Committee on Appropriations, U.S. Senate, May 13, 1994. Other speakers included representatives from the ICBL, UN, and the Department of State. The Department of Defense declined its invitation to testify or submit a statement. The hearing did receive prepared statements in support of the ban from UNICEF, the UN secretary-general, the president of the American Red Cross, and others.

29. As one of the testifying witnesses, my testimony was covered by CNN and CBS, who also conducted an interview with me in my hotel room that aired on the national evening news that night.

30. Statement of Robert Muller, executive director of the Vietnam Veterans of American Foundation, to the Subcommittee of the Committee on Appropriations, U.S. Senate, May 13, 1994. Senate Hearing 103–666 Report, 68. In introducing Muller, Sen. Leahy said that he "has done more and had more responsibility for the global campaign against landmines than anybody I know . . . So, I just want to say publicly that without not only the constant inspiration but the constant push from Bobby Muller I do not know if we would be even having this hearing today." Statement of Senator Patrick Leahy at "The Global Landmine Crisis" hearing before a Subcommittee of the Committee of Appropriations, U.S. Senate, May 13, 1994, pp. 66–67.

31. While the military was not generally supportive of the export ban, it was a sufficiently modest step to win over key individuals. But if they were really astute, they would have caught on that the moratorium affected mixed munitions, which were a combination of anti-tank and APLs. But no one was really up to date on the issue, including export-ban supporters on Capitol Hill, who also did not know that the moratorium would affect mixed munitions. If the military and other pro-use

supporters had recognized mixed munitions then it would have precluded transfer of AT mines under export ban. According to ICBL Coordinator Jody Williams, "The issue of AT and AP mines has been a quiet issue of contention in the campaign. The German campaign has always gone after all mines, as does the Italian campaign, and I think the Swedish campaign. In the U.S., we went after AP mines because we felt we could win. We knew that if we went after AT mines, we could lose and we wanted success in the early stages of the campaign." As quoted at " U.S. Group Meeting on Landmines" meeting minutes, Vietnam Veterans of America Foundation, Washington, D.C., September 26, 1994. By challenging production, Leahy was also separating congressional allies from arms production in their states.

32. Sen. John McCain letter to author, August 8, 1994.

33. For example, Sen. Paul Simon, who visited Angola and personally witnessed the landmine devastation, supported Leahy's legislation with the following comment: "I've always been somewhat interested, but having visited Angola, where they have 9 [million] to 20 million landmines, and seeing all those people missing limbs, brings it home graphically." Letter from Sen. Paul Simon to Sen. Patrick Leahy, September 9, 1994 (Dictated on September 6, 1994).

34. Boutros Boutros-Ghali, "The Global Landmine Crisis," *Foreign Affairs* 73, no. 5, (July/August, 1994):13. 1994. Highlighting the ICBL's increasing importance and respect in the global political arena, Stephen Goose of HRW Arms Project was requested to review the draft and suggest additions to the article, which was later produced in the influential *Foreign Affairs* journal.

35. *Yearbook of the United Nations 1994*. Volume 48. Department of Public Information, United Nations (The Hague, Netherlands: Martinus Nijhoff Publishers, 1994) 172.

36. United Nations Secretary-General report to the United Nations General Assembly, "Moratorium on the export of antipersonnel land-mines," A/49/275, July 27, 1994.

37. G/8/G7 Chairman's Statement, G8/G7 Naples summit, Naples, Italy. July 10, 1994.

38. Jody Williams, "Landmines and measures to eliminate them," 1995 *International Review of the Red Cross*, no 307, August 31, 1995, 375–390.

39. Ibid., 375–390.

40. Administration officials also negotiated with Leahy's office, who, in turn, consulted with HRW's Steve Goose. They were successful in having the president separate out the eventual elimination of landmines from the issue of a "humane alternative" to landmines. Tim Rieser, foreign policy aide to Sen. Leahy, as quoted at "U.S. Group Meeting on Landmines" meeting minutes, Vietnam Veterans of America Foundation, Washington, D.C., September 26, 1994.

41. Address by President William Clinton to the 49th Session of the UNGA, September 26, 1994. Press Release USUN #124-94. This regime that Clinton called for soon morphed into the U.S. and UK initiative taken to the CCW that added to the AP export mine developments the development of mines with self-destructing and—deactivating features as an eventual replacement for dumb mines. The first international meeting on this regime would be held in Budapest from June 29 to 30, 1995.

42. Letter from Sen. Patrick Leahy and Representative Lane Evans to President William Clinton, October 26, 1994.

43. In light of Leahy's leadership on the landmine issue, Senate Majority Leader George Michael selected him to serve as a member of the U.S. delegation to the UNGA, where he would lobby national delegations at the UN for support of the U.S. landmine resolution and introduce it. Letter from Sen. George Mitchell, U.S. Senate, Office of the Majority Leader, to Warren Christopher, Secretary of State, U.S. Department of State, September 19, 1994.

44. "Moratorium on the Export of Anti-Personnel Landmines," UN First Committee, A/C1/49/L19, November 3, 1994. However, Leahy had wanted to go further by calling for a "comprehensive ban," but that terminology was replaced two days earlier with the "eventual elimination" language at the request of Assistant Secretary of State Thomas McNamara, who reviewed Leahy's draft speech. The agreement was a balance, Clinton believed, between Leahy's call and U.S. military requirements. Even though he supported an eventual landmine ban, Clinton wrote Leahy that he did not "believe it feasible to achieve this in the near term" and that "[t]he only practical approach is one in which we move step by step toward our common aim." Letter from President Bill Clinton to Sen. Patrick Leahy, November 30, 1994. Letter from Thomas McNamara, assistant secretary of state, to Sen. Patrick Leahy, November 1, 1994.

45. United Nations General Assembly, 49th Session, First Committee, Agenda item 62, "Moratorium on the export of antipersonnel land-mines," November 1, 1994, A/C.1/49/L.19.

46. Ibid.

47. Yearbook of the United Nations 1994. 173.

48. "Hidden Killers: The Global Landmine Crisis," *1994 Report to the U.S. Congress on the Problem with Uncleared Landmines and the United States Strategy for Deming and Landmine Control*, Department of State publication, Bureau of Political-Military Affairs. December 1994, p. 2.

49. For example, the *1993 Hidden Killers* report estimated that landmines would injure or kill more than 150 people per week. In the 1994 report, these casualty numbers were increased based on more accurate field reporting and increased attention to the landmine problem that now suggested that 1993 report number was greatly understated. According to Col. Lawrence Machabee, a principal mover in the 1994 report's development and production, it was "an authoritative document that people could reference in terms of demining problems." Quoted in Peter J. Hager "An Interview with Lawrence Machabee, USMC: A Retrospective View of Humanitarian Demining at the Department of State," *The Journal of Humanitarian Demining*, Issue 1.1, Summer 1997.

50. Letter from Jody Williams, Coordinator, Landmines Campaign, to Landmine Campaign Supporter, May 10, 1995.

51. Letter from Wendy R. Sherman, assistant secretary, legislative affairs, Department of State, to Sen. Leahy, July 27, 1995.

52. Letter from Kristi Rollag Wangstad, vice president, public affairs, Alliant Techsystems, to David Gagne, Minnesota Fellowship of Reconciliation, March 31, 1995.

53. In January 1995, the Belgian Senate voted unanimously to ban the production, use, export, and transfer of antipersonnel mines and the House of

Representatives did the same on March 2, 1995, making Belgium the first country in the world to ban antipersonnel landmines. *Handicap International, To ban slaughtering in peace time: Facts and chronologies,* September 22, 1995, p. 43. When the twelve European Union's ministers met in Brussels to prepare for the Review Conference, HI and Medico constructed a simulated minefield in the downtown area, further drawing governmental and media attention to the landmine issue; Belgium mainly produced and exported AP mines to several countries, including Rwanda. Eddie Banks, *Brassey's Essential Guide to Anti-Personnel Landmines: Recognizing and Disarming* (Brassey's: London, 1997) 64.

54. According to the meeting's minutes, Oxfam UK agreed to organize the national campaign in Mozambique, and VVAF became committed to work with or start up campaigns in Costa Rica, Ecuador, the former Yugoslavia, and southern Africa. ICBL Landmines Campaign Rome Meeting Summary Points, March 16/17, 1995, pp. 3–4.

55. While cluster bombs are not designed to be victim-activated, their relatively high malfunction rate transforms them into a victim-activated weapon.

56. ICBL Landmines Campaign Rome Meeting Summary Points, March 16/17, 1995, p. 3.

57. Statement of Pierre Ryckmans and Vincent Stainier, Belgium Campaign to Ban Landmines and HI, at the "Networking for a Country Campaign" workshop, Cambodia Landmines Conference, June 4, 1995.

58. Besides the symbolic benefit of hosting the first landmine conference in a landmine-infested country, the Cambodia conference had goals, several salient among them, to: listen to landmine survivor stories and experience "first-hand the human and socio-economic suffering caused by mines"; encourage other NGOs to become involved in the ICBL; encourage the Cambodian government to ban landmines; encourage agencies to fund Cambodian demining programs; and raise the landmine debate among the public; draw significant media attention to the landmine issue. Coghlan and Hartke letter. Anti-Personnel mines found in Cambodia were produced in many countries, including Bulgaria, Cambodia, China, former Czechoslovakia, Germany (East), Thailand, United States, USSR, and Vietnam, Banks, 68, 69, 76, 92, 119, 211, 217, 224, and 245.

59. Letter from The Secretariat of State, Vatican City, expressing a "message from Pope John Paul II sent to the International Landmines Conference in Phnom Penh, June 2–4 1995."

60. Letter from the Anglican Archbishop of Cape Town, Desmond M. Tutu, to the "International Conference: The Socio-Economic Impact of Landmines: Towards an International Ban." [not dated]; Conference organizers also sent messages to Khmer Rouge leaders, including Pol Pot and Ieng Sary, and their followers, pleading with them to cease using landmines. The Khmer Rouges reply came several days later in a radio broadcast, asserting that for security reasons, landmines would continue to be used in their war with the government. NGO leaders responded with another letter, begging both the Khmer Rouge leaders and followers to "make the first step [toward peace] today . . . and stop laying mines." Letter from Linda J. Hartke and Denise Coghlan to Mr. Pol Pot, Mr. Khieu Samphan, Mr Ieng Sary, Mr. Ta Mok, Mr. Son Sen, and all the followers of the Khmer Rouge, June 16, 1995.

61. According to Jody Williams, during the ICBL's first few years, "the majority of the work of the ICBL was concentrated in the north, in the producer countries. While there were beginnings of campaign efforts—some very notable as with the Cambodia Campaign to Ban Landmines—in the south, the real burst of southern campaigns did not really start until after the 3rd ICBL Conference" held in Cambodia; Jody Williams e-mail to National Campaigns of the ICBL, "Process for delivering options for strengthening the ICBL structure, post-Ottawa," July 17, 1997; As a direct result of the Cambodia Conference, national campaigns were launched in Afghanistan, Cambodia, India, Kenya, Nepal, Philippines, and South Africa. "National and Regional Action Plans Decided at the Conference: Key Points," Session at the International Conference: The Socio-Economic Impact of Landmines: Towards an International Ban." June 4, 1995; The Cambodia Campaign to Ban Landmines was formed on August 8, 1995, when five NGOs—Jesuit Refugee Service, MAG, ICRC, HI and the NGO Forum—joined forces to ban landmines. E-mail correspondence from Denise Coughlan, chair, Cambodia Campaign to Ban Landmines, March 13, 2000.

62. Recorded notes from workshop discussion on "Using the Campaign as a Model for Other Issues," at the NGO Forum, Oslo, Norway, September 7, 1997, in the *ICBL Report: NGO Forum on Landmines*, Oslo, Norway, September 7–10, 1997, p. 30.

63. According to Robert Lawson, who was soon to become an important part of the movement's story as the senior advisor in the Mine Action Team in the Canadian Department of Foreign Affairs and International Trade, the "Phnom Penh formula" is a significant feature in helping to explain the ICBL's critical role in mobilizing governments to support and join a global APLB prohibition agreement. He uses the term "to describe the effective blending of the traditional NGO conference (lots of talking) with highly effective advocacy efforts that engaged local media, cultural, faith leaders, and others. In short, the conferences became 'an event' that mobilized partners and support by reaching out to various communities and the engagement of these communities (e.g., letters of support) then helped make the meeting itself a lot more than a talk shop—they became rallying points for new supporters, expanding ICBL membership. Robert Lawson e-mail correspondence with author, July 2, 2010.

64. Steve Goose, e-mail correspondence with author, July 5, 2010. According to Walker, the victim Peach Korb was 36 years old and father of three young boys when he stepped on a landmine while farming his plot on June 8. He had resigned from the military, as his salary was not enough to support his family and even though he knew his land was mined, he farmed it out of financial necessity. Susan Walker, e-mail correspondence, June 5, 2005.

65. Ibid.

66. The sessions are discussed in detail throughout the final report of the 1995 Phnom Penh Landmines Conference, "The Human and Socio-Economic Impact of Landmines: Towards an International Ban." The report was edited by Lars Negstad and printed with funds donated by the Government of Canada.

67. The first Dhammayietra took place in May 1992, when thousands of Cambodians marched from the Thai border to Phnom Penh, arriving on the day of Visa Ka bochea, the Nirvana date of the Buddha. The marchers practiced nonviolence during their walks despite traveling through areas associated with decades-old

violence. They hoped to bring peace to themselves, to those who helped or encountered the walk, and others who were touched by it.

68. The purpose of the 1992 Dhammayietra was to demonstrate support for peace after the Cambodian internal wars. The follow-up Dhammayietras in 1993 and 1994 were also devoted to various aspects of promoting peace in Cambodia.

69. Cambodia Conference Reception Packet handout, June 1995. Document retrieved in the official records of the International Campaign to Ban Landmines at Library and Archives Canada. Ottawa, Canada. Accessed by author on August 13, 2009.

70. Liz Bernstein, coordinator for the ICBL and former adviser to the Khmer Women's Center, interview with author, New York City, March 1, 2000. Liz later served as Coordinator of the ICBL from 1998 through 2004. She lived in Thailand and Cambodia for 10 years (1986–1996), where she worked with local advocacy organizations on various peace, justice, and policy issues. She co-founded the Coalition for Peace and Reconciliation and helped found the Cambodia Campaign to Ban Landmines.

71. Several of the Dhammayietra march organizers later became instrumental in the Cambodia Campaign to Ban Landmines and the ICBL itself. One of the most notable is Liz Bernstein, an American peace trainer working for the Coalition for Peace and Reconciliation, who soon became a leading force within the ICBL in expanding its membership and planning conferences and logistics. In February 1998, she was appointed ICBL co-coordinator. She also served as an advisor to the Khmer Women's Voice Centre, which, to coincide with the landmine Dhammayietra, published a magazine called *Cambodian Women's Voice Against Land-Mines* for the Fourth World Conference on Women, held in Beijing and Huairou, China, in August 1995. Through this publication, the center sought to accomplish two main objectives: First, to inform women around the world about the impact of mines, and second, to ask their support to reinforce the ban landmine movement. Preface to the *Cambodian Women's Voice Against Land-Mines*, Khmer Women's Voice Centre, May, 1995; For the Beijing Conference, the Centre also produced a video on landmines entitled "*Are We the Enemy?*" which highlighted the effects of landmine accidents on families and entire communities. After its screening in the "Women and Security" portion of the conference, the Centre was awarded a conference citation for outstanding achievement in film. Telephone interview with Liz Bernstein, Washington, D.C., March 13, 2000.

72. The ICBL did not have a Web site until March 1996, when VVAF donated some Web pages to the ICBL to house the U.S. Campaign to Ban Landmines (USCBL) coordinator. Mary Wareham, Senior Researcher, Human Rights Watch and former Coordinator, U.S. Campaign to Ban Landmines, telephone conversation with author, October 19, 1999. Also, Marissa Vitagliano, coordinator, U.S. Campaign to Ban Landmines, telephone conversation with author, VVAF, October 19, 1999. This initiative came in part from Mary Wareham, the USCBL coordinator from 1995 to 1998, who wanted a few pages to store the USCBL and ICBL Web site. Only afterwards did the major organizations in the ICBL start acquiring Web sites. At the time, very little landmine information was available on the Web, except for a UN Department of Peacekeeping Operations (UNDPKO) site. Soon, obtaining individual organizational Web sites addressing the landmine

issue became very popular among ICBL members. ICBL pamphlet, "*So you want to order resources on landmines*?" ICBL Publication, Liz Bernstein and Sue Wixley, May 1997, 10–11.

73. Williams relied on fax machines during the ICBL's initiation to the June 1995 Cambodia conference. She "wanted each to feel that what they had to say about campaign planning was important. So instead of sending letters, I'd send everyone faxes. People got in the habit of faxing back. This served two purposes—people would really have to think about what they were committing to doing before writing it down, and we have a permanent, written record of almost everything in the development of the campaign from day one." Interview with Jody Williams, "Questions frequently asked to Jody Williams," www.icbl.org, accessed March 5, 2002.

74. Adoption of the Rules of Procedure, Agenda and Organization of Work, International Meeting on Mine Clearance (Geneva, July 5–7, 1995) SG/Conf. 7/1, April 18, 1995. 2. In its invitation and promotional meeting materials, the UN estimated that "more than 110 million land-mines spread in 64 countries around the world" and the fact that "there are between 2 million and 5 million more are planted each year." Letter from Beside Tonwe, NGO liaison officer, UN Department of Humanitarian Affairs, United Nations, New York City, to NGO representatives, June 21, 1995; the Secretary-General wrote that "[i]t is estimated that there are more than 100 million land-mines spread in 64 countries around the world, and that between 2 and 5 million more are being laid each year." Report of the Secretary-General, *Assistance in Mine Clearance*, Issued as document A/49/357, September 6, 1994, p. 7. The report estimated totals for uncleared landmines in the most mine-affected countries, including Afghanistan—10 million; Angola—9–15 million; Cambodia—8–10 million; China—10 million; Egypt—22.7 million; Iraq—10 million; and Falkland Islands (Malvinas)—30,000, p. 5.

75. Press Conference given by The Honorable Cyrus R. Vance, U.S. Delegation Leader with Thomas E. McNamara, Assistant Secretary of State for Political-Military Affairs, Department of State, and Timothy G. Connolly, Principal Deputy Assistant Secretary of Defense (Special Operations and Low-Intensity Conflict) at the International Meeting on Mine Clearance, Office of Public Affairs, U.S. Mission, Geneva, July 6, 1995. Connolly eventually became an ally of the ICBL and USCBL members. According to Goose, "Connolly was our best friend in DOD and pushed hard for the U.S. to join the Mine Ban Treaty, essentially he got fired for it." Steve Goose e-mail correspondence with author, July 5, 2010. Former U.S. Secretary of State Cyrus Vance, an avowed proponent of an immediate ban on APLs, was also a member of the U.S. delegation. He was very circumspect about the newly announced U.S. APL policy and struggled to reconcile his personal views from his duty as an U.S. representative. But he was clear that he was not about to avoid stating his personal position, even though serving in head of the U.S. delegation to the UN-sponsored session, stressing that he spoke very carefully about U.S. policy while also calling for a ban even as he tried to explain why the U.S. government could not do it at the time. In response to questions about why he spoke at the conference about a production mine moratorium, "[w]hy not go for the full-out stopping of production of mines?" Vance replied that "[t]he question is, how soon or how quickly can that be done. Let me read you

what I said, and I specifically came to that point, in my speech. The particular section came on page four. I said the following: But clearing mine fields and providing rehabilitation for victims will not be enough. Our goal must be the eventual elimination of all antipersonnel land mines. We know this will take time, but personally I believe strongly this should be brought about as soon as possible. And I mean exactly what I am saying. I chose my words very carefully. I have written about it; I have spoken about it; and I believe this very deeply." Press Conference given by Vance, et al.

76. Ibid.

77. Letter from Sen. Patrick Leahy to Allen Holmes, Assistant Secretary of Defense, Special Operations/Low-Intensity Conflict, Department of Defense, July 28, 1995.

78. Letter from John Shalikashvili, Chairman of the Joint Chief of Staff, to the Honorable Ronald V. Dellums, Committee on National Security, House of Representatives. September 12, 1995.

79. The bill had 40 Democratic and 10 Republican co-sponsors. It was included on both the FY96 defense authorization bill and on the Foreign Operations Appropriations bill. Due to non-landmine reasons, the defense authorization bill was vetoed. Meanwhile, the Foreign Operations Bill, which included the Leahy-Evans legislation, passed and became law when President Clinton it on February 12, 1996. However, this provision was never implemented. Steve Goose, E-mail correspondence with author, July 5, 2010.

80. Fax from Paddy Blagden to the Office of Sen. Patrick Leahy, November 28, 1995.

81. Ibid.

82. Williams invited me to join her, Roberts, and VVAF Executive Director Bobby Muller at the news conference and to speak about being an American civilian landmine survivor. My wife, Kim, helped facilitate my participation as I just had my 8th landmine accident related surgery to save the left leg and had to travel in a wheelchair.

83. Some governments however wanted to, and tried unsuccessfully to, limit NGO participation. According to MAC's Valerie Warmington, one of the Canadian NGO leaders, "a number of delegations fought with limited success to block advancement of the status of NGOs and to downgrade the status of the ICRC within the Protocol negotiations indicate how effective a role these groups are playing despite their limited access." Valerie Warmington, "Landmine abolition: a small step forward at Geneva," *The Ploughshares Monitor,* June 1, 1996.

84. Steve Goose, Human Rights Watch Arms Project, as quoted in USCBL meeting summary, "U.S. Campaign to Ban Landmines Meeting," December 13, 1995, p. 3.

85. Steve Goose, Human Rights Watch Arms Project, as quoted in "Proceedings of the U.S. Campaign to Ban Landmines Meeting," Convened by the Women's Commission for Refugee Women and Children, Held at the Offices of Oxfam America, Boston, Massachusetts, July 24, 1995.

86. Statement of Johan Molander, president of the First Review Conference of States Parties to the Convention on the Prohibitions or Restrictions on the Use of Certain Conventional Weapons Which May Be Deemed to Be Excessively Injurious or to Have Indiscriminate Effects, September 26, 1995.

87. Since the UN Conference platform was not wheelchair-accessible, I was carried up the stairs by NGO colleagues, and an UN official carried the wheelchair in order for me to deliver my address. UN personnel had set up a microphone on the floor, but I insisted on speaking from the podium just like everyone else.

88. Statement of Ambassador Johan Molander, president of the CCW Review Conference, Vienna, September 26, 1995.

89. Message of the secretary-general of United Nations to the First Review Conference of States Parties to the Convention on the Prohibitions or Restrictions on the Use of Certain Conventional Weapons Which May Be Deemed to Be Excessively Injurious or to Have Indiscriminate Effects, September 26, 1995.

90. Gary Punch, MP, Australian Minister for Defense Science and Personnel Statement to the First Review Conference of the States Parties of the Inhumane Weapons Convention, September 26, 1995.

91. Statement of S.B. Krylov, the head of the Russian Delegation at the Conference on Prohibitions or Restrictions on the Use of Certain Conventional Weapons Which May Be Deemed to Be Excessively Injurious or to Have Indiscriminate Effects, September 26, 1995.

92. Statement by Ambassador Li Changhe, head of the Chinese Delegation at the Review Conference of States Parties to the Convention on the Prohibitions or Restrictions on the Use of Certain Conventional Weapons Which May Be Deemed to Be Excessively Injurious or to Have Indiscriminate Effects, September 27, 1995.

93. Statement of Ambassador Mark Moher, Canada's permanent representative to the United Nations for disarmament to Review Conference of States Parties to the Convention on the Prohibitions or Restrictions on the Use of Certain Conventional Weapons Which May Be Deemed to Be Excessively Injurious or to Have Indiscriminate Effects, September 26, 1995; Meanwhile back in Ottawa, Keith Martin became the first member of the Canadian Parliament to call for the government to support a comprehensive ban and announce it at the CCW. Keith Martin, "Landmines: A horror that must be banned," *Times Colonist*, October 17, 1995, A5.

94. Such simulated minefields became a standard ICBL advocacy tool at future landmine conferences.

95. "Activities of the ICBL at the CCW Review Conference," *Report on Activities: Review Conference of the Convention on Conventional Weapons, Vienna, Austria, September 25 to October 13, 1995*, International Campaign to Ban Landmines, 9.

96. On September 23, 1995, HI and other French humanitarian organizations organized a shoe pile in front of the Eifel Tower to signal their protests against the continued use of mines and to represent the thousands of mine victims.

97. "Activities of the ICBL at the CCW Review Conference," 9. In addition, four Cambodian landmine survivors, each representing one of the four military factions fighting in Cambodia, distributed copies of the Khmer Women's Voice Centre's award-winning video, *Are We the Enemy*? Denise Coughlan, chair, Cambodia Campaign to Ban Landmines, e-mail correspondence to author, March 12, 2000, and Liz Bernstein, ICBL coordinator and former adviser to the Khmer Women's Voice Centre, telephone conversation with author, March 13, 2000.

98. Jody Williams and Stephen Goose, "The International Campaign to Ban Landmines," in Maxwell A. Cameron, Robert J. Lawson, and Brian W. Tomlin,

eds., *To Walk Without Fear: The Global Movement to Ban Landmines* (Oxford University Press:Toronto, 1998) 31.

99. Ibid., 31.

100. Media coverage data shows "that whereas mine incidents were rarely reported upon before the campaign to ban landmines reached prominence, since that time they have been treated increasingly as newsworthy events deserving of political attention." Richard Price and Daniel Hope, "Media Coverage of Landmines," in *Landmine Monitor Report 1999*, 1048.

101. Jerry White was an American student at Hebrew University in Jerusalem when he stepped on a mine in April 1984. He was hiking with friends at the time. Before co-founding LSN, he worked as an Assistant Director of the Wisconsin Project on Nuclear Arms Control, where he conducted research and advocacy to stem the spread of nuclear and other weapons of mass destruction before getting involved in landmines beginning with the 1995 Vienna CCW Review Conference. White and I first met in August 1995 in Washington, D.C., where I had recently moved to start a doctorial program at Georgetown University. White informed me of area prosthetics providers, while I explained that as a landmine survivor, he was working on the wrong weapon of mass destruction as landmines have killed and maimed more people than biological, chemical, and nuclear weapons combined. Soon thereafter, White arranged for financial support for us to participate in the Vienna Review Conference. We decided to launch LSN in spring 1996 to help the hundreds of thousands of innocent and often impoverished victims of landmines who live in more than 60 countries.

102. LSN also emerged as a pioneer in peer support—building peer relationships that help transform victims into survivors, and ultimately, into fully participating citizens—by establishing six in-country landmine survivor peer support networks. In 2008, LSN changed its name to Survivor Corps, which ceased operations in 2010. The organization's leadership supported the transition of its peer to peer support resources to the Center for International Stabilization and Recovery at James Madison University in Harrisonburg, Virginia.

103. Consensus voting procedures had become a staple of international negotiations during the Cold War so as not to omit large ideological or regional blocs. Since World War II, the United States and Soviets/Russians have continued to claim that consensus rules should be applied to all international conference negotiations. In 1999, for example, the United States sought to block a Netherlands' proposal that called for substituting majority voting rules for consensus voting rules in the 1954 Hague Cultural Convention. There is a fine distinction between "consensus" and "unanimity" based negotiations. Consensus-based resolutions are adopted without a vote, while unanimity-based resolutions are passed by a vote in which all parties agree to the resolution. *Robbie Sabel, Procedure at International Conferences: A Study of the Rules of Procedure of International Inter-governmental Conferences* (Cambridge University Press: Cambridge, 1997) 285. For our current argument here, both the Hague Conferences and Ottawa Treaty negotiations used neither, and hence provide a contrast to consensus- and unanimity-based forums currently prevalent in international negotiations. The Soviet delegate to the 1946 Paris Peace Conference said that the USSR "will always be proud to defend the necessity of achieving unanimity in the settlement of international problems and considers it

inadmissible to abandon this principle." Rule 6(a), Paris Conference to Consider the Draft Treaties of Peace with Italy, Rumania, Hungary and Finland, 1946, *Collection of Documents of the Paris Peace Conference*, Verbatim Records of the 7th Plenary Meeting, C.P/Plen./7,110 (1946), quoted in ibid, p. 283.

104. Steve Goose interview, February 13, 2002. As referenced in Robert J. Lawson, *Ban Landmines: The Social Construction of the International Ban on Anti-Personnel Landmines 1991–2001*, Master Thesis, Carleton University, Ottawa, Canada, April 2002, 175.

105. Letter from Qian Qichen, vice premier of the State Council and minister of foreign affairs of the People's Republic of China, to Sen. Patrick Leahy, April 16, 1996.

106. Landmine production has been increasing in Egypt, India, Iran, Pakistan, and Ukraine, all of whom also "oppose regulation" John Mintz, "A Global Bid to Ban Land Mines: Devices Kill or Wound 26,000 People Each Year," *Washington Post*, February 4, 1996, A1.

107. Ibid., 2.

108. Statement of Cornelio Sommaruga, president of the International Committee of the Red Cross, Press Conference, Geneva, November 22, 1995 as quoted in Maresca & Maslen, 404.

109. Williams and Goose, 32.

110. "Future Landmine Campaign Activities," *Report on Activities: Review Conference of the Convention on Conventional Weapons, Vienna, Austria, September 25 to October 13, 1995*, International Campaign to Ban Landmines, 5.

111. "Assessment of the Review Conference," Ibid., 6–8.

112. Steve Goose, e-mail correspondence with author, July 5, 2010. As one of the meeting participants, I remember the Vienna conference center basement room assigned by the UN to the ICBL to conduct its meetings. Because I was in a wheelchair and the center's front entrance was inaccessible, I and the other wheelchair bound survivors had to enter the facilities through the parking garage located behind the center.

113. "Planning for Geneva," Ibid., 5.

114. Ibid., 5.

115. Also participating was Joerg Wimmers from the UN Department of Humanitarian Affairs (UNDHA) and the UN focal point for demining. He said that that "[t]he presence of NGOs at the Vienna Review Conference prevented a watered-down compromise" and that the "[s]uspension of the Conference was a 'success.' " Quoted in USCBL meeting summary, "U.S. Campaign to Ban Landmines Meeting," December 13, 1995, p. 3.

116. Goldfeld and Myers had an extraordinary working relationship since they met as freshman at Brown, where they were two of the youngest in the class, both having skipped 11th grade. Anne Goldfeld e-mail to author, June 20, 2010. Their passionate views on the humanitarian devastation caused by landmines in Cambodia were also expressed in a letter to Commission members, several of whom had strong media and political connections. Letter from Holly Myers and Anne Goldfeld to Women's Commission Members, July 5, 1995.

117. Anne Goldfeld, e-mail correspondence with author, July 4, 2010.

118. Holly Myers, e-mail correspondence with author, June 1, 2010. Goldfeld tried to bring her landmine field experience to Americans. She said that she felt

"a tremendous amount of responsibility to bring what I saw and that no one would tolerate what I saw." Anne Goldfeld interview with author, Cambridge, Massachusetts. April 15, 2008.

119. Ibid.

120. Holly Myers, seminar lecture "The International Ban on Land Mines," Ethics of Development in a Global Environment (EDGE) seminar series, Palo Alto, CA, October 4, 1995.

121. Anne Goldfeld interview with author, Cambridge, Massachusetts. April 15, 2008.

122. Holly Myers, e-mail correspondence with author, June 1, 2010.

123. "13,000 signatures" as listed in the USCBL meeting summary, "U.S. Campaign to Ban Landmines Meeting," December 13, 1995. 5. Anne Goldfeld, e-mail correspondence with author, July 1, 2010.

124. Caleb Rossiter, Project on Demilitarization & Democracy, memorandum "Dec. 13 New York Meeting on U.S. Landmines Campaign: Suggested Tasks for ATWG from the Meeting," December 20, 1995. The ATWG is the acronym for the Arms Transfer Working Group, which is a coalition of primarily Washington D.C. based groups involved in arms control, development, and human rights that are concerned about the global proliferation of conventional weaponry;

125. Steve Goose e-mail correspondence with author, July 10, 2010.

126. Ibid. According to meeting's minutes, Williams said that she was looking for a more active office to apply public pressure and "keep people moving" rather than "information clearing house."As quoted in USCBL meeting summary, "U.S. Campaign to Ban Landmines Meeting," December 13, 1995, p. 11.

127. Jody Williams e-mail to organizations involved in the United States to ban landmines, February 15, 1996.

128. Anne Goldfeld and Holly Meyers, "Ban the land mines", *Boston Globe*, December 21, 1995.

129. Jody Williams e-mail to organizations involved in the United States to ban landmines, February 15, 1996.

130. In announcing Wareham's hiring as the USCBL Coordinator to start February 20, 1996, Williams e-mailed organizations involved in the work in the United States to ban landmines that "Mary has extensive experience is [sic] coordinating landmines efforts; she is also a skilled researcher and writer; has traveled extensively in her landmines research and served as the NGO delegate on New Zealand's official delegation to the CCW." Jody Williams e-mail to organizations involved in the U.S. to ban landmines, February 15, 1996.

131. Mary Wareham e-mail correspondence with author. July 1, 2010.

132. Ibid.

133. While a program officer for Radda Barnen (Swedish Save the Children), von Essen attended the Vienna conference in the capacity of an Observer for the International Save the Children Alliance. He and Radda Banen became important members of the ICBL leadership team until the ban landmine treaty was signed in December 1997, when Radda Barnen decided to redirect its resources, including von Essen, to other humanitarian issues, such as banning child soldiers and restricting the use of small arms and light weapons.

134. Steve Goose e-mail correspondence with author, March 7, 2000.

135. USCBL meeting summary, "U.S. Campaign to Ban Landmines Meeting," December 13, 1995, p. 1.

136. "Assessment of the Review Conference," 1.

137. ICBL Press Release, "No Technological Solution to the Landmines Crisis, Groups Say," January 15, 1996.

138. Steve Goose, e-mail correspondence with author, March 7, 2000.

139. A Working Chronology of the International Movement to Ban Anti-Personnel (AP) Mines," 5.

140. Steve Goose, e-mail correspondence with author, July 7, 2010.

141. Ibid. 5. During the conference, Switzerland declared a ban on January 15th and Canada on January 17th bringing the total countries announcing a landmine ban to 22.

142. Williams and Goose, 32.

143. Those states in attendance were Austria, Belgium, Canada, Denmark, Ireland, Mexico, Norway, and Switzerland. "A Working Chronology of the International Movement to Ban Anti-Personnel (AP) Mines." 18.

144. Canadian interest in the landmine issue is partially, but not fully, derived from its global peacekeeping missions in many mine-infested areas. From 1991 to 1996, two Canadian peace-keepers had been killed and twenty-two were seriously wounded by mines. Also, many Canadian military engineers had experience with landmines during the UN operations in Cambodia. Robert Lawson conversation with author, Irvine, California, May 9, 2000.

145. Four months earlier, Lawson had been made desk officer for conventional-arms-control issues, including landmines, in the Non-Proliferation, Arms Control and Disarmament Division (IDA) of Canada's Department of Foreign Affairs and Trade (DFAIT). Before taking this post, he had worked in a range of arms control and military force positions and served for twelve years as an officer in the Canadian armed forces, which are themselves very active in peacekeeping and demining operations. Upon being assigned the landmine portfolio as part of his new responsibilities, Lawson was informed by Mark Gwozdecky, DFAIT Deputy Director, Arms Control and Disarmament Division, that the Department of National Defence (DND) would oppose any ban, and therefore it was not a policy consideration. Gwozdecky himself had been told upon taking the job in August 1995 "not to waste his time on mines" because "nobody here [IDA and DFAIT] is interested in this file, and nobody else in the world will let it go anywhere." Quoted in Brian Tomlin, "On a Fast Track to a Ban: The Canadian Policy Process," in Cameron, et al., 185–186.

146. Steve Goose e-mail correspondence with author, March 7, 2000. Lawson was especially enthused to discuss banning landmines because after taking over the mine portfolio several months before, he phoned several of his Kingston Royal Military College classmates involved in mines. According to Lawson, "they told me 'let's get rid of these god damn things.' They had especially had credibility because during this time Canadians were everywhere in the field of humanitarian demining, [such as] Angola, Afghanistan and Cambodia. Canada was very multilateral in mine clearance." Interestingly enough, Lawson discovered that Canadian military personnel were the most receptive and supportive of a ban while the civilians working in the Canadian Defense ministry were less receptive. He said,

"I found the civilians in Defense [Canada's Department of National Defense] more difficult to convince since they believed, as a matter of principle that they needed to prevent DFAIT from banning a weapon used to protect Canadian soldiers." Robert Lawson, Senior Advisor in the Mine Action Team in the Canadian Department of Foreign Affairs and International Trade, interview with author, Ottawa, Canada. August 14, 2010.

147. Lawson, 174.

148. David Atwood e-mail correspondence with author, March 2, 2000.

149. Tomlin, 194.

150. Ibid., 194.

151. Paul Hannon, Special Projects Officer at Oxfam Canada (1990–1998), interview with author, Ottawa, Canada. August 14, 2009. In 1998, Hannon became Director of Mines Action Canada and quickly became an instrumental leader in the ICBL, Landmine Monitor and Cluster Munitions Coalition.

152. Lawson interview, August 14, 2009.

153. Ibid.

154. Tomlin, 192.

155. Mark Gwozdecky, Co-coordinator of the Mine Action Team in the Canadian Department of Foreign Affairs and International Trade, interview with author, Ottawa, Canada. August 13, 2010.

156. The bill also imposed sanctions in the form of U.S. military equipment to governments that continue to allow mine exports, except when the president decides that it is in the national security interest not to do so.

157. Maresca & Maslen, 404.

158. Ariane Sand-Trigo, ICRC letter to author, March 12, 1997.

159. International Committee of the Red Cross, *Anti-Personnel Landmines—Friend or Foe?: Military Use and Effectiveness of Antipersonnel Mines* (Geneva: I.C.R.C. Publications, 1996) 7 and 71. Within two months, 55 active and retired military officers from 19 countries endorsed the report's conclusion and findings. These endorsements proved valuable as a source of support for civilian government decision-makers in supporting the ban.

160. Ibid.

161. "An Open Letter to President Clinton," Sponsored by the Vietnam Veterans of America Foundation (VVAF), *New York Times*, April 3, 1996. In addition to Gen. H. Norman Schwarzkopf, signatories to the letter included General David Jones (USAF), former Chairman of the Joint Chiefs of Staff, and General John R. Galvin (U.S. Army), former Supreme Allied Commander, and General James Hollingsworth, former commander in South Korea and architect of the Hollingsworth line.

162. H. Norman Schwarzkopf, Gen., U.S. Army, Retired, letter to Frank J. Fahrenkopf, Jr. March 2, 1996. Document retrieved in the official records of the International Campaign to Ban Landmines at Library and Archives Canada. Ottawa, Canada. Accessed by author on August 13–14, 2009. Fahrenkopf also wrote former Gen. Colin Powell, who replied that he wanted "to give Shali time to conduct this review [Administration review of its APL policy] before petitioning around him and the JCS [Joint Chiefs of Staff]." Colin C. Powell, Gen., U.S. Army (Ret.) letter to Frank J. Fahrenkopf, Jr., March 19, 1996. Document retrieved in the official records

of the International Campaign to Ban Landmines at Library and Archives Canada. Ottawa, Canada. Accessed by author on August 13–14, 2009.

163. Lora Lumpe and Jeff Donarski, *The Arms Trade Revealed: A Guide for Investigators and Activists* (Federation of American Scientists: Washington, D.C., 1998) 86.

164. Williams and Goose, 23.

165. Gallup International Opinion Research, Spring 1996, April 17, 1996.

CHAPTER 4

1. In the previous few months, the debate regarding the legality of APLs had shifted incredibly quickly. For example, in March 1996, the European Parliament passed a resolution to ban APLs.

2. Statement of Jody Williams, Vietnam Veterans of American Foundation (VVAF), representing the ICBL to the Opening Plenary Session, Review Conference of the CCW, Geneva, Switzerland, April 22, 1996.

3. Ibid.

4. Tun Channareth—or Reth as he is more commonly known—stepped on a landmine in 1982 while serving as resistance soldier on a mission near the Thai-Cambodian border. Beginning in 1998, he served as one of the ICBL's Ambassadors traveling the world urging governments to support banning mines, assisting victims, and clearing mines. Reth accepted the Nobel Peace Prize on behalf of the ICBL in December 1997. It was at this conference that the author and Jerry White launched the Landmine Survivors Network (LSN), the first organization for landmine survivors by landmine survivors.

5. As one of the event's spokespersons, I was struck by the mixed ethnicity of the audience separated by occupation, whether diplomatic, media, or NGO, but not by their compassion for landmine victims and desire to solve the global landmine crisis. The other participating landmine survivor was Tun Channarth from Cambodia, who later become an ICBL Ambassador and also accepted the Nobel Peace Prize on December 10, 1997, in Oslo, Norway, on behalf of the ICBL.

6. Today, at the location of the 1995 shoe pyramid in Geneva is a large permanent three-legged chair monument symbolizing the legs lost by landmine survivors. The monument was funded and organized by Handicap International, the NGO responsible for the shoe pyramids.

7. On April 22, the opening day of the conference, I stood among Cambodian landmine survivors, both standing and in wheelchairs, at the front of the conference door for some time before the opening plenary session. Although the delegates could not see my artificial leg and leg brace as I was dressed in a business suit whose pants covered my legs, they still took roses from my extended hand and I felt a bond with my survivor colleagues. The delegates did not disguise their contempt for being put in an uncomfortable position and later we were told that we had to wait outside.

8. Steve Goose e-mail correspondence with author, March 7, 2000.

9. At this meeting, the pro-ban core group was composed of eleven governmental representatives and individuals from the ICRC and ICBL. Before Geneva, Lawson had written and sent a report to his boss, Jill Sinclair, Director of Non-Proliferation,

Arms Control, and Disarmament Division (IDA) at DFAIT, stating that "we're coming to the final round of the CCW negotiations and it looks like there will not be much success." He then asked "do you agree?" and, "if so, I will host a meeting of the pro-ban forces to explore how to re-start movement to ban landmines." Robert Lawson, Senior Advisor in the Mine Action Team in the Canadian Department of Foreign Affairs and International Trade, interview with author, Ottawa, Canada. August 14, 2010. Before arriving at IDA in August 1994, Sinclair was the Regional Security in Peacekeeping deputy director, so she also knew the landmine issue from the broad Canadian peacekeeping experiences.

10. Robert J. Lawson, *Ban Landmines: The Social Construction of the International Ban on Anti-Personnel Landmines 1991–2001*, Master Thesis, Carleton University, Ottawa, Canada, April 2002, 195.

11. David Atwood e-mail correspondence with author, March 2, 2000.

12. Stephen Goose e-mail correspondence with author, March 7, 2000. Lawson, 195–196.

13. ICBL, *Landmine Update*, #13, July 1996, p. 2.

14. Statement of Cornelio Sommaruga, ICRC president, "International Strategy Conference Towards a Global Ban on Anti-personnel Mines," Ottawa, Canada, October 4, 1996, as reprinted in Louis Maresca & Stuart Maslen, eds., *The Banning of Anti-Personnel Landmines: The Legal Contribution of the International Committee of the Red Cross 1955–1999* (Cambridge University Press: Cambridge, United Kingdom 2000) 475.

15. Statement of Eric Roethlisberger, ICRC vice president, statement, CCW Review Conference, Third Session, Geneva, Switzerland, May 3, 1996, as reproduced in Maresca & Maslen, 447.

16. Ambassador Johan Molander in "Foreword," in Ibid., xxiv.

17. Statement by Ambassador Johan Molander, president of the Review Conference, Vienna, Austria, September 1995.

18. Statement of Cornelio Sommaruga, president of the International Committee of the Red Cross, CCW Review Session, April/May 1996, Geneva, Switzerland April 22, 1996, as reproduced in Maresca & Maslen, 427.

19. Stuart Maslan. *Anti-Personnel Mine Under Humanitarian Law: A View from the Vanishing Point* (IIntersentia: Antwerpen, 2001) 42.

20. The Canadian Ambassador in Geneva, Mark Mohler, did not want to give the statement because it was an "Ottawa thing" and he did not want to "ruffle diplomatic feathers."According to Lawson, at a BBQ at Mohler's home the Sunday before the last week of the conference, the Ambassador told him "I know you are up to shenanigans and that is your business, but my priest told me that landmines should be banned, and that we should ban them, and that I should ban them," and then gave Lawson his support to deliver the message. Lawson credits Mohler with being very good about the ban call and giving him "top cover." Lawson interview with author, August 14, 2009. Subsequently, Lawson, then a relatively minor foreign ministry official, made the front page of Canada's largest paper, *The Toronto Globe Mail*, leading Foreign Minister Lloyd Axworthy to ask "Who is Bob Lawson?" Ibid.

21. Letter from Sen. Patrick Leahy to Anthony Lake, National Security Adviser, May 3, 1996.

22. Letter from Sen. Patrick Leahy to President William J. Clinton, April 11, 1996.

23. As quoted in Tim Weiner, "U.S. Is Wary of Ban on Land Mines," *New York Times*, June 17, 1997. A10.

24. This VVAF advertisement was briefly discussed at the end of chapter three in the context of providing a complementary strategy with the ICRC efforts to engaged the support of military leaders to support a ban.

25. Letter from Sen. Patrick Leahy to William Perry, secretary of defense, April 19, 1996.

26. Letter from Sen. Patrick Leahy to Walter B. Slocombe, undersecretary for policy, department of defense, May 7, 1996. Letter from Sen. Patrick Leahy to Warren Christopher, secretary of state, June 20, 1996.

27. As the administration's landmine policy was being developed for the May 16 announcement, Sen. Leahy provided guidance, which, ultimately, was not followed. He realized that halting U.S. use of APL in February 1999 "may not provide adequate time for the Pentagon," he recommended "essential elements of any new U.S. policy." These essentials included: "an unequivocal, total renunciation of anti-personnel mines, which would take effect by the end of the Clinton administration (by the year 2001)." Letter from Sen. Patrick Leahy to Warren Christopher, secretary of state, May 7, 1996.

28. Letter from President Clinton to the Senate, January 7, 1997. White House Press Release, January 8, 1997.

29. Remarks by Senior Defense Official, Background Briefing by Office of the Secretary of Defense (Public Affairs) on Landmines, May 16, 1996.

30. Letter from Sen. Patrick Leahy to William Perry, secretary of defense, June 27, 1997.

31. Even though President Clinton in 1994 called for "the eventual elimination" of landmines in a speech at the UNGA, the United States did not commit to banning them immediately.

32. Lawson, 213.

33. Ibid., 212.

34. Ibid., 211.

35. President Clinton remarks to the UNGA, General Assembly Hall, UN Headquarters, September 24, 1996. In September 1996, clearance began on the APL and AT landmines around the naval base at Guantanamo Bay, Cuba, at the order of President Clinton. The clearance operation was finished in 1999.

36. Lawson, 215. MAC is a coalition of over 100 Canadian NGOs committed to banning landmines. Appreciation to the ICBL was also included in Axworthy's opening address, when he stated to the country representatives that "[w]e should recognize that much of the impetus for the ban has come from those, be they victims, NGOs, or international agencies, working in the field." Statement of the Canadian minister of foreign affairs, Lloyd Axworthy, to the International Strategy Conference "Towards a Global Ban on Anti-Personnel Mines," October 3, 1996. In fact, the title for one of the conference's strategy sessions was "NGO and Parliamentarian Agenda for Action," and twelve of the scheduled twenty-five presenters were representatives of NGOs. Conference Agenda, Towards a Global Ban on Anti-Personnel Mines, International Strategy Conference, October 3–5, 1996.

37. Mark Gwozdecky, Coordinator of the Mine Action Team in the Canadian Department of Foreign Affairs and International Trade, interview with author, Ottawa, Canada. August 13, 2010.

38. Ibid.

39. At the time, Sen. Patrick Leahy informed the U.S. secretary of state Warren Christopher that the United States should attend as a full participant because he had confidence that within a relatively short period of time the Ottawa Declaration would have over one hundred states on board. Pressure would then rapidly build on the holdouts, who could then be brought into a negotiation in the CD, CCW, or some other forum. Letter from Sen. Patrick Leahy to Warren Christopher, secretary of state, June 20, 1996.

40. In an October meeting at the National Security Council (NSC), the author and two other USCBL representatives, Caleb Rossiter, Project on Demilitarization & Democracy, and Mary Wareham, VVAF and USCBL coordinator, were informed by NSC officials, including Nancy Soderberg, Anne Witkowsky, and Richard Reagan that the United States was going to take the landmine issue to the CD. The United Kingdom may have been the first country to take the landmine issue to the CD, when in CD discussions in 1994 it "proposed that United States should consider applying a code of conduct to the transfer of anti-personnel landmines." United Nations secretary-general report to the United Nations General Assembly, "Moratorium on the export of anti-personnel land-mines," A/49/275, July 27, 1994.

41. France also announced that it would renounce the use of mines except in cases of self-defense. As the ICBL representative, Jody Williams, immediately asked for the floor after the French announcement to criticize it—"your policy is contradictory, you are saying you want to ban landmines, except when you want to use them." Quoted in Brian W. Tomlin "On a Fast Track to a Ban: The Canadian Policy Process," in Maxwell A. Cameron, Robert J. Lawson, and Brian W. Tomlin, eds., *To Walk Without Fear: The Global Movement to Ban Landmines* (Oxford University Press:Toronto, 1998), 201.

42. Ibid., 203–205. Mark Gwozdecky, Coordinator of the Mine Action Team in the Canadian Department of Foreign Affairs and International Trade, interview with author, Ottawa, Canada. e-mail with author, June 21, 2010.

43. Tomlin, 204.

44. Lawson interview with author, August 14, 2009.

45. Lawson, 219.

46. Lloyd Axworthy, "Canada and Antipersonnel Landmines: Human Security as a Foreign Policy Priority" in Steve Smith, Amelia Hadfield, Tim Dunne, eds., *Foreign Policy: Theories, Actors, Cases* (Oxford: Oxford University Press, 2008) 237–241. Tomlin, 205.

47. Axworthy had already received the blessing of UN Secretary-General Boutros Boutros-Ghali for creating a separate negotiating track to ban landmines. Axworthy, 238.

48. Ambassador McNamera, head of the U.S. team, already had left the conference to return to Washington, D.C., when Axworthy made his announcement. Even with the announcement, the Canadians kept their promise to the Americans by keeping a time-deadline out of the Ottawa Declaration.

49. Statement by Mark Gwozdecky, government of Canada, to the Regional Conference on Landmines, Budapest, Hungary, March 27, 1998. ICBL Report: Regional Conference on Landmines, International Campaign to Ban Landmines, Budapest, Hungary, March 26–28, 1998, 50.

50. Gwozdecky interview.

51. Robert J. Lawson, Mark Gwozdecky, Jill Sinclair, and Ralph Lysyshyn in Cameron, et al. 161. These authors are Canadian diplomats and all played important roles during the Mine Ban Treaty drafting process and networking with NGOs and the UN.

52. Ekos Research Associates, Inc., "Ban Convention on Anti-Personnel Mines: Government Representative Focus Group," as part of the *A Global Ban on Landmines: Survey of Participants*, Technical Report, December 22, 1997, 1.

53. All *Track I* meetings would take place in Europe. In contrast, all *Track II* meetings, except for one held in Sweden, were outside of Europe.

54. Williams and Wareham were employed by VVAF. ICBL did not have employed staff until 1998. From 1995, many of the national campaigns to ban landmines were established largely by Liz Bernstein on behalf of Cambodia Campaign and then working for VVAF as the ICBL's Mozambique conference organizer in 1996–1997. She had help in Africa from ICBL members Alex Vines (HRW) and Graham Saul (Oxfam). Mary Wareham, Human Rights Watch and former coordinator, U.S. Campaign to Ban Landmines, e-mail correspondence with the author. July 1, 2010.

55. Mary Wareham, senior researcher, Human Rights Watch and former coordinator, U.S. Campaign to Ban Landmines, telephone interview with the author, October 12, 1999. It was not until mid-1998 that use of e-mail took off in Europe, especially among governments.

56. In 1995, in the U.S. Department of Defense, for example, some employees were refused outside lines for the Internet, for security reasons. Ann Peters, Director, Landmines Project at the Open Society Institute, conversation with author, Washington, D.C., October 5, 1999.

57. Dr. Andrew Bennett, associate professor of government, Georgetown University, written correspondence with author, June 7, 2000. In 1995, Dr. Bennett worked on the staff of the secretary of defense.

58. Gwozdecky, interview with author, Ottawa, Canada. August 13, 2010.

59. Statement by Ambassador Madeleine K. Albright, U.S. representative to the United Nations, to the First Committee, November 4, 1996.

60. Jim Wurst, Disarmament Times, e-mail to Mary Wareham, USCBL Coordinator, "Quotes from Delegates to the UN First Committee Disarmament on Land Mines and Other Conventional Weapons Issues," October 1996. NGO Committee on Disarmament. November 12, 1996.

61. Ibid.

62. Statement by Ambassador Grigory V. Berdennikev, representative of the Russian Federation in the First Committee of the 51st UN General Assembly. November 7. 1996.

63. The ten governments abstaining from the vote were Belarus, China, Cuba, Democratic Republic of Korea, Israel, Pakistan, Republic of Korea, Russian Federation, Syria and Turkey. Their objections were diverse, including the fact that

the resolution did not include the right to self-defense, discussion of alternatives to APLs, lack of controls on non-state actor or terrorist use of mines, and/or failure to mention that the issue should be discussed in the CD. UNGA 51/45S, An International Agreement to Ban Anti-Personnel Landmines, Adopted December 10, 1996.

64. Letter from Barbara Larkin, assistant secretary of state, Bureau of Legislative Affairs, Department of State, to Sen. Patrick Leahy. Not dated.

65. Robert Bell, national security adviser, White House Press Conference, January 17, 1997. White House Press Release, January 17, 1997.

66. As quoted in Mary Wareham, "Rhetoric and Policy Realities in the United States," in Cameron, et al., 228.

67. Sen. Patrick Leahy, "Land Mines: Nothing Less Than a Ban," *Washington Post*, January 19, 1997. C7.

68. As quoted in Dana Priest, "U.S. Holds Key to Ban of Mines: Clinton Set to Decide On Options for Talks, *Washington Post*, January 2, 1997, A16. Both Leahy and the ICBL decided not to oppose the introduction of landmines in the CD unless it conflicted with the fast track process of the Ottawa Process.

69. Lawson, 235.

70. Thomas Hajnoczi, Thomas Desch, and Deborah Chatsis, "The Ban Treaty," in Cameron, et al, p. 294. The previous month, the core group met informally in Geneva. During the Vienna conference, four governments—South Africa, Germany, Philippines, and the Netherlands—were added to the group to increase diplomatic strength and broaden geographical diversity.

71. In Vienna, the ICRC announced that in the sixteen months since the end of the CCW Review Conference in May 1996, which adopted the Landmines Protocol, "[a]t least 13,000 people are thought to have been killed by mines during these months; more than 20,000 have suffered unspeakable injustices." Statement of the International Committee of the Red Cross, February 12, 1997, reproduced in Maresca Maslen, 503.

72. Statement of Diana, Princess of Wales, to the "Responding to Landmines: A Modern Tragedy and its Solutions," Seminar hosted by the Mines Advisory Group and Landmine Survivors Network at the Royal Geographical Society, London, England, June 12, 1997.

73. Statement of Jody Williams, ICBL coordinator, to the "A Global Ban on Landmines—treaty signing conference and mine action forum," December 3, 1997.

74. Another notable change was that anti-vehicle mines with anti-handling devices were specifically eliminated from the treaty draft.

75. ICRC Position Paper No. 4, "Landmines: Crucial Decisions 1997", December, 1997. Maresca & Maslen, 498. In a harbinger of future negotiating challenges, the U.S. Defense Department opposed removing the world "primarily" from the APL definition because it would classify a significant portion of its anti-tank inventory unusable and possibly affect other munitions. Letter from Judith A. Miller, general counsel of the Department of Defense, to Sen. Patrick Leahy, June 16, 1997.

76. As referenced and quoted in Lawson, 193, footnote 104.

77. Jody Williams, ICBL coordinator, broadcast on "Talk to America," Voice of America Radio Service, December 4, 1998; Statement of Jody Williams, coordinator, ICBL, to the Expert Meeting on the Text of a Convention to Ban

Anti-Personnel Landmines, Vienna, Austria, February 12, 1997, in *An Explosion Every Twenty Minutes—Conference Report: Brussels International Conference for a Total Ban on Anti-Personnel Landmines*, June 24–27, 1997, p. 9.

78. Statement of South African Deputy President Mbeki, at the opening session of the "Landmines Free Africa: The OAU and the Legacy of Anti-Personnel Mines Conference, Kempton Park, South Africa May 19–22, 1997.

79. Williams invited me to serve as a representative, joining the other five representatives, who were all from the southern Africa region. As I was civilian who had lost legs to a mine in Africa, it was thought appropriate to join the delegation to highlight the indiscriminate and international negative effects of the landmine devastation in Africa, which is the world's most mine infested continent.

80. South African Defense Minister Joe Modise, Conversation with author, Alkantapan military testing range, Northern Cape Province, South Africa, May 21, 1997. The VVAF advertisement was an open letter to President Clinton signed by fifteen retired generals and admirals urging him to "support a permanent and total international ban on the production, stockpiling, sale and use of this weapon." "An Open Letter to President Clinton," *New York Times*, April 3, 1996. In addition to General Schwarzkopf, signatories included General David Jones, former Chairman of the Joint Staffs, and General John R. Galvin, former Supreme Allied Commander of NATO.

81. Plan of Action of the First Continental Conference of African Experts on Landmines, "Landmines Free Africa: The OAU and the Legacy of Anti-Personnel Mines, Kempton Park, South Africa, May 21, 1997.

82. Lawson, 243.

83. Jody Williams, Opening Statement, Brussels Conference on Antipersonnel Mines, June 24, 1997.

84. New Zealand Campaign Against Landmines (CALM) Newsletter, Number 5, July 1997.

85. Williams and Goose, 37.

86. Many of the currently deployed landmines in Africa were used during World War II by British and German troops in northern Africa, during the Cold War by surrogate African states of the major powers and during the post-Cold War era in internal and regional conflicts in the Horn of Africa and Central Africa.

87. Noel Stott, "The South African Campaign," in Cameron, et al., 72.

88. Ibid., 68 and 74.

89. As quoted in "SACBL Launched on July 24, 1995, with Nobel Peace Laureate Bishop Desmond Tutu," Reuters Ltd, July 25, 1995. Document retrieved in the official records of the International Campaign to Ban Landmines at Library and Archives Canada. Ottawa, Canada. Accessed by author on August 13, 2009.

90. "Landmine Conference ends with a call to sign Ottawa Treaty in December," ICBL news release, Maputo, Mozambique, February 28, 1997.

91. Ibid.

92. Lawson, 248.

93. Turkmenistan, "Final Communiqué of the Ashgabat Central Asia Regional Conference on a Global Ban on Anti-Personnel Mines," July 12, 1997.

94. Maresca and Maslen, 338.

95. Organization of American States, General Assembly resolution AG/RES. 1411 XXVI-O/96, The Western Hemisphere as Anti-Personnel Land Mine-Free Zone, June 7, 1996 as referenced in Lawson, 244.

96. Ibid., 245.

97. As Leahy and Hegal were introducing the landmine legislation, the House of Representatives, led by Rep. Lane Evans (IL), sent a letter, signed by over 160 Representatives, to Clinton urging full U.S. participation in the Ottawa process. VVAF Executive Director Bobby Muller also helped recruit Rep. Evans to carry the House version of Leahy's legislation. Muller knew Evans as they were both ex-Marines. He expected to introduce legislation similar to the new Leahy-Hagel landmines bill in the House to bring flexibility for the United States if it joined the Ottawa process.

98. Letter from Sen. Jesse Helms to Senate colleagues, June 27, 1997. Of course, this is not true. Millions of American deployed mines are still in place around the world, including Vietnam.

99. Letter from Sen. Jesse Helms to Senate colleagues, June 27, 1997.

100. Letter from John Salikashvili, chairman of the Joint Chiefs of Staff, to Sen. Strom Thurmond, Chairman of the Armed Services Committee, June 17, 1997. The Pentagon had estimated "that U.S. casualties will increase by 15 percent during the initial phase of a conflict in the Persian Gulf region if this legislation is enacted. United States casualty rates could reach as high as 30 percent in a North-East Asian contingency, and 35 percent in various European theaters." Letter from Sen. Jesse Helms to Senate Colleagues, June 27, 1997.

101. Letter from U.S. Army Chief of Staff, Dennis J. Reimer, to Sen. Storm Thurmond, June 19, 1997. 1997 Report to Congress, submitted May 14, 1997, 1, paragraph A. In addition, the Pentagon also argued that the moratorium would result in the loss of two-thirds of its self-destructing landmine inventory and 100 percent of its "deep" mining capability. Ibid.

102. Sen. Leahy had hoped that since there was no significant progress in the CD that the United States would "take its place at the negotiating table in Brussels and put is full weight behind the Canadian initiative." Letter from Sen. Patrick Leahy to John D. Holum, U.S. Arms and Control and Disarmament Agency, January 27, 1997.

103. Don Hubert, *The Landmine Ban: A Case Study in Humanitarian Advocacy* (Occasional Paper #42 in the Thomas J. Watson Jr., Institute for International Studies, Brown University, Providence, Rhode Island) 20.

104. "Mexico Blocks Conclave on World Land-Mine Ban," *Washington Post*, June 13, 1997, A33.

105. The Labor Party won 418 seats, the most seats the party had ever held, while the Conservative Party won only 165 seats, the fewest seats they have held in nearly 100 years. On May 21, the UK Foreign Secretary Robin Cook and Defense Secretary George Robertson announced that the UK would ban the use of APLs by 2005 and continue as a participant in the Ottawa Process and CD.

106. Tim Butcher, "Labour bans landmines from 2005," *Electronic Telegraph*, Issue 727, May 22, 1997.

107. Fred Barbash, "Royal Spin; Princess Diana, Since Leaving the British Royal Family, Has Won a Following as a Benevolent Alternative Monarch," *Washington Post*, February 14, 1997, p. A23.

108. Robert Hardman, "Princess calls for greater efforts to clear landmines," *The Daily Telegraph*, June 13, 1997, p. 10.

109. Ibid.

110. The following month, Princess Diana asked LSN Co-Founders, Jerry White and the author, to plan secretly an August trip to Bosnia to meet landmine survivors. Diana, Princess of Wales, conversation with Ken Rutherford and Jerry White, Kensington Palace, London. July 27, 1997.

111. See Oslo Conference opening statements discussed at the beginning of Chapter Five.

112. Sean Sutton, photographer, Mines Advisory Group (MAG), conversation with author. North Atlantic on the Queen Mary II. May 4, 2007 and e-mail correspondence with author, July 5, 2010. Sutton first documented the issue in 1989 in Burma and began working with MAG full time in 1997. He had previously worked with MAG in the field in Lao, Cambodia and Angola and with Halo in Angola and Afghanistan. Renowned veteran Vietnam era photojournalist Tim Page describes Sutton as "the ultimate battlefield archeologist."

113. Sean Sutton, photographer, Mines Advisory Group (MAG), conversation with author. North Atlantic on the Queen Mary II. May 4, 2007 and e-mail correspondence with author, July 5, 2010.

114. "Banishing Land Mines," Editorial, *New York Times*, August 12, 1997.

115. Department of Defense news briefing, August 12, 1997.

116. White House Statement, Office of the Press Secretary (Martha's Vineyard, Massachusetts) August 18, 1997.

117. Among the administration's alarm regarding eliminating U.S. APL use in Korea, there were two major concerns. First, military commanders were seriously apprehensive about a conventional war with North Korea because it would not be short, albeit it was winnable without APLs but at a higher casualty cost. The second concern was that geographic channels from North Korea to South Korea provided invasion routes. The application of APLs could channel enemy forces rather than allowing them to move more broadly, which, in turn is more dangerous, especially at the early stages of a war.

118. Letter from Madeleine Albright, U.S. secretary of state, to ministers of the countries who are members of the Ottawa Core Group. August 20, 1997.

119. Ibid.

120. Strangely, but not surprisingly, two core group countries proposed reintroducing the world "primarily" in the definition of a landmine and "In one case in order to keep some antitank mines that would be excluded under the present draft." e-mail from Paul Vermeulen, Handicap International-Switzerland, to Jody Williams, "Today's core group meeting in Geneva," August 22, 1997.

121. E-mail from Jody Williams to selected ICBL members "ICBL Letter to Core Group Meeting," August 21, 1997.

122. Letter from Jody Williams, coordinator, ICBL and Steve Goose, Chairman, Steering Committee, U.S. Campaign to Ban Landmines, to Core Group Representatives, August 21, 1997.

123. Ibid.

124. Steve Goose note via e-mail from Jody Williams to selected USCBL members, August 22, 1997.

CHAPTER 5

1. Oslo conference participation was limited to those states that signed onto the Brussels Declaration.

2. The Canadians had presented the idea of chairing the ban-APL treaty drafting conference to Ambassador Selibi in November 1996 in Geneva, where he "had distinguished himself as an independent thinker capable of dealing effectively with the larger nuclear powers." Later, the Core Group would ask him to chair the Oslo September conference, because Canada did not want a Canadian to host it as it would not be a "good perception." Robert J. Lawson, interview with author, Irvine, California, May 9, 2000, and Robert J. Lawson, *Ban Landmines: The Social Construction of the International Ban on Anti-Personnel Landmines 1991–2001*, Master Thesis, Carleton University, Ottawa, Canada, April 2002, 238.

3. Mark Gwozdecky, Coordinator of the Mine Action Team in the Canadian Department of Foreign Affairs and International Trade, interview with author, Ottawa, Canada. August 13, 2010.

4. Diana, Princes of Wales, letter to Mr. and Mrs. Brian Isfeld, July 10, 1997. The Isfeld's son, Master Corporal Mark R. Isfeld, was killed on June 21, 1994, while clearing landmines in Croatia. He was serving with the *1st Combat Engineer Regiment* of the *Canadian Military Engineers*, on his third UN Peacekeeping tour. Known as "Izzy" by all his regimental brothers, Mrs. Isfeld crocheted miniature woolen dolls, called 'Izzy dolls,' by the Canadian military forces, with blue berets that her son and other Canadian military forces would give to children while on peacekeeping missions. Isfeld was buried at Little Mountain Royal Canadian Legion cemetery, Chilliwack, British Colombia on June 27, 1994. The Mark R. Isfeld Secondary School in Courtenay, British Columbia was officially inaugurated on October 22, 2001. Princess Diana wrote that "As a mother myself, I cannot begin to imagine our heartache of having lost your wonderful son, who was obviously so brave and dedicated. I truly believe anyone who are [*sic*] undertakes the horrendous task of demining, must indeed be a very special and courageous person." Ibid. In one of his last letters, Corporal Isfeld recorded that "My troop in the 5 weeks we have been here have lifted or destroyed approx. 600 Mines" and that he had "been doing a lot of mine lift supervision or overseeing, recording data, negotiating, communicating concerns and encouraging the lifting of mines and minefields that are not necessarily on our patrol routes, in the hopes of saving lives of soldiers, civilians and animals." Mark Isfeld letter to Brian and Carol Isfeld, May 18, 1994 (written from Smilcic, Croatia).

5. "The Land Mine Cause," *Christian Science Monitor*, September 8, 1997, p. 20. The *USA Today* said that "Princess Diana's death may ultimately achieve what she had fought for much of her adult life: new limits or even a global ban on land mines."Jack Kelly and William M. Welch, "Death could be impetus for land mine ban," *USA Today*, September 2, 1997, p. 20A.

6. Much of the on the ground financial support and transportation logistics for Princess Diana's visit was provided by Norwegian People's Aid (NPA), one of the world's leading NGOs clearing minefields, while Princess Diana and her small group arrived in Sarajevo from London in a private plane borrowed from billionaire investor and global philanthropist George Soros. White and I were in Bosnia conducting an analysis of landmine victim rehabilitative services for the U.S. State

Department's Office of Transition Initiative. On our way from Washington, D.C. to Bosnia, we arrived in London on July 27 to update Princess Diana and her staff at Kensington Palace on our activities, including the upcoming trip to Bosnia.

7. Diana, Princess of Wales conversation with author, Tuzla, Bosnia. August 8, 1997.

8. Diana, Princes of Wales letter to author. August 12, 1997. At the invitation of Princess Diana's staff, White and I attended Princess Diana's September 6th funeral in London and flew to Oslo the following day to join the conference, which had started the previous week. Since we were attending the funeral service in Westminster Abbey, we could not also march in the funeral procession to honor her work for landmine victims, so we helped facilitate the participation of three landmine survivors, comprised of a Bosnian Muslim, Croatian Catholic, and Serbian Orthodox, that Princess Diana had met in Bosnia.

9. Quoted in Kelly and Welch, 20A.

10. Statement of Sen. Patrick Leahy, "Seize This Moment," to the NGO Forum, Oslo, Norway, September 7, 1997 in the ICBL Report: NGO Forum on Landmines, Oslo, Norway, September 7–10, 1997, p. 17.

11. Statement by Robin Cook, UK foreign secretary, Foreign and Commonwealth Office, Daily Bulletin, September 18, 1997. *Disarmament Diplomacy,* September 1997, p. 19.

12. Lawson, p. 262.

13. Jody Williams and Stephen Goose, "The International Campaign to Ban Landmines," in Maxwell A. Cameron, Robert J. Lawson, and Brian W. Tomlin, eds., *To Walk Without Fear: The Global Movement to Ban Landmines* (Oxford University Press:Toronto, 1998) 43; Robert O. Mueller, "New Partnerships for a New World Order: NGOs, State Actors, and International Law in the Post-Cold War World," *Hofstra Law Review,* Fall 1998, p. 1.

14. Statement by Kofi Annan, the United Nations Secretary-General to the Diplomatic Conference on Landmines, Oslo, Norway, September 3, 1997. Press Release SG/SM/6313.

15. Peter Herby telephone conversation with author, January 29, 1999.

16. Steve Goose, Panel Discussion on U.S. Landmine Policy and Verification, The American Bar Association; Section of International Law and Practice, October 23, 1997.

17. With the American Congress and public, the idea that the military utility of landmines in the sensitive Korean peninsula was an easy sell. The Americans argued that it has a unique security problem with over 100,000 forces serving in Europe alone and more internationally. Thus, no one in Oslo had the security problems that the United States has, they said. The mines currently deployed in the demilitarized zone (DMZ) and stockpiled in South Korea are used for deterrence; slow progress of enemy, and to protective obstacle belts.

18. The Americans argued they needed the anti-tank (AT) systems to protect light infantry, such as the 82nd Airborne in the Gulf War, until the mechanized forces arrive, usually in about seven to ten days. During that time, the Americans said, infantry face threats from heavily mechanized enemy forces and thus need the AT systems to protect themselves. Near the conference start, the U.S. delegation distributed a background sheet providing a summary of "U.S. Anti-Amour

Landmine Systems," noting that they are not anti-personnel weapons but are "anti-tank mine systems [that] are constructed with anti-personnel components." Delegation of the United States to the Oslo Diplomatic Conference, Background sheet: "Summary of U.S. Anti-Armor Landmine Systems," September 4, 1997. Until the lead up to the Oslo meeting, the administration and Pentagon had always labeled these "anti-personnel components" as antipersonnel mines (APLs) including in the president's January remarks concerning capping the U.S. landmine inventory. The American RADAM system, for example, is a mixed system that combines seven remote-anti-armor-mine (RAAM) AT mines and five area-denial-artillery-munitions (ADAM) or APLs in one 155 shell. Because of the AP component, this mixed system is not Ottawa compliant. U.S. Army Engineer Systems Handbook, May 2001 as quoted in *Military Operations: Information on U.S. Use of Land Mines in the Persian Gulf War,* U.S. General Accounting Office Report to the Honorable Lane Evans, House of Representatives, GAO-02-1003, September 2002, p. 55, footnote 7.

19. The ICBL Action Plan concluded by outlining the post-treaty signing strategies into three categories: Ratification, Implementation, and Monitoring and Universalization. While these strategies are beyond the scope of this analysis, it is important to note that the ICBL was already gearing up to produce a momentum that would ensure the treaty would enter into force, that it would be global, and that governments would implement its provisions. "Entry Into Force Before the Year 2000, ICBL Action Plan for the Ratification, Implementation, Monitoring and Universalization of the International Treaty Banning Antipersonnel Landmines and for the Eradication of the Weapon, and Assistance to Mine Victims," Presented to the Oslo Diplomatic Conference, September 18, 1997, described in *The ICBL Report: NGO Forum on Landmines,* Oslo, Norway, September 7–10, 1997, pp. 62–64. The ICBL submitted their action plan to the Government Diplomatic Conference on September 18, to make government delegations aware of ICBL activities.

20. The action plan's first goal focused on securing signatures from governments to the treaty, by encouraging national campaigns and NGOs to perform six tasks over the next three months: (1) requesting meetings with their governments "to discuss plans for signature to the treaty and national implementation measures"; (2) targeting countries that endorsed the Brussels Declaration but did not sign the treaty; (3) national campaigns based in non-participating countries should request meetings with their governments to lobby for treaty signing in Ottawa in December; (4) neighboring national campaigns will start ban landmine activities and lobbying to those countries that do not have national campaigns; (5) ICBL representatives will meet with state delegations at the UN in New York "to discuss signature and implementation of the treaty; and (6) national campaigns will push for landmine survivor and de-mining assistance in all meetings with governmental delegations. Ibid, p. 62.

21. Quoted in *Disarmament: The Future of Disarmament,* edited transcripts of the forums held in the UN on April 10, September 23, and October 21–23, 1997, by the NGO Committee on Disarmament, in cooperation with the UN Centre for Disarmament Affairs and the UN Department of Public Information, and the NGO presentations made during the NPT PrepCom on April 16, 1997 (United Nations: New York, 1998) 115.

22. An anti-handling device is distinctively designed to thwart mine-lifting and -tampering. When disturbed, the device detonates itself or the mine maiming or killing the individual performing the action (or anyone close by).

23. Colin King, *Legislation and the Landmine*, Jane's Intelligence Review, Special Report No. 16, November 1997, p. 19.

24. According to Robert Sherman, director, Advanced Projects, Arms Control and Disarmament Agency at the Department of State and a member of U.S. delegations to CCW Review Conference and the Oslo Diplomatic, "The American delegation seemed ready to approve the (Ottawa Treaty) but was highly influenced by a letter in favor [*sic*] of landmines sent to president [*sic*] Clinton by ten high rank generals headed by gen. Alexander Haig." E-mail from Robert Sherman, director, Advanced Projects, Arms Control and Disarmament Agency, Department of State and member of U.S. delegations to CCW Review Conference and the Oslo Diplomatic Conference to MGM Demining Network, March 20, 2002.

25. As quoted in "U.S. Is Alone in Seeking Loophole in Ban on Mines," *New York Times*, September 4, 1997, p. A10.

26. Ibid., A10.

27. Letter from twenty-five representatives to President William Clinton, September 11, 1997.

28. Letter from Senators Chuck Hagel and Patrick Leahy to President William Clinton, September 16, 1997.

29. ICBL Press Release, "U.S. to Make Final Attempt to Maim Landmine Ban Treaty," September 15, 1997.

30. Leahy wrote Clinton before the signing conference to say that his leadership on this issue was critical and suggesting a possible way for him to do it. In consultation with Sen. Hagel, they suggested "that the administration announce that it intends to sign the treaty once the mixed mines problem is solved, and is undertaking an aggressive program to solve it. The advantages to such an approach would be considerable. By linking our signature to solving this problem the United States would once again be in a leadership position, the administration would have the support of Congress, and the Pentagon would be assured of an effective anti-tank mine capability or some suitable replacement technology." Letter from Sen. Patrick Leahy to President Bill Clinton, November 12, 1997. In the end, Clinton did not follow Leahy's guidance.

31. Mark Gwozdecky, co-coordinator of the Mine Action Team in the Canadian Department of Foreign Affairs and International Trade, interview with author, Ottawa, Canada. August 13, 2010.

32. Robert Lawson, senior advisor in the Mine Action Team in the Canadian Department of Foreign Affairs and International Trade, interview with author, Ottawa, Canada. August 14, 2010.

33. Legal scholars have argued that legal norms should be consistent to be effective. Such norms require uniform application in every possible action. Thomas M. Franck, *Fairness in International Law and Institutions* (Oxford University Press: Oxford, 1995) 121–122.

34. Sen. Patrick Leahy, "Seize the Moment," *ICBL Ban Treaty News*, September 9, 1997, p. 1. Quoted in Robert J. Lawson, Mark Gwozdecky, Jill Sinclair, and Ralph

Lysyshyn, "The Ottawa Process and the International Movement to Ban Anti-Personnel Mines," in Cameron, et al., 178.

35. Franck, 30–31. For example, a *Washington Post* story covering the Oslo Conference and American demands for exceptions led with the question "When is an antipersonnel land mine—a fist-sized object designed to blow up a human being—no longer an antipersonnel land mine?" and respective answer "When the president of the United States says so."Dana Priest, "Clinton Directive on Mines: New Form, Old Function, *Washington Post*, September 24, 1997, A19.

36. President Bill Clinton, "Remarks by the President on Land Mines," The Roosevelt Room, The White House, Office of the Press Secretary, September 17, 1997.

37. Joint Chiefs of Staff Vice Chairman, General Joseph W. Ralston as quoted in Priest, A22.

38. Letter from William Cohen, the secretary of defense, to Sen. Patrick J. Leahy, January 12, 1988.

39. William S. Cohen, "Necessary and Right," *Washington Post*, September 19, 1997, A23.

40. William Cohen, conversation with author, Missouri State University, Springfield, Missouri. October 3, 2006.

41. Bill Clinton, *My Life* (Alfred A. Knopf: New York, 2004) 765.

42. Letter from President Bill Clinton to Members of the U.S. Campaign to Ban Landmines, February 4, 1998.

43. Sen. Patrick Leahy address to the U.S. Senate, "A Lost Chance for U.S. Leadership," September 23, 1997.

44. Ibid.

45. Letter from Sen. Patrick Leahy to President Bill Clinton, November 12, 1997.

46. As quoted in Peter Baker, "A Dispute Between Neighbors: Clinton Heatedly Restates Opposition to Canada's Move to Ban Antipersonnel Land Mines," *Washington Post*, A20, November 24, 1997.

47. As quoted from President Clinton, Voice of America radio report, November 23, 1997.

48. The Nobel Peace Prize for 1997 official announcement, The Norwegian Nobel Institute, October 10, 1997. Ironically, Alfred Nobel's father owned and operated a successful armaments factory in St. Petersburg, Russia, that produced landmines for the Tsar's army during the Crimean War. Another irony is that when landmines were being used for the first time on a wide regional scale during the American Civil War, Alfred produced his "promising blend of nitroglycerine and black powder, which he marketed as 'blasting oil'" and planned to tap the lucrative industrial exploitation of the mixture on the way to inventing dynamite that would produced the income to endow the Nobel Awards. http://nobelpeaceprize.org/en_GB/alfred-nobel The Norwegian Nobel Institute, accessed August 20, 2009.

49. The Norwegian Nobel Committee on its decision to award the Nobel Prize for Peace for 1997, October 10, 1997.

50. The Nobel Committee's decision to recognize Williams and the ICBL closely followed the nomination letter for the ICBL to be awarded the Peace Prize as submitted by Congressman James McGovern (D-MA) to Mr. Geir Lundestad,

Director, The Norwegian Nobel Committee, January 13, 1997. Rep. McGovern wrote that "[t]he ICBL was initiated at the end of 1991 by Ms. Williams for VVAF and Medico International." Document retrieved in the official records of the International Campaign to Ban Landmines at Library and Archives Canada. Ottawa, Canada. Accessed by author on August 13, 2009. Ironically, Williams said somewhat later said it was risky for her to trust to governments because: "I cut my teeth on the Reagan-Bush wars in Central America and the Salvadorian Government wanted to kill me, so I didn't trust governments." But, she wanted governments to get beyond the word "eventual" in banning APL and she and the ICBL needed them to be partners. "Let's be real," she said, "Governments negotiate international treaties, while the ICBL and I can't." Jody Williams speech, Des Moines, Iowa. January 8, 2000.

51. Lawson, 296.

52. Several delegates stated that they could not sign the treaty due to their territory being occupied or threatened by hostile neighbors. For example, the Georgia representative stated that his country "remains occupied by separatists and their supporters in Abkhazia," while the Armenian representatives stated his country's concern "by recent Azerbaijani statements excluding any Azerbaijani accession to the ban" and the heavily mined borders between them. Statement of H.E. Tedo Japaridze, Ambassador of Georgia, to the Signing Ceremony of the Anti-Personnel Mines Convention, Ottawa, Canada. December 34, 1997; and Statement by the Armenian Delegation to the Signing Ceremony of the Anti-Personnel Mines Convention, Ottawa, Canada. December 4, 1997.

53. For example, the day before the conference opening on December 2, 1997, Venezuela announced that it would sign, while during the previous week, Japan and Poland announced they would sign.

54. United Nations Secretary General Kofi Annan upon the occasion of the Ottawa Treaty signing, United Nations Department of Information, SG/SM/633B, DC/2591, September 26, 1997.

55. According to the United Nations, the MBT was not only "remarkable because of its speed—approximately 14 months—but also because of the motivation of the principal players and the negotiating procedures they followed." *The United Nations Disarmament Yearbook*, Volume 22: 1997, (United Nations Publications: United States, 1998) 107.

56. It was also decided that the next ICBL meeting would convene in Frankfurt, Germany, in February 1998 to further develop ICBL strategy and possibly re-organize the ICBL in light of the convention being signed. Mine Ban Campaign Praises Treaty, Challenges Governments to Ratify Now," ICBL Press Release, December 1, 1997.

57. Ekos Research Associates, Inc., "Ban Convention on Anti-Personnel Mines: Government Representative Focus Group," as part of the *A Global Ban on Landmines: Survey of Participants*. Technical Report, December 22, 1997, p. 1.

58. Swiss diplomat's remarks at the Ottawa Process Forum, Ottawa, Canada. December 5, 1997.

59. Ekos Research Associates, Inc., 1.

60. Statement by Robert Lawson, Government of Canada, to the Workshop on Ratification and Implementation of the Mine Ban Treaty, Regional Conference on

Landmines, Budapest, Hungary, March 27, 1998. Report: Regional Conference on Landmines, International Campaign to Ban Landmines, Budapest, Hungary, March 26–28, 1998, p. 53.

61. Lawson, et al. in Cameron, et al., 163.

62. Statement by Lloyd Axworthy, Canadian Foreign Minister, to the NGO Forum on Banning Anti-Personnel Landmines, Oslo, Norway, September 7, 1997.

63. Ibid.

64. Statement of Ambassador Karl F. Inderfurth, Special Representative to the President and Secretary of State for Global Humanitarian Demining, "Coordination of Resources for Mine Action" Roundtable, Ottawa, Canada, December 4, 1997. As Special Representative, Inderfurth's duties included bringing together donors, deminers, and the mine-affected governments, international organizations, non-governmental organizations and the private sector in order to expand substantially and to make more effective the global humanitarian demining effort.

65. Bobby Muller, interview, Canada. "Ban Landmines: Canada and the Global Movement to Ban Landmines," CD-ROM produced by the Government of Canada. This CD-ROM was the winner of a gold medal award from the International Television and Video Association for excellence in multimedia.

66. Professor Francis Sejersted, Chairman of the Norwegian Nobel Committee, on the occasion of the award of he Nobel Peace Prize for 1997, Oslo, Norway, December 10, 1997.

67. Torbjoern Pedersen, *The Boston Globe*, "Leading foe of mines quits, keeps prize," February 10, 1998.

68. Quoted in Carlye Murphy, "The Nobel Prize Fight," *Washington Post*, March 22, 1998, p. F4.

69. Letter from Sen. Patrick Leahy to William Cohen, Secretary of Defense. February 6, 1998.

70. Letter from President Bill Clinton to Sen. Patrick Leahy, December 19, 1997.

CHAPTER 6

1. Statement by UN Secretary-General Boutros Boutros-Ghali to the Review Conference of States Parties to the Convention on Prohibitions or Restrictions on the Use of Certain Conventional Weapons Which May Be Deemed to Be Excessively Injurious Or to Have Indiscriminate Effects, Vienna, Austria, September 1995.

2. John M. Shalikashvili, chairman of the Joint Chiefs of Staffs, in letter to MG Nicholas Krawciw, United States (Ret), president, The Dupay Institute, February 6, 1997.

3. "AP Mine Ban: Progress Report," A Regular Report Provided by Canada on the Anti-personnel Mine Ban. Number 1, February 1997.

4. Robert Lawson, senior advisor in the Mine Action Team in the Canadian Department of Foreign Affairs and International Trade, interview with author, Ottawa, Canada. August 14, 2010.

5. John Borrie, Senior Researcher & Project Manager, UNIDIR, e-mail correspondence with author, June 2, 2010.

6. Norwegian Nobel Committee press release, October 10, 1997.

7. Statement by Bernard Miyet, Under Secretary General Peacekeeping Operations, to the Ottawa Workshop on Mine Action Co-ordination, Ottawa Canada, March 23–24, 1998.

8. Statement by UN Under-Secretary General, at the Tokyo Land Mines Conference.

9. Statement by UN Secretary-General, Kofi Annan, to the Signing Ceremony of the Anti-Personnel Mines Convention, Ottawa, Canada, December 3, 1997. In 1997, the UN Mine Action Service (UNMAS) was created within the UN Department of Peacekeeping Operations (DPKO). Meanwhile, the UN Development Program (UNDP) and UNICEF played—and still play—key roles in the Inter-Agency Standing Group on Mine Action chaired by UNMAS. UNICEF is the lead UN agency on mine risk education and UNDP supports many mine action programs. So Annan's statement is only relevant in the sense that UN Secretariat functions were merged in DPKO, although this was not total either. For example, interaction and support for the MBT at the treaty secretariat level would continue to fall to the UN Department for Disarmament Affairs (DDA), although the MBT would have its own implementation support unit (ISU). I would like to thank John Borrie for suggesting this point and providing the aforementioned information. John Borrie, Senior Researcher & Project Manager, UNIDIR, e-mail correspondence with author, June 2, 2010.

10. Statement by the Honorable Lloyd Axworthy, Minister of Foreign Affairs, at the closing session of the International Strategy Conference, "Towards a Global Ban on Anti-Personnel Mines," Ottawa, Canada, October 5, 1996.

11. David C. Atwood, Associate Representative, Disarmament and Peace, Friends World Committee and Consultation, Quaker United Nations Office, Geneva, "Banning Landmines: Observations on the Role of Civil Society," Paper prepared for the volume *Peace Politics of Civil Society*, June 1998, p. 9.

12. Richard Price, "Reversing the Gun Sights: Transnational Civil Society Targets Land Mines." *International Organization*, 52. Summer 1998, pp. 627–631.

13. Robert Lawson, senior advisor in the Mine Action Team in the Canadian Department of Foreign Affairs and International Trade, personal communication with author, Ottawa, Canada. June 15, 2010. The survey of participants at the December 1997 MBT signing ceremony, as mentioned by Lawson, forms the basis for some of this book's analysis. This survey is referenced in previous chapters.

14. Ibid., 86.

15. Office of Weapons Removal and Abatement, Bureau of Political-Military Affairs, U.S. Department of State, *To Walk the Earth in Safety*, 9th Edition, July 2010.

16. Office of Weapons Removal and Abatement, Bureau of Political-Military Affairs, U.S. Department of State, *To Walk the Earth in Safety*, 8th Edition, July 2009 and *To Walk the Earth in Safety*, 9th Edition. Special credit for the U.S. leadership as the world's largest supporter for global landmine victim assistance and humanitarian demining programs goes to the U.S. State Department's Office of Weapons Removal for Abatement (WRA) in the Bureau of Political-Military Affairs. Current and former WRA long-time staff members helping people to "walk the earth in safety" includes Mark Adams, Steve Costner, Stacy Davis, Dennis Hadrick, James Lawrence, Pat Patierno, and John Stevens. Exceptional recognition for the U.S. leadership position in global humanitarian demining also goes to Paul Arcangeli,

Staff Director of the House Armed Services Committee, who, as a former U.S. Army Ordinance Corps officer and commander of the 176th Explosive Ordnance Disposal Detachment in Alaska, participated in and supported missions to Vietnam, Laos and Cambodia with the Joint Task Force—Full Accounting. He then applied his skills as Director of the Humanitarian Demining Training Center (HDTC) personnel at Ft. Leonard Wood (FLW), which helps mine-affected countries develop an effective national humanitarian mine action capacity. As HDTC Director, he encouraged and supported my Missouri State University students to get engaged in mine action through internships and overnight fields trips to HDTC (see photo A-1). U.S. support of mine action would not be possible without bi-partisan support in Congress, and the leadership of the three Special Representatives for Humanitarian Demining, which include the Special Representative of President Clinton for Global Humanitarian Demining Ambassador Karl Inderfurth, Special Representative of Presidents Bush and Clinton for Global Humanitarian Demining Ambassador Donald Steinberg, and Special Representative of President Bush for Global Humanitarian Demining Ambassador Lincoln Bloomfield.

17. Mary Wareham, "The Role of *Landmine Monitor* in Promoting and Monitoring Compliance with the 1997 Anti-Personnel Mine Ban Convention," in John Borrie and V. Martin Randin, eds., *Disarmament as Humanitarian Action: From Perspective to Practice* (United Nations: UN Institute for Disarmament Research, 2006) 83. Wareham and Steve Goose oversaw the creation of the *Landmine Monitor,* and remain part of its Ban Policy thematic research team.

18. For example, the first report, *Landmine Monitor* Report *1999* was 1,071 pages with thirteen additional pages of charts, while *Landmine Monitor* Report *2009* is 1,253 pages. International Campaign to Ban Landmines. *Landmine Monitor Report 1999: Toward a Mine-Free World.* Washington DC: Human Rights Watch. 1999 and International Campaign to Ban Landmines. *Landmine Monitor Report 2009: Toward a Mine-Free World.* Ottawa: Mines Action Canada, 2009.

19. Wareham, 84.

20. ICBL Press Release, "Landmine Campaign Details Global Progress and Problems at Opening of Diplomatic Conference in Mozambique," May 3, 1999.

21. International Campaign to Ban Landmines, *Landmine Monitor Report 2000: Toward a Mine-Free World.* Washington DC: Human Rights Watch. 2000. Executive Summary, 5.

22. The European Commission, "Land Mines: The Plight, The International Commitments, the reinforcement of the contribution of the European Union," http://eu-mine-actions.jrc.cec.eu.int/policy/background_1.htm.

23. Statement by Chris Patten, Commissioner, European Commission, to the Second Meeting of the States Parties to the Ottawa Convention, Geneva, September 11–15, 2000. http://demining.jrc.it/aris/news/ottawa_commissioner.htm (September 14, 2000).

Bibliography

BOOKS

Africa Watch. *Landmines in Angola*. New York: Africa Watch, 1993.

Albright, Madeleine. *Madam Secretary: A Memoir*. New York: Miramax, 2003.

Asia Watch and Physicians for Human Rights. *Land Mines in Cambodia: The Coward's War*. United States: Asia Watch and Physicians for Human Rights, September 1991.

Banks, Eddie. *Brassey's Essential Guide to Anti-Personnel Landmines: Recognizing and Disarming*. London: Brassey's, 1997.

Best, Geoffrey. *War and Law Since 1945*. Oxford: Clarendon Press, 1994.

Bolton, Mathew. *Foreign Aid and Landmine Clearance: Governance, Politics and Security in Afghanistan, Bosnia and Sudan*. New York: I.B. Tauris & Co Ltd. 2010.

Borrie, John. *Unacceptable Harm: A History of How the Treaty to Ban Cluster Munitions was Won*. Geneva, Switzerland: United Nations Institute for Disarmament Research, 2009.

Cameron, Maxwell A., Robert J. Lawson, and Brian W. Tomlin, eds. *To Walk Without Fear: The Global Movement to Ban Landmines*. Toronto: Oxford University Press, 1998.

Clinton, Bill. *My Life*. New York: Alfred A. Knopf, 2004.

Croll, Mike. *The History of Landmines*. Barnsley, South Yorkshire, United Kingdom: Leo Cooper an imprint of Pen and Sword Military Books Ltd., 1998.

Croll, Mike. *Landmines in War and Peace: From Origin to Present Day*. Barnsley, South Yorkshire, United Kingdom: Pen and Sword Military an imprint of Pen and Sword Military Books Ltd., 2008.

Davies, Paul. *War of the Mines: Cambodia, Landmines and the Impoverishment of a Nation*. With photographs by Nic Dunlap. London: Pluto Press, 1994.

Franck, Thomas M. *Fairness in International Law and Institutions.* Oxford: Oxford University Press, 1995.

Handicap International. *Antipersonnel Landmines: For the Banning of Massacres of Civilians in Time of Peace—Facts and Chronologies.* 2nd ed., Lyon, France: Handicap International.

Hartman, Gregory K. *Weapons That Wait: Mine Warfare in the U.S. Navy.* Annapolis, MD: Naval Institute Press, 1979.

Higgins, Rosalyn. *Problems and Process: International Law and How We Use It.* Oxford: Oxford University Press, 1995.

Human Rights Watch Arms Project. *Landmines in Mozambique.* New York: Human Rights Watch, 1994.

Human Rights Watch Arms Project. *Still Killing: Landmines in Southern Africa.* New York: Human Rights Watch, 1997.

Human Rights Watch Arms Project—and Physicians for Human Rights. *Landmines: A Deadly Legacy.* New York: Human Rights Watch, 1993.

Lumpe, Lora, and Jeff Donarski. *The Arms Trade Revealed: A Guide for Investigators and Activists.* Washington, D.C.: Federation of American Scientists, 1998.

Maresca, Louis, and Stuart Maslen, eds. *The Banning of Anti-Personnel Landmines: The Legal Contribution of the International Committee of the Red Cross 1955–1999.* Cambridge, UK: Cambridge University Press, 2000.

Maslen, Stuart. *Commentaries on Arms Control Treaties, Vol. 1, The Convention on the Prohibition of the Use, Stockpiling Production, and Transfer of Anti-Personnel Mines and on Their Destruction.* Oxford, UK: Oxford University Press, 2004.

Maslen, Stuart. *Anti-Personnel Mines Under Humanitarian Law: A View from the Vanishing Point.* Antwerpen: Iintersentia, 2001.

Matthew, Richard, Byron McDonald, and Kenneth R. Rutherford, eds. *Landmines and Human Security: International Politics and War's Hidden Legacy.* Albany, NY: State University of New York Press, 2004.

McDonald, Jacqueline, ed. *Alternatives for Landmine Detection.* Santa Monica, CA, RAND: 2003.

McGrath, Rae. *Landmines: Legacy of Conflict: A Manual for Development Workers.* United Kingdom: Oxfam, 1994.

Organization for the Prohibition of Chemical Weapons, *Chemical Disarmament: Basic Facts.* Organization for the Prohibition of Chemical Weapons: The Hague, 1998.

Prokosch, Eric. *The Technology of Killing: A Military and Political History of Antipersonnel Weapons.* London: Zed Books, 1995.

Roberts, Shawn, and Jody Williams. *After the Guns Fall Silent: The Enduring Legacy of Landmines.* Washington, D.C.: Vietnam Veterans of America Foundation, 1995.

Scott, James Brown. *The Reports to the Hague Conferences of 1899 and 1907.* Oxford: Clarendon Press, 1917.

Sigal, Leon V. *Negotiating Minefield: The Landmines Ban in American Politics.* New York: Routledge, 2006.

Smith, David. *Sherman's March to the Sea 1964: From Atlanta to Savannah.* London. Osprey Publishing, 2007.

Waltz, Kenneth N. *Theory of International Politics.* New York: McGraw Hill, 1979.

Williams, Jody, Steve Goose, and Mary Wareham, eds. *Banning Landmines: Disarmament, Citizen Diplomacy and Human Security.* Lanham, MD: Rowman & Littlefield, 2008.

Youngblood, Norman E. *The Development of Mine Warfare: A Most Murderous and Barbarous Conduct: War, Technology, and History.* Westport, CT: Praeger Press, 2006.

BOOK CHAPTERS

Axworthy, Lloyd. "Canada and Antipersonnel Landmines: Human Security as a Foreign Policy Priority." In *Foreign Policy: Theories, Cases*, edited by Steve Smith, Amelia Hadfield, Tim Dunne. Oxford: Oxford University Press, 2008.

Blagden, Patrick. "The Use of Mines and the Impact of Technology." In *Clearing the Fields: Solutions to the Global Land Mine Crisis*, edited by Kevin M. Cahill, 112–123. New York: Council of Foreign Relations, Basic Books, 1995.

Boutros-Ghali, Boutros. "Forward." In *Clearing the Fields: Solutions to the Global Land Mine Crisis*, edited by Kevin M. Cahill, xii–xiv. New York: Council of Foreign Relations, Basic Books, 1995.

Cahill, Kevin M. "Introduction." In *Clearing the Fields: Solutions to the Global Land Mine Crisis*, edited by Kevin M. Cahill, 1–14. New York: Council of Foreign Relations, Basic Books, 1995.

Cameron, Maxwell A., Robert J. Lawson, and Brian W. Tomlin. "To Walk Without Fear." In *To Walk Without Fear: The Global Movement to Ban Landmines*, edited by Maxwell A. Cameron, Robert J. Lawson, and Brian W. Tomlin, 1–19. Toronto: Oxford University Press, 1998.

Chabasse, Philippe. "The French Campaign." In *To Walk Without Fear: The Global Movement to Ban Landmines*, edited by Maxwell A. Cameron, Robert J. Lawson, and Brian W. Tomlin, 60–67. Toronto: Oxford University Press, 1998.

Eliasson, Jan. "An International Approach Toward Humanitarian Assistance and Economic Development of Countries Affected by Land Mines." In *Clearing the Fields: Solutions to the Global Land Mine Crisis*, edited by Kevin M. Cahill, 165–178. New York: Council of Foreign Relations, Basic Books, 1995.

Giannour, Chris, and J. Jack Geiger. "The Medical Lessons of Land Mine Injuries." In *Clearing the Fields: Solutions to the Global Land Mine Crisis*, edited by Kevin M. Cahill, 138–147. New York: Council of Foreign Relations, Basic Books, 1995.

Hajnoczi, Thomas, Thomas Desch, and Deborah Chatsis. "The Ban Treaty." In *To Walk Without Fear: The Global Movement to Ban Landmines*, edited by Maxwell A. Cameron, Robert J. Lawson, and Brian W. Tomlin, 68–75. Toronto: Oxford University Press, 1998.

Long, David, and Laird Hindle. "Europe and the Ottawa Process: An Overview" In *To Walk Without Fear: The Global Movement to Ban Landmines*, edited by Maxwell A. Cameron, Robert J. Lawson, and Brian W. Tomlin, 185–211. Toronto: Oxford University Press, 1998.

Mearshimer, John. "The False Promise of Institutions." In *The Perils of Anarchy: Contemporary Realism and International Security*, edited by Michael E. Brown, Sean M. Lynn Jones, and Steven Miller. Cambridge. The MIT Press, 1995.

Stott, Noel. "The South African Campaign." In *To Walk Without Fear: The Global Movement to Ban Landmines*, edited by Maxwell A. Cameron, Robert J. Lawson, and Brian W. Tomlin, 68–75. Toronto: Oxford University Press, 1998.

Tomlin, Brian W. "On a Fast Track to a Ban: The Canadian Policy Process." In *To Walk Without Fear: The Global Movement to Ban Landmines*, edited by Maxwell A. Cameron, Robert J. Lawson, and Brian W. Tomlin, 185–211. Toronto: Oxford University Press, 1998.

Vance, Cyrus, and Herbert S. Okun. "Eliminating the Threat of Land Mines: A New U.S. Policy." In *Clearing the Fields: Solutions to the Global Land Mine Crisis*, edited by Kevin M. Cahill, 198–210. New York: Council of Foreign Relations, Basic Books, 1995.

Waltz, Kenneth N. "The Origins of War in Neo-Realist Theory." In *Conflict After the Cold War: Arguments on Causes of Peace*, edited by Richard K. Betts. Boston: Allyn and Bacon, 1994.

Wareham, Mary. "Rhetoric and Policy Realities in the United States." In *To Walk Without Fear: The Global Movement to Ban Landmines*, edited by Maxwell A. Cameron, Robert J. Lawson, and Brian W. Tomlin, 99–117. Toronto: Oxford University Press, 1998.

Wareham, Mary. "The Role of the Landmine Monitor in Promoting and Monitoring Compliance with the 1997 Anti-Personnel Mine Ban Convention." In *Disarmament as Humanitarian Action: From Perspective to Practice*, edited by John Borrie and V. Martin Randin. United Nations: UN Institute for Disarmament Research, 2006.

Warmington, Valerie, and Celina Tuttle. "The Canadian Campaign." In *To Walk Without Fear: The Global Movement to Ban Landmines*, edited by Maxwell A. Cameron, Robert J. Lawson, and Brian W. Tomlin, 48–59. Toronto: Oxford University Press, 1998.

White, Jerry, and Ken Rutherford. "The Role of the Landmine Survivors Network." In *To Walk Without Fear: The Global Movement to Ban Landmines*, edited by Maxwell A. Cameron, Robert J. Lawson, and Brian W. Tomlin, 99–117. Toronto: Oxford University Press, 1998.

Williams, Jody, and Stephen Goose. "The International Campaign to Ban Landmines." In *To Walk Without Fear: The Global Movement to Ban Landmines*, edited by Maxwell A. Cameron, Robert J. Lawson, and Brian W. Tomlin, 20–47. Toronto: Oxford University Press, 1998.

JOURNAL ARTICLES

Anderson, Kenneth, and Monica Schurtman. "Symposium: The United Nations Family: Challenges of Law and Development: The United Nations Response to the Crisis of Landmines in the Developing World." *Harvard International Law Journal* 36 (Spring, 1995: 359–371).

Andersson, Neil, Cesar Palha de Sousa, and Sergio Paredes. "Social Cost of Land Mines in Four Countries: Afghanistan, Bosnia, Cambodia and Mozambique." *British Medical Journal* 311 (September 16, 1995): 718–721.

Ascherio, Alberto, Robin Biellik, Andy Epstein, Gail Snetro, Steve Gloyd, Barbara Ayotte, and Paul R. Epstein. "Deaths and Injuries Caused by Land Mines in Mozambique." *The Lancet* (September 16, 1995): 721–724.

Askin, Steve, and Stephen Goose. "The Market for Anti-Personnel Landmines—A Global Survey." *Jane's Intelligence Review* (September 1994): 425–431.

Aubert, Maurice. "The International Committee of the Red Cross and the Problem of Excessively Injurious or Indiscriminate Weapons." *International Review of the Red Cross* 279 (November/December 1990): 483.

Bisenkov, L. N., and N. A. Tynyakkin. "Osobennosti okazaniya khirugicheskoy pomoshchi postradavshim s minnovsryvnymi raneniyami v armii respubliki Afghanistan." [Providing special surgical care to land mine casualties in the army of the Republic of Afghanistan.] *Voenno-medisinkiy zhurnal (VMZ) [Military medical journal]* (January 1992).

Boutros-Ghali, Boutros. "The Land Mine Crisis: A Humanitarian Disaster." *Foreign Affairs* (September/October 1994): 8–13.

Brem, Stefan, and Kenneth R. Rutherford. "The Landmine Ban and the Debate on Small Arms and Light Weapons: Walking Together and Divided Agenda?" *Security Dialogue* 32, no. 2 (June 2001): 169–186.

Carnahan, Lieutenant Colonel Burris M. "The Law of Land Mine Warfare: Protocol II To The United Nations Convention on Certain Conventional Weapons." *Military Law Review* 105, no. 73 (Summer, 1984): 73–96.

Clegg, Liz. "NGOs Take Aim." *The Bulletin of the Atomic Scientists* 55 (January/February 1999): 49.

Colby, James C. "Medical Complications of Antipersonnel Land Mines." *Bulletin of the American College of Surgeons* 81, no. 8 (August 1996): 9–11.

Colby, James C., Eric Stover, and Jonathan Fine, M. D. "Civilian Injuries due to War Mines." *Technologies in Orthopedics* 10, no. 3 (1995): 259–264.

Coupland, Robin M., and Adriaan Korver. "Injuries from Antipersonnel Landmines: The Experience of the International Committee of the Red Cross." *British Medical Journal* (December 14, 1991): 1509–1512.

Coupland, Robin M., and Hans O. Samnegaard. "Effect of Type and Transfer of Conventional Weapons on Civilian Injuries: Retrospective Analysis of Prospective Data from Red Cross Hospital." *British Medical Journal* 319 (August 14, 1999): 410–412.

Coupland, Robin M., and Remi Russbach. "Injuries from Anti-Personnel Mines: What is Being Done?"*Medicine and Global Survival* 1, no. 1 (March 1994): 18–22.

Ekberg, Peter J. "Remotely Delivered Land Mines and International Law." *Columbia Journal of Transnational Law* 33, no. 1 (1995).

Eshaya-Chauvin, B., and R. M. Coupland. "Transfusion Requirements for the Management of War Injured: The Experience of the International Committee of the Red Cross." *British Journal of Anesthesia* 68 (1992): 221–223.

Grau, Lester W. "Mine Warfare and Counterinsurgency: The Russian View." *Professional Bulletin of Army Engineers* 29, no. 1 (March 1999): 2–7.

Grau, Lester W., and William A. Jorgensen. "Guerilla Warfare and Landmine Casualties Remain Inseparable." U.S. Army Medical Department Journal (October–December 1998).

Hager, Peter J. "An Interview with Lawrence Machabee, USMC: A Retrospective View of Humanitarian Demining at the Department of State." *The Journal of Humanitarian Demining*, no. 1.1 (Summer 1997).

Jeffrey, Sue J. "Antipersonnel Mines: Who Are the Victims?" *Journal of Accident & Emergency Medicine* 13, no. 5 (September 1996): 343–346.

Johnson, D., J. Crum, and S. Lumjiak. "Medical Consequences of the Various Weapons Systems Used in Combat in Thailand." *Military Medicine* 146 (1981): 632–34.

Joyner, Christopher C. "Crossing the Great Divide: Views of a Political Scientist Wandering in the World of International Law." American Society of International Law *1987 Proceedings* (1990).

Joyner, Christopher C. "UN General Assembly Resolutions and International Law: Rethinking the Contemporary Dynamics of Norm-Creation." *California Western International Law Journal* 11 (Summer 1989).

Joyner, Christopher C., and John C. Dettling. "Bridging the Cultural Chasm: Cultural Relativism and the Future of International Law." *California Western International Law Journal* 20 (1989–1990).

King, Colin. "Legislation and the Landmine." *Jane's Intelligence Review*, Special Report no. 16, (November, 1997): 4.

Meddings, David R., and Stephaine M. O'Connor. "Circumstances Around Weapon Injury in Cambodia After Departure of a Peacekeeping Force: Prospective Cohort Study." *British Medical Journal* 319 (August 14, 1999): 412–413.

Mueller, Robert O. "New Partnerships for a New World Order: NGOs, State Actors, and International Law in the Post-Cold War World." *Hofstra Law Review* (Fall 1998): 1. . . .http://web.lexis.nexis.com/univers. . .ae68bc 5b69828b8cc037e6&taggedDoca> October 13, 1999.

Paavolainen, J. Rautio. "Afghan War Wounded: Experience with 200 Cases." *Journal of Trauma* (1988): 523–525.

Physicians for Human Rights. "One Doctor's Crusade." *Record* 11, no. 1 (April 1998): 6.

Price, Richard. "Reversing the Gun Sights: Transnational Civil Society Targets Land Mines." *International Organization* 52 (Summer 1998).

Rutherford, Kenneth R. "A Theoretical Examination of Disarming States: NGOs and Anti-Personnel Landmines." *Journal of International Politics* 37, no. 4 (December 2000): 457–477.

Rutherford, Kenneth R. "The Hague and Ottawa Conventions: A Model for Future Weapon Ban Regimes?" *Nonproliferation Review* 6, no. 3 (Spring–Summer 1999): 36–50.

Williams, Jody. "Landmines and Measures to Eliminate Them." *International Review of the Red Cross* 307 (August 31, 1995): 375–390.

Winslow, Philip C. "The Case Against Landmines." *Red Cross, Red Crescent* 2 (1997).

Wurst, Jim. "Ten Million Tragedies, One Step at a Time." *The Bulletin of the Atomic Scientists* (July/August 1993): 14–21.

MAGAZINES AND NEWSPAPERS

"An Open Letter to President Clinton." *New York Times*, April 3, 1996.

Baker, Peter. "A Dispute Between Neighbors: Clinton Heatedly Restates Opposition to Canada's Move to Ban Antipersonnel Land Mines." *Washington Post*, November 24, 1997, A20.

Bandler, James. "Laureate in a Minefield." *The Boston Globe Magazine*, June 7, 1998.

"Banishing Land Mines." Editorial, *New York Times*, August 12, 1997.

Barbash, Fred. "Royal Spin." *Washington Post*, February 14, 1997, A23.

Bonner, Raymond. "Pentagon Weighs Ending Opposition to a Ban on Mines: Public Review Ordered." *New York Times*, March 17, 1996, 1A.

Browne, Malcolm W. "Land Mines Called a World Menace." *New York Times*, November 15, 1993, A9.

Butcher, Tim. "Labour Bans Landmines from 2005," *Electronic Telegraph*, no. 727, May 22, 1997.

Charny, Joel R., and Anne Goldfeld. "Cambodia: Don't Look Away." *New York Times*. May 10, 1990.

"China Prototypes Minelayer System." *Jane's Defence Weekly*, July 3, 1993, 24.

Cohen, William S. "Necessary and Right." *Washington Post*, September 19, 1997, A23.

Clines, Francis X. "28-Year Quest to Abolish Land Mines Pays Off for Veteran, Who Fights On." *New York Times*, December 3, 1997, A10.

Friend, Tim. "Millions of Land Mines Hinder Afghan Recovery: 2-Decade Legacy Hurts Workforce, Farmland." *USA Today*, November 28, 2001, 1A and 10A.

Goldfeld, Anne. "The Dying Fields: New Horror in Cambodia." *New York Times*, June 4, 1991.

Goldfeld, Anne. "Killers in the Earth." *Washington Post*, July 9, 1996, C1.

Goldfeld, Anne. "A Weapon We Can Live Without." *Boston Globe*, September 22, 1996.

Goldfeld, Anne, and Holly Myers. "Halting the Hidden Killers: The Effort to Ban Land Mines." *Boston Globe*. June 2, 1994.

Goldfeld, Anne, and Holly Myers. "Ban the Land Mines." *Boston Globe*. December 21, 1995.

Hardman, Robert. "Princess Calls for Greater Efforts to Clear Landmines." *The Daily Telegraph*, June 13, 1997, 10.

"India Calls for Int'l Consensus on Banning Landmines." *Xinhua English Newswire*, November, 15, 1998.

Kelly, Jack, and William M. Welch. "Death Could Be Impetus for Land Mine Ban." *USA Today*, September 2, 1997, 20A.

"The Land Mine Cause." *Christian Science Monitor*, September 8, 1997, 20.

Leahy, Senator Patrick J. "Land Mines: Nothing Less Than a Ban." *Washington Post*, January 19, 1997, C7.

Leahy, Senator Patrick J. Letter to the *New York Times*, January 13, 1994.

"Lifting the Land Mine Curse." *New York Times*, February 8, 1995.

Martin, Keith. "Landmines: A Horror That Must Be Banned." *Times Colonist*, October 17, 1995, A5.

"Mexico Blocks Conclave on World Land-Mine Ban." *Washington Post*, June 13, 1997, A33.

Mintz, John. "A Global Bid to Ban Land Mines: Devices Kill or Wound 26,000 People Each Year." *Washington Post*, February 4, 1996, A1.

Murphy, Caryle. "The Nobel Prize Fight." *Washington Post*, March 22, 1998.

Pedersen, Torbjoern. "Leading Foe of Mines Quits, Keeps Prize." *The Boston Globe*, February 10, 1998.

Priest, Dana. "Clinton Directive on Mines: New Form, Old Function." *Washington Post*, September 24, 1997, A19.

Priest, Dana. "U.S. Holds Key to Ban of Mines: Clinton Set to Decide on Options for Talks." *Washington Post*, January 2, 1997, AO1, A1, A6, and A16.

Priest, Dana. "White House to Take U.N. Route Toward Global Land Mine Ban: Rival Canadian-Led Effort For Earlier Treaty Rejected." *Washington Post*, January 18, 1997, A2.

Reed, Susan, and Andrea Pawlyna. "A Marine's Reparation: Thanks to a Vietnam Vet, Cambodia Amputees Have New Legs and Jobs." *PEOPLE* 44, no. 24 (December 11, 1995), 103.

"SACBL Launched on July 24, 1995 with Nobel Peace Laureate Bishop Desmond Tutu." Reuters Ltd., July 25 1995. Document retrieved in the official records of the International Campaign to Ban Landmines at Library and Archives Canada. Ottawa, Canada. Accessed by author on August 13, 2009.

Stover, Eric, and Dan Charles. "The Killing Minefields of Cambodia." *New Scientist*, October 19, 1991, 27.

Strada, Gino. "The Horror of Land Mines." *Scientific American*, May 1996, 42.

Swanson, K. C. "Pentagon's Fighting a Ban on Mines." *National Journal*, February 17, 1996, 370–371.

Taylor, Michael. "Pentagon Looking for Ways to Avoid Mines in Bosnia." *San Francisco Chronicle*, November 29, 1995, A20.

"U.S. Is Alone in Seeking Loophole in Ban on Mines." *New York Times*, September 4, 1997, A10.

Wallace, Charles P. "Land Mines Take Toll on Cambodian Peace." *Los Angeles Times*, December 14, 1991, A4.

Webster, Donovan. "It's the Little Bombs That Kill You." *The New York Times Magazine*, January 23, 1994, 27–32.

Weiner, Tim. "U.S. Is Wary of Ban on Land Mines." *New York Times*, June 17, 1997, A10.

"Why Red Cross Opposes a Partial Ban on Land Mines." *Christian Science Monitor*, September 27, 1995, 6.

Wren, Christopher S. "U.N.-Backed Drive to Restrict Land Mines Fails at Talks." *New York Times*, October 13, 1995, A6.

"Yeltsin Affirms Support for Ban on Mines." *Reuters*, October 29, 1997.

PUBLIC STATEMENTS

Albright, Ambassador Madeleine K. U.S. Representative to the United Nations. United Nations First Committee. New York, NY. November 4, 1996.

Anderson, Kenneth. Director, Arms Project, Human Rights Watch. Subcommittee of the Committee on Appropriations, United States Senate, May 13, 1994. Senate Hearing "The Global Landmine Crisis." 103–666 Report.

Annan, Kofi. United Nations Secretary-General, to the Diplomatic Conference on Landmines. Oslo, Norway. September 3, 1997. Press Release SG/SM/6313.

Annan, Kofi. United Nations Secretary-General, to the Signing Ceremony of the Anti-Personnel Mines Convention. Ottawa, Canada. December 3, 1997.

Armenian Delegation. Signing Ceremony of the MBT. Ottawa, Canada. December 4, 1997.

Axworthy, Honorable Lloyd. Minister of Foreign Affairs. Closing Session of the International Strategy Conference, "Towards a Global Ban on Anti-Personal Mines." Ottawa, Canada. October 5, 1996.

Axworthy, Honorable Lloyd. Minister of Foreign Affairs to the NGO Forum on Banning Anti-Personnel Landmines. Oslo, Norway, September 7, 1997.

Berdennikev, Ambassador Grigory V. Representative of the Russian Federation. First Committee of the 51st UN General Assembly. New York, NY. November 7, 1996.

Boutros-Ghali, Boutros. UN Secretary-General. Review Conference of States Parties to the Convention on Prohibitions or Restrictions on the Use of Certain Conventional Weapons Which May Be Deemed to Be Excessively Injurious Or to Have Indiscriminate Effects. Vienna, Austria. September 1995.

Chabasse, Philippe. Handicap International. "The French Campaign," at the Second NGO Conference on Landmines. Report of Proceedings. Geneva, Switzerland. May 9–11, 1994.

Changhe, Ambassador Li. Head of the Chinese Delegation at the Review Conference of States Parties to the Convention on the Prohibitions or Restrictions on the Use of Certain Conventional Weapons Which May be Deemed to be Excessively Injurious or to have Indiscriminate Effects. Vienna, Austria. September 27, 1995.

Chretien, Canadian Prime Minister Jean. Signing Conference for the Ottawa Convention. Ottawa, Canada. December 3, 1977.

Clinton, President William. 49th Session of the UNGA. September 26, 1994. Press Release. USUN #124-94.

Cook, Robin. United Kingdom Foreign Secretary. Diplomatic Conference on an International Total Ban on Anti-Personnel Land Mines. Oslo, Norway. Foreign and Commonwealth Office. September 2, 1997.

Diana, Princess of Wales. "Responding to Landmines: A Modern Tragedy and its Solutions." Seminar hosted by the Mines Advisory Group and Landmine Survivors Network at the Royal Geographical Society. London, England. June 12, 1997.

Duncan, Ambassador John. Head of the United Kingdom Delegation to the 8th Meeting of States Parties to the Convention on the Prohibition of the Use, Stockpiling, Production and Transfer of Anti-Personnel Mines and their Destruction. Amman, Jordan. November 18, 2007.

Fowler, Ambassador Robert B. Canadian Representative to the UN. UNSC Discussion on Landmines. New York, NY. As quoted in e-mail "UN Security Council Discusses Mines: Part 2," from David Isenbenberg, Center for Defense Information to the arms trade email network. August 26, 1996.

Gebauer, Thomas. Director, MEDIO International. "On the Way from a Legal Pprohibition to an Effective Abolition of Mines: Remarks on Integrating Mine Action." Oslo Landmines NGO-Forum. September 7–10, 1997.

Godal, Bjoern Tore. Norwegian Foreign Minister. Diplomatic Conference on an International Total Ban on Anti-Personnel Land Mines. Oslo, Norway. September 2, 1997.

Goldfeld, Anne. Board Member, Women's Commission for Refugees. Asia Pacific Sub-Committee of the House Foreign Affairs Committee. Washington, D.C. April 10, 1991.

Goose, Stephen. Washington Director, The Arms Project of Human Rights Watch. Senate Appropriations Subcommittee on Foreign Operations. Washington, D.C. June 15, 1993.

Goose, Steve. Human Rights Watch. Regional Conference on Landmines, Budapest, Hungary. March 27, 1998. Report: Regional Conference on Landmines, International Campaign to Ban Landmines. Budapest, Hungary. March 26–28, 1998.

Goose, Steve. Panel Discussion on U.S. Landmine Policy and Verification, The American Bar Association; Section of International Law and Practice. Washington, D.C. October 23, 1997. (Author Notes).

Gwozdecky, Mark. Coordinator of the Mine Action Team in the Canadian Department of Foreign Affairs and International Trade. Ottawa Process Forum. Ottawa, Canada. December 5, 1997. (Author notes).

Gwozdecky, Mark. Government of Canada, Regional Conference on Landmines. Budapest, Hungary. March 27, 1998.

Inderfurth, Ambassador Karl F., Special Representative to the President and Secretary of State for Global Humanitarian Demining, "Coordination of Resources for Mine Action" Roundtable. Ottawa, Canada. December 4, 1997.

Japaridze, Ambassador H. E. Tedo. Georgia. Signing Ceremony of the Anti-Personnel Mines Convention. Ottawa, Canada. December 3–4, 1997.

Krylov, S. B. Head of the Russian Delegation at the Conference on Prohibitions or Restrictions on the Use of Certain Conventional Weapons Which May be Deemed to be Excessively Injurious or to have Indiscriminate Effects. Vienna, Austria. September 26, 1995.

Lauber, Jurg. Diplomatic Adviser, Switzerland Ministry of Foreign Affairs. Ottawa Process Forum. Ottawa, Canada. December 5, 1997. (Author Notes).

Lawson, Robert. Government of Canada, to the Workshop on Ratification and Implementation of the Mine Ban Treaty, Regional Conference on Landmines. Budapest, Hungary. March 27, 1998.

Leahy, Senator Patrick. Address to the U.S. Senate, "A Lost Chance For U.S. Leadership," U.S. Senate. Washington, D.C. September 23, 1997.

Leahy, Senator Patrick. "Seize this Moment," to the NGO Forum. Oslo, Norway. September 7, 1997.

Leahy, Senator Patrick. Subcommittee of the Committee on Appropriations, United States Senate, May 13, 1994. Senate Hearing "The Global Landmine Crisis." Washington, D.C. 103–666 Report.

Leahy, Senator Patrick. United Nations General Assembly's First Committee on Disarmament and International Security. New York, NY. November 30, 1993.

Matheson, Ambassador Michael J. Delegation of the United States of American to the Plenary Session of the Review Conference on the Convention of Conventional Weapons. Vienna, Austria. September 27, 1995.

Mbeki, South African Deputy President. Opening Session of the "Landmines Free Africa: The OAU and the Legacy of Anti-Personnel Mines Conference. Kempton Park, South Africa. May 19–22, 1997.

Miyet, Bernard. Under Secretary General Peacekeeping Operations, to the Ottawa Workshop on Mine Action Co-ordination. Ottawa, Canada. March 23–24, 1998.

Moher, Ambassador Mark. Canada's Permanent Representative to the United Nations for Disarmament to Review Conference of States Parties to the

Convention on the Prohibitions or Restrictions on the Use of Certain Conventional Weapons Which May be Deemed to be Excessively Injurious or to have Indiscriminate Effects. Vienna, Austria. September 26, 1995.

Molander, Johan. Chairman of the Group of Governmental Experts, UN First Committee. New York, NY. November 3, 1994.

Molander, Johan. President of the First Review Conference of States Parties to the Convention on the Prohibitions or Restrictions on the Use of Certain Conventional Weapons Which May be Deemed to be Excessively Injurious or to have Indiscriminate Effects. Vienna, Austria. September 26, 1995.

Moon, Chris. Opening Session of the Ottawa Conference. Ottawa, Canada. October 3, 1996.

Muller, Robert. Executive Director, Vietnam Veterans of American Foundation. Subcommittee of the Committee on Appropriations, United States Senate, May 13, 1994. Senate Hearing "The Global Landmine Crisis." Washington, D.C. 103–666 Report.

Muller, Robert O., Executive Director, Vietnam Veterans of American Foundation. Keynote Presentation "The International Campaign to Ban Landmines: Where Do We Go From Here?" at the Second NGO Conference on Landmines. Report of Proceedings. Geneva, Switzerland. May 9–11, 1994.

Myers, Holly. USCBL. Seminar lecture "The International Ban on Land Mines," Ethics of Development in a Global Environment (EDGE) seminar series. Palo Alto, CA. October 4, 1995.

Palwankar, Umesh. ICRC legal department. "International Committee of the Red Cross: The Review Process of the 1980 Convention," at the Second NGO Conference on Landmines. Report of Proceedings. Geneva, Switzerland. May 9–11, 1994.

Patierno, Pat. Director, Office of Humanitarian Demining, Bureau of Political-Military Affairs. Department of State, at the "Landmines: Human Rights and National Security Conference." Harvard Club. New York, NY. May 15, 2000.

Patten, Chris. Commissioner. European Commission. Second Meeting of the States Parties to the Ottawa Convention. Geneva, Switzerland. September 11–15, 2000.

Punch, Gary. Australian Minister for Defense Science and Personnel. First Review Conference of States Parties to the Convention on the Prohibitions or Restrictions on the Use of Certain Conventional Weapons Which May be Deemed to be Excessively Injurious or to have Indiscriminate Effects. Vienna, Austria. September 26, 1995.

Roethlisberger, Eric. ICRC Vice President. CCW Review Conference, Third Session. Geneva, Switzerland. May 3, 1996.

Rutherford, Ken. Subcommittee of the Committee on Appropriations, United States Senate, May 13, 1994. Senate Hearing "The Global Landmine Crisis." Washington, D.C. 103–666 Report.

Ryckmans, Pierre, and Vincent Stainier. Belgium Campaign to Ban Landmines and Handicap International. "Networking for a Country Campaign" workshop, Cambodia Landmines Conference. June 4, 1995.

Sejersted, Professor Francis. Chairman of the Norwegian Nobel Committee, on the occasion of the award of the Nobel Peace Prize for 1997. Oslo, Norway. December 10, 1997.

Sommaruga, Cornelio. President of the International Committee of the Red Cross. Review Conference of States Parties to the Convention on the Prohibitions or Restrictions on the Use of Certain Conventional Weapons Which May be Deemed to be Excessively Injurious or to have Indiscriminate Effects. Vienna, Austria. September 26, 1995.

Sommaruga, Cornelio. President of the International Committee of the Red Cross. "International Strategy Conference Towards a Global Ban on Antipersonnel Mines." Ottawa, Canada. October 4, 1996.

Von Essen, Carl. Closing Plenary Speech, on behalf of the ICBL, CCW Review Conference. Vienna, Austria. October 13, 1995.

Walker, Susan. ICBL Co-Coordinator, at the "Ceremony to mark Entry into Force of the Mine Ban Convention." Geneva, Switzerland. March 1, 1999.

Williams, Jody. ICBL Ambassador, at the USCBL Grassroots meetings associated with the 2000 Presidential Primaries in Iowa. Des Moines, Iowa. January 8, 2000.

Williams, Jody. Vietnam Veterans of American Foundation (VVAF), Chair of the International Campaign to Ban Landmines. Plenary Session of "International Conference: The Socio-Economic Impact of Landmines: Towards an International Ban." June 2, 1995.

Williams, Jody. VVAF, ICBL Coordinator. Opening Plenary Session, Review Conference of the Convention on Conventional Weapons. Geneva, Switzerland. April 22, 1996.

Williams, Jody. VVAF, ICBL Coordinator. Opening Statement, Brussels Conference on Antipersonnel Mines. Brussels, Belgium. June 24, 1997.

Williams, Jody. VVAF, ICBL Coordinator. "A Global Ban on Landmines—Treaty Signing Conference and Mine Action Forum." Ottawa, Canada. December 3, 1997.

Williams, Jody. VVAF, ICBL Coordinator. Nobel Peace Prize Acceptance Speech. Oslo, Norway. December 10, 1997.

WRITTEN CORRESPONDENCE (LETTERS OTHERWISE NOTED AS FAX OR E-MAIL)

Albright, Madeleine. Madeleine Albright, U.S. Ambassador to the UN, to Senator Patrick J. Leahy, October 6, 1993.

Albright, Madeleine. Madeleine Albright, U.S. Ambassador to the UN, to Senator Patrick J. Leahy, January 21, 1994.

Albright, Madeleine. Madeleine Albright, U.S. Ambassador to the UN, to Senator Patrick J. Leahy, February 20, 1996.

Andreani, Jacques. Jacques Andreani, French Ambassador to the United States, to Senator Patrick Leahy, March 7, 1994.

Bell, Peter D. Peter D. Bell, President, CARE to Anthony Lake, Assistant to the President for National Security Affairs, May 3, 1996.

Blagden, Paddy. Paddy Blagden fax to the Office of Senator Patrick Leahy, November 28, 1995.

Carstairs, Tim. Tim Carstairs. Landmines campaign officer, Handicap International, to Jody Williams, ICBL Coordinator, June 19, 1992.

Carstairs, Tim. Tim Carstairs, Landmines campaign officer, Handicap International, to Senator Patrick J. Leahy, October 28, 1993.

Chabasse, Dr. Philippe, and Tim Carstairs. Dr. Philippe Chabasse and Tim Carstairs, Handicap International to Senator Patrick Leahy, February 17, 1993.

Clinton, President William J. President William J. Clinton to Senator Patrick Leahy, February 22, 1994.

Clinton, President William J. President William J. Clinton to Senator Patrick Leahy, November 30, 1994.

Clinton, President William J. President William J. Clinton to Senator Patrick Leahy, April 2, 1997.

Clinton, President William J. President William J. Clinton to Members of the United States Campaign to Ban Landmines, February 4, 1998.

Clinton, President William J. President William J. Clinton to Marissa A. Vitagliano, USCBL Coordinator, August 31, 1998.

Clinton, President William J. William J. Clinton to Senator Patrick Leahy, July 6, 1997.

Clinton, President William J. William J. Clinton to Senator Patrick Leahy, December 19, 1997.

Coughlan, Denise. Denise Coughlan. Chair, Cambodia Campaign to Ban Landmines. E-mail to ICBL. March 13, 2000.

Daschle, Senator Thomas. Senator Thomas Daschle to Senator Patrick Leahy, December 9, 1992.

Davies, Peter J. Peter J. Davies, President and CEO, InterAction, to Senator Patrick J. Leahy, August 7, 1992.

Davis, Terry. Terry Davis to Will Davis, Bureau of Politico-Military Affairs, Office of Defense Trade Controls, Department of State, August 5, 1993.

de Silva, Geetha. Geeth de Silva, Charge d' Affaires, Embassy of Sri Lanka in the United States, to Senator Patrick Leahy, July 24, 1997.

Diana, Princes of Wales. Diana, Princess of Wales letter to Mr. and Mrs. Brian Isfeld. July 10, 1997.

Doubleday, Captain Michael. U.S. Defense Department at Defense Department regular briefing. August 19, 1997.

Evans, Lane, and Senator Patrick J. Leahy to Secretary of State Warren, Secretary of Defense William Perry, and Arms Control and Disarmament Director John Holum, April 11, 1995.

Goose, Steve. Steve Goose, Human Rights Watch and Chairman, Steering Committee, US Campaign to Ban Landmine Note via E-mail from Jody Williams, ICBL Coordinator, to selected USCBL members, August 22, 1997.

Hagel, Senator Chuck and Senator Patrick Leahy. Senator Chuck Hagel and Patrick J. Leahy to President William Clinton, September 16, 1997.

Hartke, Linda J., and Denise Coghlan. Linda J. Hartke and Denise Coghlan to His Excellency Samdech Hun Sen, Second Prime Minister, Royal Government of Cambodia, June 4, 1995.

Hartke, Linda J., and Denise Coghlan. Linda J. Hartke and Denise Coghlan to His Royal Highness Norodom Ranariddh, First Prime Minister, Royal Government of Cambodia, June 4, 1995.

Hartke, Linda J., and Denise Coghlan. Linda J. Hartke and Denise Coghlan to Mr. Pol Pot, Mr. Khieu Samphan, Mr Ieng Sary, Mr. Ta Mok, Mr. Son Sen, and all the followers of the Khmer Rouge, June 4, 1995.

Hartke, Linda J., and Denise Coghlan. Linda J. Hartke and Denise Coghlan to Mr. Pol Pot, Mr. Khieu Samphan, Mr. Ieng Sary, Mr. Ta Mok, Mr. Son Sen, and all the followers of the Khmer Rouge, June 16, 1995.

Helms, Senator Jesse. Senator Jesse Helms to Senate Colleagues, June 27, 1997.

Hogg, Douglas. Douglas Hogg, Foreign and Commonwealth Office, Minister of State, United Kingdom, to Chris Mullen, MP, House of Commons, United Kingdom, January 22, 1993.

Holmes, H. Allen. H. Allen Holmes, Assistant Secretary of Defense, to Senator Leahy, November 7, 1996.

Holum, John D. John D. Holum. Director, U.S. Arms Control and Disarmament Agency, to Senator Patrick J. Leahy, February 10, 1997.

Inderfurth, Karl. Karl Inderfurth, Ambassador, Office of the US Representative at the UN, fax entitled "Angola and Landmines" to Senator Patrick Leahy, April 25, 1996. Fax entitled "Angola and Landmines."

International Campaign to Ban Landmines. International Campaign to Ban Landmines to Johan Molander, Chairman, Expert Group, Preparatory to the Review Conference of the 1980 Conference of the 1980 Conventional Weapons Convention," May 19, 1994.

Ipsen, Peter. Peter Ipsen, DSAA/LPD Fax to Tim Rieser, Senior Policy Aide to Senator Patrick Leahy, June 14, 1993.

"Landmine export moratorium demarche." Telegram from Department of State to US missions in landmine producing countries, December 7, 1993.

Larkin, Barbara. Barbara Larkin, Assistant Secretary of State, Bureau of Legislative Affairs, Department of State, on behalf of Secretary of State Madeline Albright, to Senator Patrick J. Leahy, March 2, 1998.

Larkin, Barbara. Barbara Larkin, Assistant Secretary of State, Bureau of Legislative Affairs, Department of State, to Senator Leahy, March 17, 1997.

Leahy, Senator Patrick J. Senator Patrick J. Leahy and thirty-four Senators to Senate Colleagues, July 22, 1993.

Leahy, Senator Patrick J. Senator Patrick J. Leahy letters to Senators Hank Brown, John Kerry, and Thomas Daschle, November 30, 1992.

Leahy, Senator Patrick J. Senator Patrick J. Leahy to Allen Holmes, Assistant Secretary of Defense, Special Operations/Low-Intensity Conflict, Department of Defense, July 28, 1995.

Leahy, Senator Patrick J. Senator Patrick J. Leahy to Ambassador Madeleine Albright, October 25, 1993.

Leahy, Senator Patrick J. Senator Patrick J. Leahy to Anthony Lake, National Security Advisor, May 3, 1996.

Leahy, Senator Patrick J. Senator Patrick J. Leahy to Handicap International. January 28, 1993.

Leahy, Senator Patrick J. Senator Patrick J. Leahy to John D. Holum, US Arms and Control and Disarmament Agency, January 27, 1997.

Leahy, Senator Patrick J. Senator Patrick J. Leahy to Karl Inderfurth, Alternate Representative to the United Nations, January 16, 1994.

Leahy, Senator Patrick J. Senator Patrick J. Leahy to President Bill Clinton, October 23, 1997.

Leahy, Senator Patrick J. Senator Patrick J. Leahy to President Bill Clinton, October 24, 1997.

Leahy, Senator Patrick J. Senator Patrick J. Leahy to William Cohen, Secretary of Defense. February 6, 1998.

Leahy, Senator Patrick J. Senator Patrick J. Leahy to President William Clinton, April 16, 1997.

Leahy, Senator Patrick J. Senator Patrick J. Leahy to President William J. Clinton, December 23, 1993.

Leahy, Senator Patrick J. Senator Patrick J. Leahy to Secretary of State Warren Christopher, February 25, 1994.

Leahy, Senator Patrick J. Senator Patrick J. Leahy to Senator Paul Simon, September 16, 1994.

Leahy, Senator Patrick J. Senator Patrick J. Leahy to Walter B. Slocombe, Under Secretary for Policy, Department of Defense, May 7, 1996.

Leahy, Senator Patrick J. Senator Patrick J. Leahy to Warren Christopher, Secretary of State, May 7, 1996.

Leahy, Senator Patrick J. Senator Patrick J. Leahy to Warren Christopher, Secretary of State, June 20, 1996.

Leahy, Senator Patrick J. Senator Patrick J. Leahy to William Perry, Secretary of Defense, June 27, 1996.

Leahy, Senator Patrick J. Senator Patrick J. Leahy to William Perry, Secretary of Defense, November 25, 1996.

Leahy, Senator Patrick J. Patrick J. Leahy to President William J. Clinton, April 11, 1996.

Leahy, Senator Patrick J. Patrick J. Leahy to William Perry, Secretary of Defense, April 19, 1996.

Leahy, Senator Patrick J. Senator Patrick Leahy to Mr. Richard Schwartz, President/CEO, Alliant Techsystems, Inc., July 18, 1995.

Leahy, Senator Patrick J. Senator Patrick Leahy to President Bill Clinton, November 12, 1997.

Leahy, Senator Patrick J., and Representative Land Evans. Senator Patrick J. Leahy and Representative Lane Evans to President William J. Clinton, October 26, 1994.

Letter from twenty-five representatives to President William Jefferson Clinton, September 11, 1997.

McGrath, Lou. Lou McGrath, Executive Director, Mines Advisory Group (MAG). Welcoming visitors to the MAG website: www.mag.uk.org.

McNamara, Thomas E. Thomas E McNamara, Assistant Secretary of State, to Senator Patrick J. Leahy, November 1, 1994.

Miller, Judith A. Judith A. Miller, General Counsel of the Department of Defense, to Senator Patrick J. Leahy, June 16, 1997.

Mitchell, Senator George J. Senator George Mitchell to Warren Christopher, Secretary of State, U.S. Department of State, September 19, 1994.

Muller, Robert O. Robert O. Muller, Executive Director, Vietnam Veterans of America Foundation to Senators, August 4, 1992.

Myers, Holly and Anne Goldfeld. Holly Myers and Anne Goldfeld to U.S. Campaign to Ban Landmines, August 4, 1995.

Ogun-Bassani, Bilge, Deputy Director UNICEF, to Stuart Maslen, Vietnam Veterans of America Foundation, August 16, 1993.

Perry, William. William Perry, Secretary of Defense, to Senator Patrick J. Leahy, June 5, 1996.

Perry, William, and Warren Christopher. William Perry, Secretary of Defense, and Warren Christopher, Secretary of State, to Senator Patrick J. Leahy, June 28, 1994.

Powell, Gen. Colin C. Gen. Colin C. Powell. US Army (Ret.) letter to Frank J. Fahrenkopf, Jr., March 19, 1996.Document retrieved in the official records of the International Campaign to Ban Landmines at Library and Archives Canada. Ottawa, Canada. Accessed by author on August 13–14, 2009.

Qichen, Qian. Qian Qichen. Vice Premier of the State Council and Minister of Foreign Affairs of the People's Republic of China, to Senator Patrick Leahy, April 16, 1996.

Reimer, Dennis. Dennis Reimer, U.S. Army Chief of Staff, Dennis J. Reimer to Senator Storm Thurmond, June 19, 1997.

Renwick, Ambassador Robin. Ambassador Robin Renwick, British Embassy-Washington, to Senator Patrick J. Leahy, November 3, 1994.

Riggs, John M. John M. Riggs, MG, USA Director of Requirements Correspondence "Modified VOLCANO Mine Canister Procurement," amendment from to PEO ASM with. Attention to SPAE ASM, Warren, MI. May 8, 1996.

Rossiter, Caleb. Project on Demilitarization & Democracy, memorandum to individuals involved in the December 13, 1995 U.S. meeting on landmines. "Dec. 13 New York Meeting on U.S. Landmines Campaign: Suggested Tasks for ATWG from the Meeting," December 20, 1995.

Schwartz, Richard. Richard Schwartz, President and Chief Executive Officer, Alliant Techsystems, to Senator Leahy, July 26, 1995.

Schwarzkopf, H. Norman Gen., U.S. Army, Retired, to Frank J. Fahrenkopf, Jr. March 2, 1996. Document retrieved in the official records of the International Campaign to Ban Landmines at Library and Archives Canada. Ottawa, Canada. Accessed by author on August 13–14, 2009.

Secretariat of State, Vatican City, expressing a "message from Pope John Paul II sent to the International Landmines Conference in Phnom Penh, June 2, 1995.

Shalikashvili, John. John Shalikashvili, Chairman of the Joint Chief of Staff, to the Honorable Ronald V. Dellums, Committee on National Security, House of Representatives, September 12, 1995.

Shalikashvili, John. John Shalikashvili, Chairman of the Joint Chiefs of Staffs, to MG Nicholas Krawciw, USA (Ret), President, The Dupay Institute, February 6, 1997.

Shalikashvili, John. John Shalikashvili, Chairman of the Joint Chiefs of Staff, to Senator Strom Thurmond, Chairman of the Armed Services Committee, June 17, 1997.

Sherman, Robert. Robert Sherman, Director, Advanced Projects, Arms Control and Disarmament Agency, Department of State and member of US delegations to CCW Review Conference and the Oslo Diplomatic Conference E-mail to MGM Demining Network, March 20, 2002.

Sherman, Wendy R. Wendy R. Sherman, Assistant Secretary, Legislative Affairs, U.S. Department of State, to Senator Patrick J. Leahy, May 3, 1994.

Sherman, Wendy R. Wendy R. Sherman, Assistant Secretary, Legislative Affairs, U.S. Department of State, to Senator Patrick J. Leahy, July 27, 1995.

Simon, Senator Paul. Senator Paul Simon to Senator Patrick J. Leahy, September 9, 1994. (Dictated on September 6, 1994).

Slocombe, Walter B. Walter B. Slocombe, Under Secretary for Defense, to Senator Patrick Leahy, April 25, 2000.

Soros, George. George Soros, President, Open Society Institute, to Vice-President Albert Gore, Jr., July 23, 1997.

Steinberg, Donald K. Donald K. Steinber, U.S. Ambassador to Angola, to Senator Patrick Leahy, April 29, 1996.

Tonwe, Beside. Beside Tonwe, NGO Liaison Officer, UN Department of Humanitarian Affairs, United Nations, New York City, to NGO representatives, June 21, 1995.

Tutu, Desmond M. Desmond M. Tutu, Anglican Archbishop of Cape Town, to the "International Conference: The Socio-Economic Impact of Landmines: Towards an International Ban," n.d.

Twenty-five representatives to President William Jefferson Clinton, September 11, 1997.

U.S. Senior Defense Public Affairs Official. Remarks on Landmines at Background Briefing by Office of the Secretary of Defense. May 16, 1996.

Vermeulen, Paul. Paul Vermeulen. Handicap International-Switzerland, E-mail to JodyWilliams, ICBL Coordinator. "Today's core group meeting in Geneva," August 22, 1997.

Wangstad, Kristi Rollag. Kristi Rollag Wangstad, Vice President, Public Affairs, Alliant Techsystems, to David Gagne, Minnesota Fellowship of Reconciliation, March 31, 1995.

Welch, C. M. C. M. Welch, Chairman Executive Committee, Mohawk Electrical Systems, Inc to Senator Leahy, August 12, 1993.

Welch, C. M. C. M. Welch, Chairman Executive Committee, Mohawk Electrical Systems, Inc to Senator Leahy, September 8, 1993.

Williams, Jody. Jody Williams, Coordinator, Landmines Campaign, to Landmine Campaign Supporter, May 10, 1995.

Williams, Jody. Jody Williams, Coordinator, Landmines Campaign, to Mary Anne Schwabe, Staff Director, Women's Commission for Refugee Women and Children, June 25, 1993.

Williams, Jody. Jody Williams, Coordinator, Landmines Campaign, to Senator Patrick Leahy, July 30, 1992.

Williams, Jody Williams. Jody Williams, ICBL Coordinator. E-mail to selected ICBL members. ICBL Letter to Core Group Meeting," August 21, 1997.

Williams, Jody. Jody Williams, ICBL Coordinator. E-mail to National Campaigns of the ICBL. "Process for delivering options for strengthening the ICBL structure, post-Ottawa," July 17, 1997.

Williams, Jody. Jody Williams. ICBL Coordinator. E-mail to organizations involved in the US to ban landmines, February 15, 1996.

Williams, Jody. Jody Williams. ICBL Coordinator. ICBL and Steve Goose, Chairman, Steering Committee, US Campaign to Ban Landmines, to Core Group Representatives, August 21, 1997.

Williams, Jody, Kenneth Anderson, and Stephen Goose. Jody Williams, Coordinator, Landmine Campaign and Vietnam Veterans of American Foundation, Kenneth Anderson, Director, Arms Project of Human Rights Watch, and Stephen Goose, Washington Director, Arms Project of Human Rights Watch, to Mr. Sohrab Kheradi, Secretary of the Review Conference and Deputy-Director, Center for Disarmament Affairs, United Nations, February 22, 1994.

Wurst, Jim. Jim Wurst. Disarmament Times, to Mary Wareham, USCBL Coordinator, "Quotes from Delegates to the UN First Committee Disarmament on Land Mines and Other Conventional Weapons Issues," October 1996. NGO Committee on Disarmament. November 12, 1996.

INTERNATIONAL CAMPAIGN TO BAN LANDMINES (ICBL) AND UNITED STATES CAMPAIGN TO BAN LANDMINES (USCBL) DOCUMENTS

"Activities of the ICBL at the CCW Review Conference," *Report on Activities: Review Conference of the Convention on Conventional Weapons, Vienna, Austria, September 25 to October 13, 1995*, International Campaign to Ban Landmines.

Benesch, Susan, Glenn McGory, Christina Rodriguez, and Robert Sloane. "International Customary Law and Antipersonnel Landmines: Emergence of a New Customary Norm." *Landmine Monitor Report 1999.*

Bernstein, Liz, and Sue Wixley. "So You Want to Order Resources on Landmines?" *ICBL Pamphlet*, May 1997, 10–11.

An Explosion Every Twenty Minutes—Conference Report: Brussels International Conference for a Total Ban on Anti-Personnel Landmines, June 24–27, 1997.

"International Campaign Advances Call to Ban Landmines, Says Landmine Protocol is a Failure," International Campaign to Ban Landmines, press release, May 11, 1994.

"International Campaign Advances Call to Ban Landmines, Says Landmine Protocol is a Failure," press release, May 11, 1994.

International Campaign to Ban Landmines. Landmine Monitor Report 1999: Toward a Mine-Free World. Washington D.C.: Human Rights Watch. 1999.

International Campaign to Ban Landmines. Landmine Monitor Report 2000: Toward a Mine-Free World. Washington D.C.: Human Rights Watch. 2000.

International Campaign to Ban Landmines. Landmine Monitor Report 2009: Toward a Mine-Free World. Ottawa: Mines Action Canada, 2009.

"Landmines: The Plight, The International Commitments, the Reinforcement of the Contribution of the European Union," *The European Commission*, http://eu-mine-actions.jrc.cec.eu.int/policy/background_1.htm.

"Landmine Campaign Details Global Progress and Problems at Opening of Diplomatic Conference in Mozambique," ICBL press release, May 3, 1999.

Landmines Campaign Rome Meeting Summary Points, March 16/17, 1995.

"Landmine Conference Ends with a Call to Sign Ottawa Treaty in December," ICBL press release, Maputo, Mozambique, February 28, 1997.

Landmine Update #13, July 1996.

"Mine Ban Campaign Praises Treaty, Challenges Governments to Ratify Now," ICBL press release, December 1, 1997.

"Mine Ban Movement Accelerates Into New Phase," ICBL press release, October 1, 1998.

"Mine Campaign Wins Nobel Peace Prize!" ICBL press release, October 10, 1997.

NGO Forum on Landmines, ICBL Report. Oslo, Norway. September 7–10, 1997.

"No Technological Solution to the Landmines Crisis, Groups Say," ICBL press release, January 15, 1996.

"Organizations Working to Ban Landmines," December 1997.

Price, Richard, and Daniel Hope. "Media Coverage of Landmines." *Landmine Monitor Report 1999.*

Proceedings of the US Campaign to Ban Landmine meeting, "Convened by the Women's Commission for Refugee Women and Children, Held at the Offices of Oxfam American, Boston, Massachusetts, July 24, 1995.

Record of the 6 October 1992 meeting of the founding members of the ICBL.

Regional Conference on Landmines. International Campaign to Ban Landmines. Budapest, Hungary. March 26–28, 1998.

Report of the Final Plenary Session," NGO Conference on Antipersonnel Mines, London, May 26, 1993.

Report of Working Group 3: Promoting the Ban: Countering the Opposition," at the Second NGO Conference on Landmines, Report of Proceedings. Geneva. May 9–11, 1994.

"Report on Activities: Review Conference on the Convention on Conventional Weapons" held in Vienna, Austria.

Senator Patrick Leahy. "Seize the Moment." *ICBL Ban Treaty News*, September 9, 1997.

United States Campaign to Ban Landmines. "When is an Antipersonnel Landmine not a Mine?—When it is American." press release, September 9, 1997.

"U.S. Campaign to Ban Landmines Bulletin," Issue 3, March 1996.

U.S. Campaign to Ban Landmines Meeting Minutes. New York. December 13, 1995.

"US Group Meeting on Landmines" meeting minutes, *Vietnam Veterans of America Foundation*, Washington, D.C., September 26, 1994.

"U.S. To Make Final Attempt to Maim Landmine Ban Treaty," ICBL Press Release. September 15, 1997.

"Where Do We Go from Here: Broadening the Campaign," Second NGO Conference on Landmines, Report of Working Group 4. Geneva. May 9–11, 1994.

Williams, Jody. "Brief Assessment and Chronology of the Movement to Ban Landmines," Vietnam Veterans of America Foundation document, n.d.

Williams, Jody. "Questions Frequently Asked to Jody Williams." *International Campaign to Ban Landmines*, http://www.icbl.org/cgi-bin/faq/landmines/index.cgi?subject=99624475 (accessed March 5, 2002).

Williams, Jody. "Response to draft of talking points," Memorandum. April 9, 1992.

Williams, Jody. "Talk to America," Voice of America Radio Service, December 4, 1998.

INTERNATIONAL COMMITTEE FOR THE RED CROSS (ICRC) DOCUMENTS

Anti-personnel Landmines: Friend or Foe? A Study of the military use and effectiveness of anti-personnel landmines." International Committee for the Red Cross. Geneva. March 1996.

"ICRC Calls for Examination of the Military Use of Anti-Personnel Landmines." ICRC press release, January 13, 1994.

ICRC Position Paper No. 4. "Landmines: Crucial Decisions 1997." December, 1997.

Landmines Must Be Stopped: The Worldwide Epidemic of Landmine Injuries: The ICRC's health oriented approach. Report, International Committee for the Red Cross. September 1995.

"Final Communiqué of the Ashgabat Central Asia Regional Conference on a Global Ban on Anti-Personnel Mines." Turkmenistan. July 12, 1997.

Final Declaration. "Regional Seminar on Land-mines and the 1980 Convention on Conventional Weapons." Addis Ababa. February 23–24, 1995.

Gray, Dr. Robin. ICRC Surgical Coordinator. *Humanitarian Consequences of Mine Usage,* report presented to the ICRC Symposium on Anti-Personnel Landmines, April 1993.

"Mines and Humanitarian Activities." Report presented by Jean-Michel Monod, *Montreux Symposium on Anti-Personnel Mines Report,*. International Committee of the Red Cross, Montreux, Switzerland. April 21–23, 1993.

A Perverse Use of Technology: Mines, ICRC. 1992.

Report on the Work of Experts. "Weapons that may Cause Unnecessary Suffering or have Indiscriminate Effects." ICRC. Geneva, Switzerland. 1973.

Report to the International Committee of the Red Cross for the Review Conference of the CCW. International Committee for the Red Cross. February 1994.

"Symposium on Anti-personnel Mines." International Committee of the Red Cross, Montreux, Switzerland. April 21–23, 1993.

UNITED NATIONS (UN) DOCUMENTS

1977 Additional Protocol I to the 1945 Geneva Convention, Article 51 (4). "Moratorium on the Export of Anti-Personnel Landmines," UN First Committee, A/C1/49/L19, November 3, 1994.

Abramson, Bruce. *Landmines: UNHCR's Efforts to Protect Returnees and Assist their Rehabilitation,* UNHCR Programme and Technical Support Section. Geneva. September 1993.

Adoption of the Rules of Procedure, Agenda and Organization of Work, International Meeting on Mine Clearance. Geneva, Switzerland. July 5–7, 1995. SG/Conf. 7/1, April 18, 1995.

"*Afghanistan: The Development of Indigenous Mine Action Capabilities.*" A study prepared by Robert Eaton, Chris Horwood, and Norah Niland. Lessons Learned Unit, United Nations Department of Humanitarian Affairs. United Nations. n.d.

Assistance in Mine Clearance. Report of the Secretary-General. United Nations General Assembly. 49th Session, A/49/357/Add.1 September 20, 1994.

Bornmann, Gerhard. UNHCR Demining Officer. *Programme For Protection Against Explosive Land Mines.* In connection with the tasks of UNHCR, March 1993.

Boutros-Ghali, Boutros. *An Agenda for Peace* A/47/277. 1992.

"*Cambodia: The Development of Indigenous Mine Action Capacities.*" A study prepared by Robert Eaton, Chris Horwood, and Norah Niland. Lessons Learned Unit, United Nations Department of Humanitarian Affairs. United Nations. n.d.

Hansen, Peter. UN Under-Secretary-General for Humanitarian Affairs, to the Review Conference of States Parties to the Convention on the Prohibitions or Restrictions on the Use of Certain Conventional Weapons Which May be Deemed to be Excessively Injurious or to have Indiscriminate Effects. September 27, 1995.

Mine Action Programme for Afghanistan: Workplan 1999. United Nations Office for the Coordination of Humanitarian Assistance to Afghanistan (UNOCHA), Mine Action Center for Afghanistan. n.d.

Pinder, Martin. Senior Organisation and Methods Officer. *Landmines and UNHCR persons of concern*, a draft discussion paper on possible UNHCR study, prepared for the Liaison Unit, Southern Africa Operations. UNHCR Geneva, June 10, 1997.

"Speakers Urge Imposition of Global Ban on Anti-Personnel Mines, as Security Council Discusses Demining in Peace-Keeping Context." SC/6257. Press Release, August 15, 1996.

UN Department of Humanitarian Affairs. Informal Policy Paper for the Review Conference of States Parties to the Convention on the Prohibitions or Restrictions on the Use of Certain Conventional Weapons Which May be Deemed to be Excessively Injurious or to have Indiscriminate Effects (CCW). Vienna. September 25 to October 13, 1995.

UNHCR Statement to the Group of Governmental Experts to Prepare the Review Conference of the States Parties to the Convention on Prohibition or Restrictions on the use of Certain Conventional Weapons Which May Be Deemed to be Excessively Injurious or to have Indiscriminate Effects. Geneva, Switzerland. January 1995.

UNICEF. *Anti-Personnel Land-Mines: A Scourge on Children. UNICEF House, New York, 1994.*

United Nations Disarmament Yearbook. Department of Disarmament Affairs. New York, 1997.

United Nations Environment Programme. *A Rapid Assessment of the Impacts of the Iraq-Kuwait Conflict on Territorial Ecosystems*. 1991.

United Nations General Assembly, 49th Session, First Committee, Agenda item 62, "Moratorium on the export of anti-personnel land-mines," November 1, 1994, A/C.1/49/L.19.

United Nations General Assembly. 49th Session. UNGA First Committee. Official Records, 5th Meeting. October 18, 1994. A/C.1/49/PV.5.

United Nations General Assembly. 49th Session, UNGA First Committee. Official Records, 8th Meeting. October 21, 1994. A/C.1/49/PV.8.

United Nations General Assembly. 49th Session, UNGA First Committee. Official Records, 9th Meeting. October 24, 1994, A/C.1/49/PV.9.

United Nations General Assembly. 49th Session, UNGA First Committee. Official Records, 10th meeting, October 24, 1994, A/C.1/49/PV.10.

United Nations General Assembly. 49th Session, UNGA First Committee. Official Records, 19th meeting, November 14, 1994, A/C.1/49/PV.19.

United Nations General Assembly. Agenda Item 70, A/RES/50/70, January 15, 1996.

United Nations General Assembly. Document A/C.1/48/L.42.

United Nations General Assembly. Document A/Conference 95/15 and Corr. 1–5; 19 International Legal Materials 1534 (1980).

United Nations High Commissioner for Refugees. "UNHCR Supports Mine Ban; Plans Boycott of Producers." Press Release. July 6, 1995.

United Nations Institute for Training and Research. "Remnants of War," International Symposium held by the Libyan Institute for International Relations and the United Nations Institute for Training and Research (UNITAR) on "The Problem of the Material Remnants of the Second World War in general and in Libya in particular." April 28 to May 1, 1981.

United Nations Office for the Coordination of Humanitarian Assistance to Afghanistan (UNOCHA). *Mine Action Programme: Afghanistan*. United Nations, 1999.

United Nations Secretary-General Report to the United Nations General Assembly, "Moratorium on the Export of Anti-Personnel Land-Mines" A/49/275, July 27, 1994.

Yearbook of the United Nations 1994. Vol. 48. Department of Public Information, United Nations. The Hague, Netherlands: Martinus Nijhoff Publishers, 1994.

U.S. GOVERNMENT DOCUMENTS

"1998 Hidden Killers: The Global Landmine Crisis." United States Department of State, Bureau of Political-Military Affairs (December 1998).

Bell, Robert. National Security Advisor, White House Press Conference. White House Press Release. January 17, 1997.

Clinton, President William. Address to the 49th Session of the UNGA, USUN #124-94. Press Release. September 26, 1994.

Clinton, President William. Letter to the Senate, January 7, 1997. White House Press Release. January 8, 1997.

Clinton, President William. "Remarks by the President on Land Mines," The Roosevelt Room, The White House. Office of the Press Secretary. September 17, 1997.

Delegation of the United States to the Oslo Diplomatic Conference, Background sheet: "Summary of U.S. Anti-Armor Landmine Systems," September 4, 1997.

"Department of Defense Actions on Landmine Proliferation." Office of Assistant Secretary of Defense. *News Release*. December 21, 1993.

Department of Defense news briefing. August 12 1997.

"Hidden Killers: The Global Landmine Crisis." A Report to the U.S. Congress on the Problem with Uncleared Landmines and the United States Strategy for Deming and Landmine Control. Department of State Publication. Bureau of Political-Military Affairs, Washington, D.C. December 1994.

"Hidden Killers: The Global Problem with Uncleared Landmines." A Report to the U.S. Congress on the Problem with Uncleared Landmines and the United States Strategy for Deming and Landmine Control. Department of State Publication, Bureau of Political-Military Affairs. Washington, D.C., July 1993.

"Milestones in Humanitarian Demining: Development of the Landmine Threat and the Discipline of Humanitarian Demining." *Fact Sheet*. Bureau of Political-Military Affairs, U.S. State Department. April 15, 2002.

Military Operations: Information on U.S. Use of Land Mines in the Persian Gulf War, United States General Accounting Office Report to the Honorable Lane Evans, House of Representatives. GAO-02-1003. September 2002.

Office of Weapons Removal and Abatement, Bureau of Political-Military Affairs, United States Department of State, *To Walk the Earth in Safety.* 8th ed. July 2009.

Office of Weapons Removal and Abatement, Bureau of Political-Military Affairs, United States Department of State. *To Walk the Earth in Safety.* 9th ed. July 2010.

"Portfolio Synopsis: Patrick J. Leahy War Victims Fund." USAID Document. October 1997.

Statement by the Press Secretary on "Anti-Personnel Landmines." The White House. May 16, 1997.

"Suspension of Transfers of Anti-Personnel Mines." U.S. National Defense Authorization Act for Fiscal Year 1993. U.S. Federal Register, Volume 57. Washington, D.C.: U.S. Government Printing Office, November 25, 1992.

U.S. National Defense Authorization Act for Fiscal Year 1993, Publication No. 102-484, sec. 1365, Washington, D.C.: U.S. Government Printing Office, 1993.

Vance, Cyrus, United States Delegation Leader and former Secretary of State with Thomas E. McNamara, Assistant Secretary of State for Political-Military Affairs, Department of State, and Timothy G. Connolly, Principal Deputy Assistant Secretary of Defense (Special Operations and Low-Intensity Conflict) Press Conference given by The Honorable Cyrus R. Vance, at the International Meeting on Mine Clearance, Office of Public Affairs. United States Mission. Geneva, Switzerland. July 6, 1995.

White House. "Fact Sheet: U.S. Policy on a Landmine Control Regime." Press Release. September 26, 1994.

White House Statement, Office of the Press Secretary. Martha's Vineyard, Massachusetts. August 18, 1997.

REPORTS (NON-ICBL, ICRC, UNITED NATIONS AND U.S. GOVERNMENT)

"AP Mine Ban: Progress Report." A Regular Report Provided by Canadian Government on the Anti-personnel Mine Ban, Number 1, February 1997.

"Ban Convention on Anti-Personnel Mines: Government Representative Focus Group," Ekos Research Associates, Inc., as part of the *A Global Ban on Landmines: Survey of Participants*, Technical Report, December 22, 1997.

Biddle, Stephen D. Julia L. Klare, and Jason Rosenfield. "The Military Utility for Landmines: Implications For Arms Control," *Institute For Defense Analyses*, IDA Document D-1559, June 1994.

Blagden, Patrick. United Nations Demining Expert, Preparatory Report "Summary of United Nations Demining," *Montreux Symposium on Anti-Personnel Mines Report*, International Committee of the Red Cross. Montreux, Switzerland. April 21–23, 1993.

"Cambodia—On the Brink of Peace," Report from a delegation of The Women's Commission for Refugee Women and Children delegation visit to Cambodia, January 1–8, 1991.

"Deming—An Operators View," Report by Brian Haiwell and L. Malin, British Aerospace Defence Ltd., Royal Ordnance Division, *Montreux Symposium on Anti-Personnel Mines Report*, International Committee of the Red Cross. Montreux, Switzerland. April 21–23, 1993.

Ekos Research Associates, Inc., "Ban Convention on Anti-Personnel Mines: Government Representative Focus Group," as part of the *A Global Ban on Landmines: Survey of Participants*, Technical Report, December 22, 1997.

Essen, Carl von. *Sweden's Landmine Defence*, Radda Barnen: Swedish Save the Children. Stockholm, Sweden. March 1996.

"Exposing the Source: U.S. Companies and the Production of Antipersonnel Mines," Human Rights Watch Report, *Human Rights Watch Arms Project* 9, no. 2. (April 1997).

Goldfield, Anne E. End of tour report sent to Karen Elshazly, Director of International Programs, American Refugee Committee and Bob Medrala, American Refugee Committee Country Director, Thailand, July 14, 1990.

Goose, Steve. "Global Production & Trade in Landmines," Report presented by Steve Goose, Director, Arms Project of Human Rights Watch, Washington, *Montreux Symposium on Anti-Personnel Mines Report*, International Committee of the Red Cross. Montreux, Switzerland. April 21–23, 1993.

"*In Its Own Words: The U.S. Army and Antipersonnel Mines in the Korean and Vietnam Wars*." Human Rights Watch Arms Project and Vietnam Veterans of America Foundation. July 1997.

"The Issue of Anti-Personnel Landmines." China National Defense White Paper, Information Office of the States Council. The Peoples Republic of China. July 27, 1998.

"Making the World Unsafe for Landmines: A Timetable for Developing alternatives and Implementing a worldwide Ban on the Smallest Weapon of Mass Destruction," The Project on Demilitarization and Democracy. Submitted to the Under-Secretary of State for Arms Control and International Security Affairs. U.S. Department of State, June 1995.

McGrath, Rae. *The Reality of the Present Use of Mines by Military Forces*, report presented to the ICRC Symposium on Anti-Personnel Landmines, April 1993.

"Military Consequences of Landmine Restrictions." A Study by The Dupuy Institute. McLean, Virginia, April 1996.

Project on Demilitarization and Democracy. *Making the World Unsafe for Landmines: A Timetable for Developing Military Alternatives and Implementing a Worldwide Ban on the Smallest Weapon of Mass Destruction*. Submitted to the Under-Secretary of State for Arms Control and International Security Affairs. U.S. Department of State, June 1995.

Rogers, Brigadier A. P. V. British Army of the Rhine, *The Mines Protocol: Negotiating History*. Report presented to the ICRC Symposium on Anti-Personnel Landmines, April 1993.

Rutherford, Ken, and Sue Eitel. *Landmine Awareness in Bosnia: General Overview.* Report prepared for U.S. Department of Defense under a contract with the Landmine Survivors Network, April 1998.

"UN Coordination Central to Kosovo Clearance." *Safelane: Canada's Landmine Ban Report* 10, no. 4 (Winter 1999–2000).

CONFERENCES

Cambodian Women's Voice Against Land-Mines, Khmer Women's Voice Centre, Fourth World Conference on Women. Beijing-Huairou. May 1995.

Eblagh, K. "Practical Problems in Demining and their Solutions," UNOCHA Mine Clearance Programme-Afghanistan, presentation at the Convention of National Societies of Electrical Engineers of Europe (EUREL) International Conference "The Detection of Abandoned Land Mines: A Humanitarian Imperative Seeking a Technical Solution," October 7–9, 1996. Edinburgh, United Kingdom. Conference publication.

McAslan, Colonel A. R. R. "The Countermine Challenge: An Evolving Requirements," Deputy Director Operational Requirements (Land Systems), UK Ministry of Defence, paper presented at the Convention of National Societies of Electrical Engineers of Europe (EUREL) International Conference: The Detection of Abandoned Land Mines: A Humanitarian Imperative Seeking a Technical Solution," October 7–9, 1996. Edinburgh, United Kingdom.

Organization of American States, General Assembly Resolution AG/RES. 1411 XXVI-O/96, The Western Hemisphere as Anti-Personnel Land Mine-Free Zone, June 7, 1996.

Panel "Controlling Weapons: Ethical and Practical Issues," at the 1999 International Studies Association Annual Conference. Washington, D.C. February 17, 1999.

Panel Discussion on U.S. Landmine Policy and Verification. The American Bar Association; Section of International Law and Practice. Washington, D.C. October 23, 1997.

Plan of Action of the First Continental Conference of African Experts on Landmines, "Landmines Free Africa: The OAU and the Legacy of Anti-Personnel Mines. Kempton Park, South Africa. May 21, 1997.

Walker, John K. "*Air Scatterable Land Mines as an Air Force Munition*." Paper presented at the 1978 Air University Airpower Symposium, Battlefield Support in the 1980s, Air War College, Maxwell Air Force Base, Alabama, February 14, 1978 and published by the Rand Corporation, P-5955.

PERSONAL COMMUNICATIONS WITH AUTHOR*

*Note that job titles reflect former or current position(s).

Atwood, David. Associate Representative, Disarmament and Peace, Friends World Committee and Consultation, Quaker United Nations Office, Geneva. E-mail to author. March 2, 2000.

Baaser, Sharif. Program Specialist, Mine Action and Small Arms Child Protection, Programme Division UNICEF. E-mail to author. June 21, 2010.

Barlow (US Army Ret.), COL. Dennis. E-mail correspondence with author June 29 and July 1, 2010. Barlow was the Director of Humanitarian Policy in the Office of the Secretary of Defense and the first leader of the Humanitarian Demining Task Force in the Pentagon. He also established the Mine Action Information Center and Center for International Stabilization at James Madison University, Harrisonburg, Virginia.

Bennett, Dr. Andew. Associate Professor of Government, Georgetown University, written correspondence, June 7, 2000. In 1995, Dr. Bennett worked on the staff of the secretary of defense. Conversation with author.

Bernstein, Liz. Coordinator for the ICBL (1998–2004) and co-founder Coalition for Peace and Reconciliation and helped found the Cambodia Campaign to Ban Landmines former adviser to the Khmer Women's Center, interview with author, New York. March 1, 2000.

Bernstein, Liz. Coordinator for the ICBL and former adviser to the Khmer Women's Center, telephone interview with author. March 13, 2000.

Borrie, John. Senior Researcher & Project Manager, UNIDIR. E-mail correspondence with author. June 2, 2010.

Brinkert, Kerry. Director of the MBT's Implementation Support Unit (ISU). E-mail correspondence with author, June 16, 2010. Housed at the International Center for Humanitarian Demining (GICHD) in Geneva, the ISU was created 2001 based on an agreement of MBT States Parties with the purpose to further enhance the MBT's operation and implementation. Between 1998 and 2002, Brinkert worked for the Mine Action Team of Canada's Department of Foreign Affairs and International Trade where he served as the Section Head of Research, Policy and Communications.

Campbell, Senator Ben Nighthorse. Letter to author. June 20, 1994.

Cohen, William. U.S. Secretary of Defense (1997–2001). Conversation with author. Missouri State University, Springfield, Missouri. October 3, 2006.

Coughlan, Denise. Chair, Cambodia Campaign to Ban Landmines. E-mail to author. March 12, 2000.

Diana, Princess of Wales. Letter to author. August 12, 1997.

Diana, Princess of Wales, conversation with author. Hotel Bristol, Tuzla, Bosnia. August 8, 1997.

Diana, Princess of Wales, conversation with author, Kensington Palace, London. July 27, 1997.

Goldfeld, Dr. Anne. E-mail correspondence with author, June 20, June 30, July 1, and July 4, 2010.

Goldfeld, Dr. Anne. Medical Coordinator for the American Refugee Committee on the Thai-Cambodian border at Site II in 1989 and in 1994, and Professor of Medicine at Harvard Medical School and Professor of Immunology and Infectious Disease at the Harvard School of Public Health. Interview with author. Cambridge, Massachusetts. April 15, 2008.

Goose, Steve. Director, Human Rights Watch Arms Division and Chair, US Campaign to Ban Landmines. E-mail correspondence with author. March 7, 2000, and July 5, 2010.

Gwozdecky, Mark. Coordinator of the Mine Action Team in the Canadian Department of Foreign Affairs and International Trade. E-mail to author. June 21, 2010.

Gwozdecky, Mark. Coordinator of the Mine Action Team in the Canadian Department of Foreign Affairs and International Trade. Interview with author. Ottawa, Canada. August 13, 2010.

Hannon, Paul. Special Projects Officer at Oxfam Canada (1990–1998) and current Director, Mines Action Canada. Interview with author. Ottawa, Canada. August 14, 2010.

Herby, Peter. Head, Mines-Arms Unit, Legal Division, International Committee for the Red Cross (ICRC). Telephone interview with author. January 29, 1999.

Inderfurth, Ambassador Karl. Ambassador Inderfurth served as Assistant Secretary of State for South Asian Affairs (1997–2001), Special Representative of the President and Secretary of State for Global Humanitarian Demining (1997–98) and U.S. Representative for Special Political Affairs to the United Nations, with ambassadorial rank, where he also served as Deputy U.S. Representative on the U.N. Security Council (1993–1997) Interview with author. Washington, D.C. May 15, 2001.

Inderfurth, Ambassador Karl. E-mail to author. June 19, 2010.

Khun, Ratana. Chief of Secretariat for the Public, Cambodian Mine Action Center. Interview with author. James Madison University, Harrisonburg, Virginia. June 1, 2010.

Kongstad, Steffen. Deputy Director General, Royal Norwegian Ministry of Foreign Affairs. Conversation with author. Amman, Jordan. June 7, 2005.

Lawson, Robert. Deputy Director, Canadian Mine Action Team. Interview with author. University of California at Irvine. Irvine, California. May 9, 2000.

Lawson, Robert. Senior Advisor in the Mine Action Team in the Canadian Department of Foreign Affairs and International Trade. E-mail correspondence with author, July 2, 2010.

Lawson, Robert. Senior Advisor in the Mine Action Team in the Canadian Department of Foreign Affairs and International Trade. Interview with author. Ottawa, Canada. August 14, 2010.

Modise, Joe. South African Minister of Defense. Conversation with author. Alkantapan military testing range, Northern Cape Province, South Africa. May 21, 1997.

Moran, Joe. Air Pilot, African Medical and Research Foundation. Conversation with author, Dublin, Ireland. May 28, 2008.

Morgan, Tamara. Trauma Nurse, African Medical and Research Foundation. E-mail correspondence with author. July 3, 2010.

McCain, Senator John. Letter to author. August 8, 1994.

Myers, Holly. U.S. Campaign to Ban Landmines Coordinator for Public Awareness and Education. E-mail correspondence with author. June 1, 2010.

Peters, Ann. Open Society Institute. Telephone interview with author. Washington, D.C. October 5, 1999.

Rieser, Tim. Foreign Policy Aide to Senator Patrick Leahy. Interview with author. Washington, D.C. October 29, 1998.

Rieser, Tim. Foreign Policy Aide to Senator Patrick Leahy. Letter to author. October 3, 1994.

Sand-Trigo, Ariane. International Committee for the Red Cross (ICRC) Delegation to the United Nations. Letter to author. March 3, 1997.

Sutton, Sean. Photographer, Mines Advisory Group (MAG). Conversation with author. North Atlantic on the Queen Mary II. May 4, 2007.

Sutton, Sean. Photographer, Mines Advisory Group (MAG). E-mail correspondence with author. July 5, 2010.

Walker, Susan. Handicap International and International Campaign to Ban Landmines. E-mail to selected ICBL members, including the author. June 2, 2005.

Wareham, Mary. Senior Researcher, Human Rights Watch and former Coordinator, US Campaign to Ban Landmines. E-mail correspondence with author. July 1, 2010.

Wareham, Mary. Senior Researcher, Human Rights Watch and former Coordinator, US Campaign to Ban Landmines. Telephone interview with author. October 12 and 19, 1999.

Marissa Vitagliano, Coordinator, US Campaign to Ban Landmines. Telephone interview with author. October 19, 1999.

OTHER REFERENCES

"Antipersonnel Landmine Use and Policy," *Alliant Fact Sheet*, ca. July 1995.

"*Are We the Enemy*," Video, produced by the Khmer Women's Voice Centre, May, 1995.

Atwood, David C., Associate Representative, Disarmament and Peace, Friends World Committee and Consultation, Quaker United Nations Office, Geneva, "Banning Landmines: Observations on the Role of Civil Society." Paper prepared for the volume *Peace Politics of Civil Society*, June 1998.

Ban Landmines: The Ottawa Process and the International Movement to Ban Landmines. CD-ROM. Canadian Department of Foreign Affairs and International Trade, 1998.

Cambodia Conference Reception Packet handout, June 1995. Document retrieved in the official records of the International Campaign to Ban Landmines at Library and Archives Canada. Ottawa, Canada. Accessed by author on August 13, 2009.

"Campaign for a Landmine Free World . . . turning tragedy into hope," Vietnam Veterans of America brochure.

D'Aria, Dorian. U.S. Army Engineer Center, Fort Leonard Wood, Missouri and Mr. Lester W. Grau, Foreign Military Studies Office, Fort Leavenworth, Kansas. "Instant Obstacles: Russian Remotely Delivered Mines." *Red Thrust Star.* U.S. Forces Command OPFOR Training Program, S-2, 11th Armored Cavalry Regiment, Fort Irwin, CA 92310-5031, January 1996.

Declaration of the Voice of Cambodian Women Against The Use of Landmines in Cambodia, Khmer Women's Voice Centre letter, February 23, 1995.

"Foreign Mine Handbook (Balkan States)," *Department of the Army, Training Circular.* No. 20-32-3. August 15, 1997.

Gallup International Opinion Research, Spring 1996, April 17, 1996.

Gibbs, Rick. Presentation at a public meeting of the Committee on Alternative Technologies to Replace Anti-Personnel Landmines. Meeting Notes complied by Vietnam Veterans of America Foundation, December 10, 1999.

Hubert, Don. *The Landmine Ban: A Case Study in Humanitarian Advocacy: Occasional Paper #42.* Providence, Rhode Island: Thomas J. Watson Jr. Institute for International Studies, 2000.

Kelemen, Michelle. "Russia/Landmines." Voice of America, May 27, 1998.

"Land Mines: The Plight, The International Commitments, the Reinforcement of the Contribution of the European Union," The European Commission. http://eu-mine-actions.jrc.cec.eu.int/policy/background_1.htm.

"Landmines: A Princess Legacy," produced by British Broadcasting Corporation (BBC)—Bristol. 1998.

Lawson, Robert J. "Ban Landmines: The Social Construction of the International Ban on Anti-Personnel Landmines 1991–2001," Master's thesis, Carleton University, Ottawa, Canada, April 2002.

New Zealand Campaign Against Landmines (CALM) Newsletter, Number 5, July 1997.

Norwegian Nobel Committee, Press Release on the announcement of the awarding of the 1997 Peace Price to the ICBL and its coordinator, Jody Williams. October 10, 1997.

Price, Tom. "A Lever to Move the World." *Foundation for Public Affairs,* October 7, 1999, 7.

Tuttle, Celina. "Ottawa Landmines Conference a Highlight: Landmine Ban Proposed." *The Ploughshares Monitor* 17, no. 4 (December 1996).

Warmington, Valerie. "Landmine Abolition: A Small Step Forward at Geneva." *The Ploughshares Monitor,* June 1, 1996.

Women's Commission for Refugee Women and Children. Proceedings of the U.S. Campaign to Ban Landmine meeting. Held at the Offices of Oxfam American, Boston, Massachusetts. July 24, 1995.

A Working Chronology of the International Movement to Ban Anti-Personnel (AP) Mines, published by the Centre for Negotiation and Dispute Resolution, The Norman Paterson School of International Affairs, Carleton University, Ottawa, Canada. n.d.

Index

About the Author

KENNETH R. RUTHERFORD is Director of the Center for International Stabilization and Recovery and Professor of Political Science at James Madison University. He is the author of *Humanitarianism Under Fire: The US and UN Intervention in Somalia* and has co-edited two books: *Landmines and Human Security: International Politics and War's Hidden Legacy* and *Reframing the Agenda: The Impact of NGO and Middle Power Cooperation in International Security Policy.*

He has worked for international aid agencies in Bosnia, Kenya, Mauritania, Senegal, and Somalia, and served as Fulbright Professor in Jordan. After losing his legs to a landmine, he co-founded the Landmine Survivors Network, a leading member of the International Campaign to Ban Landmines, which was awarded the 1997 Nobel Peace Prize, and the Cluster Munitions Coalition that helped achieve the Convention on Cluster Munitions. His story has been profiled in *Reader's Digest* and on television, including the BBC, *The View,* and *Oprah*. He was the recipient of the United Nations Association-USA humanitarian award by Sir Paul and Heather Mills McCartney and the Leadership in International Rehabilitation Award by Northwestern University.

Dr. Rutherford earned his Ph.D. at Georgetown University, and BA and MBA degrees from the University of Colorado where he was football letterman and inducted in its Hall of Fame for distinguished alumni. He lives in Harrisonburg, Virginia with his wife Kimberly and their four children, Hayden, Campbell, Duncan, and Lucie.

CPSIA information can be obtained at www.ICGtesting.com
Printed in the USA
LVOW10*0456210214

374648LV00002B/6/P

9 780313 393969